THE CONSPIRACY

An Innocent Priest

with
Anthology of Reviews

Monsignor William McCarthy

iUniverse, Inc.
New York   Bloomington

The Conspiracy
An Innocent Priest

Edited by Cliff Carle

iUniverse books may be ordered through booksellers or by contacting:

iUniverse
1663 Liberty Drive
Bloomington, IN 47403
www.iuniverse.com
1-800-Authors (1-800-288-4677)

ISBN: 978-1-4502-3964-6 (sc)
ISBN: 978-1-4502-3965-3 (dj)
ISBN: 978-1-4502-3966-0 (ebook)

Library of Congress Control Number: 2010909150

Printed in the United States of America

iUniverse rev. date: 06/11/2012

DEDICATION

Since June 19, 2009 to June 10, 2010 is the year for priests, I dedicate this book to St. John Vianney, the Cure of Ars. He too was accused falsely of preposterous nonsense, mainly because of his penitential lifestyle; often attacked by the devil himself, leaving him bruised and bloodied.

PURPOSE OF THIS BOOK

I am a survivor of the pedophile witch hunt in the Church at the end of the 1990s. For me the hunt began the year 2003 and ended in 2008. "Those who do not remember the past are destined to repeat it." This book is an attempt to stop the insanity in the Church from ever happening again, by remembering and recalling the past. As outlined in my story within these pages, they say knowledge is power -- and that knowledge is also offered in this book for a priest to protect himself from a false accusation and the horrible consequences that follow.

It is also my hope and intention that this book shall be an inspiration to everyone who is against the type of injustice that myself and other innocent priests have suffered; and who wish to be of help by taking appropriate action when necessary, or simply offering comfort when needed.

DISCLAIMER –
NAMES & PLACES

Some of the people who are involved in my story have graciously given me verbal permission to use their names. In other instances, I was either not able to, or chose not to obtain verbal permission. Thus I have had to change certain names due to a variety of reasons; such as the person is deceased, or I no longer have contact information, or the incident I describe could possibly bring discredit to the person's name. It is absolutely not my intent to retaliate and cause any harm to, or bring into disrepute the name of any individual who, for any reason, has attempted to hurt me, my name, and/or my reputation.

In other instances, I have used my own discretion in choosing whether to use either the real name of a participant, or to create a fictitious name. However, in all instances, the events that I describe are to the best of my ability true and accurate.

Also, in a few instances, certain locations where events took place have been either changed or omitted in order to protect the privacy of an individual, a family, or a place of business.

Similarities to situations in this book or to names you may know are completely coincidental.

A NOTE TO READERS

At the onset of my harrowing ordeal, my dear friend, Sil Grassman, said to me, "Keeping a journal will help you keep your sanity." This book is the result of her sage advice. In my time of exile, sometimes daily, sometimes weekly I would write a combination of what I was thinking, experiencing, remembering, reading, watching, and what was happening in the world around me. I wrote in a stream of consciousness style; as a result you will find repeats of certain facts and details of my case. To varying degrees, the unfairness of the conspiracy haunted me daily. So please bear with me when you come across any repetition. Additionally, the verb tense will alternate between present and past at times, depending on where my mind was at while I was writing.

At the end of five years, my journal weighed in at 800+ handwritten pages. I knew that would be too long and too much to ask of you kind readers, and thus I have removed approximately 400 of those pages. Perhaps someday I will include those musings in a second book, God willing and if the Spirit so moves me.

HOW TO USE THIS BOOK

As you read, please keep either a yellow highlighter, or a pen or pencil handy to mark certain passages that "speak to you" or inspire you. If at some time in your life you ever have to go through a major life altering experience, it is my hope that you will be able to call upon these passages as a guide. I entreat you to compare the desolation and despair of my situation with yours, and see the solutions that came to me through the blessings of God. Then reread the thoughts you highlighted that brought comfort to me in my darkest hours of need, and that brought me back whole again. It is my prayer that reading this book will be as beneficial to you as writing it was for me.

Table of Contents

YEAR THREE (2005)

YEAR FOUR (2006)

YEAR FIVE (2007)

YEAR SIX (2008)

YEAR SEVEN (2009)

YEAR ONE (2003)

CHAPTER 1

THE ACCUSATION

On February 3, 2003, Detective Michael Reedy from a New Jersey prosecutors' office came to my office and said to me: "You have been accused of molesting two little sisters, Nora and Mary in 1980."

I could not have been more shocked by such an outrageous accusation. "I certainly did not," I said emphatically and without hesitation.

"Well," Detective Reedy remarked, "you don't remember because it was too painful and you buried it—but you did do it."

After the detective left I was in complete shock. *Surely the detective will go back and discover he is chasing after a lead that is based on false information,* I thought to myself, *and my name will be cleared.* But this was not to be the case.

A few days later I was called to the prosecutors' office. When I arrived there, Detective Reedy informed me that the family did not accuse me. Rather, two unrelated women came to his office and did so. Again I categorically denied that I had touched or done anything inappropriate to the sisters. I asked him, "*Where* did this alleged crime happen, and *how* did it happen?"

He said matter-of-factly, "You sat down on the couch in the Snedo home and you took the little sisters on your lap and touched them." Then he demonstrated to me that I touched their thighs and breasts.

I looked him squarely in the eyes and said, "First of all, I have no recollection of seeing them in their house. Even if they were there, they would not go near me. I didn't know them and they didn't know me. After all, I was only in the parish a few months."

Detective Reedy continued to investigate me for several more weeks and he finally called me to come in and "wrap things up." When I got there, he ambushed me: "Well now, it comes down to two things. Either you sign a confession or you take a polygraph test."

"I will be happy to take a lie detector test and finally have a chance to clear myself," I said eagerly, seeing the opportunity for vindication.

As if on cue, the operator came into the room, quickly hooked me up to the polygraph machine, and proceeded to ask me questions. At the end he abruptly said, "You failed and you are guilty."

I was flabbergasted; I knew something wasn't right. "I want a second opinion," I insisted.

He gave me the name of another operator; then Detective Reedy called me out of the room. He brought me through dark corridors, rattling keys while we walked, and took me into another dingy, dark room where we sat down. With a certain amount of satisfaction, he proceeded to tell me that they now had all the evidence in the world that I did this terrible thing.

When I protested, he ordered me to sign a confession. I refused and said defiantly, "I will not sign my name to a lie."

After at least two more hours of interrogation, I informed him that I had to go home as I had to conduct a Pre Cana weekend. I shook his hand, left him, and drove home in a snow storm.

I knew this was not going to go away without a fight. The following week I retained Gerry Rooney as my lawyer. He interviewed me and checked whether my case fell under the statute of limitations. He informed me that it did not, and that's the reason why the detective had gone this far. Then he asked me to take another polygraph test. I asked him the name of the operator. It turned out to be the same operator that Detective Reedy's operator had recommended to me for a second opinion. I refused to have anything to do with a friend of Reedy's operator.

A few days later, my attorney referred me to the prestigious Argus Investigative firm in Scotch Plains, NJ, for a balanced and unbiased polygraph test. This time, the results showed that I conclusively passed—that I was innocent. The results were sent to my civil and canon lawyers, and were later presented at my Ecclesiastical trial (which would not come to be until four more interminable years).

A little while after the initial criminal investigation ended, it was late at night and I was upstairs in the rectory when I heard a noise downstairs that frightened me, since I was the only person in the rectory at the time. I called the police who arrived in about fifteen minutes to the parking lot of the rectory, with their lights flashing. I stuck my head out of the window and within minutes the policemen were laughing good-naturedly. I went downstairs and they informed me that the noise had been made by Mr. Al Betwinas, from bingo; he had been bringing the bingo change to the rectory.

2

The next day, rumors ran wild throughout the community. Some of them had me arrested and put in jail, which caused a great number of people to call the parish office, the police department, and the town hall. The next day I mailed a letter to all my parishioners to explain to them what had actually happened.

* * *

A CLARIFYING STATEMENT FROM MONSIGNOR WILLIAM MCCARTHY

Dear Parishioners:

This Tuesday night, March 25, 2003, at about 11:00 p.m., I was in my bedroom in the rectory preparing to sleep for the night. I heard footsteps downstairs; since I was the only one in the rectory, I felt there was a prowler in the house. I called the police. The police went around to the parish center and met with Al Batwinas and the bingo leaders in Fahey Hall. They mentioned that I called the police to check the rectory for a possible intruder. Al Batwinas told them, "That was just me bringing the bingo coin (not the Bingo receipts) into the rectory for next week." The police officers, Berres and Froisland, brought their cars around to the rectory. I stuck my head out the window and asked them why they were not inside checking the rectory. They were amused at me and told me it was Al Batwinas. I was embarrassed, but they were angels and just laughed and took off to continue more important work.

Some people seeing two police cars at the rectory let their imagination run wild with them, all kinds of rumors surfaced such as:
1. Father McCarthy died;
2. Father McCarthy collapsed;
3. Father McCarthy was arrested;
4. There was a robbery; etc.

All of which were totally false and somewhat amusing. I never knew I was so important (just kidding). Since I announced my "move up" retirement date, it looks like a psychological bomb has landed in the middle of East Hanover and caused a massive ripple wave of unsettlement and rumor around the parish. Maybe it is a way of getting their minds off the war that can be unbearable to watch on TV or to even think about. So please spread the word that all these wild rumors are totally untrue and also please refrain from calling on the phone or coming to the office. It is very stressful on the secretaries and others in the office.

Thank you for your concern. I will keep you updated as to the results of my medical testing and what will eventually be done to correct my problem.

Signed: William M. McCarthy

∗   ∗   ∗

The records of my case were sent to my bishop, whose name I am withholding. Hereafter, I shall refer to him as either "my bishop" or "my former bishop" so as not to confuse him with his successor, Bishop Serratelli, whose name is frequently mentioned within these pages.

My bishop wrote to me informing me that he was putting me under censure. This meant I was not allowed to say a public mass, or dress as a priest, or perform priestly duties. I was crushed. I could not believe what was happening to me in light of charges that were in my mind unfounded—and in all cases, were as yet unsubstantiated and unproven. The diocese then reported my case to the media, which further traumatized me. The diocese claimed that I had sent a letter to the East Hanover community telling them of my exoneration, and that was why they were compelled to go to the media. The fact is, the letter I sent to the community had nothing to do with either the investigation or exoneration. The letter I sent (as you just read) was to quell the rumors that were rampant, and to bring peace to the community.

I did not understand why my bishop took such an aggressive course of action. This was clearly above and beyond standard procedure in treating an unverified *allegation*. As I later discovered: Months prior to the accusation against me, my bishop had attended a meeting of all the bishops of the USA in Dallas, Texas. It was assembled shortly after the first major instance of priest pedophilia hit the headlines. The bishops developed a charter on how to deal with any future accusations of child abuse by priests that might possibly surface. Basically, the mandate was "guilty till proven innocent." Even one accusation and the priest shall be removed. It was a "one strike and you're out" policy.

*   *   *

Eventually I went back to my lawyer, Mr. Rooney, for a final meeting; he did not show me the file, but paraphrased an anonymous letter that was sent to the diocese accusing me of molesting two little sisters in 1980. The letter was signed with a fictitious name, but the detective failed to find the author of the anonymous letter. That was all he told me. I left the office and came home.

The statement of Detective Reedy that the family did not accuse me of this act, rather a couple of women who came to his office and made the accusation stayed on my mind. I was baffled as to who those women were. I was on my way by airplane with my friend Dr. Hoagland to Alabama to go to EWTN (Eternal Word Television Network). When thousands of feet in the air, I prayed that God would reveal to me who "these women" were. Suddenly like a flash of lightening two names popped up in my mind. I knew instantly that they were my accusers. These two women had a vendetta against me and were determined to bring me down.

CHAPTER 2

THE WILL

The history of my conflict with the two women who falsely accused me stems way back. In my capacity as pastor of St. Rose of Lima Church, I ministered to an elderly lady. She became very fond of me and even visited my family in Ireland. This 87-year-old woman, Mrs. Murphy, had not spoken to her daughter for twenty years. She told me she was bequeathing all her assets to the diocese of Paterson, except for $25,000 which she was leaving to me. She spoke about that very freely with other people. As a result of this, Mrs. Cain, a busybody who was a brief acquaintance of Mrs. Snedo, and a friend of Mrs. Murphy's daughter, decided to involve herself. Mrs. Cain visited the elderly Mrs. Murphy and told her, "Do not to leave Father McCarthy any money. He is mean and doesn't care about you."

A few weeks later I visited Mrs. Murphy and she confirmed that Mrs. Cain said mean things about me; told her not to leave me any money in her will, and took her to a lawyer.

I invited Mrs. Cain to come and see me. I asked her, "Why did you say those things to Mrs. Murphy?" Mrs. Cain denied ever saying anything of the sort to Mrs. Murphy. When I informed Mrs. Murphy of Mrs. Cain's denial, she pounded her chair and yelled, "Yes she did, she absolutely did!"

I saw Mrs. Cain again and this time she became irate, walked out of my office, and left the parish. Then she got in contact with Mrs. Murphy's daughter and they joined forces against me, and demanded a meeting with my bishop.

We all met with the Vicar General at the Chancery Office. They demanded that I be removed as pastor of St. Rose, claiming that I "manipulated old people to put me in their will." They got no satisfaction and everybody went home.

During the many years of my friendship with Mrs. Murphy, she often said to me, "Monsignor McCarthy, don't ever let anyone put me in a nursing home." While Mrs. Murphy was recovering in the rehabilitation center, I called her daughter to meet me there. I brought her to the bedside of Mrs. Murphy and was able to get them to reconcile with each other.

However, shortly after this, her daughter got her attorney to declare her mother mentally incompetent and succeeded in getting power of attorney. Next, her daughter put her mother in a nursing home and proceeded to put her mother's home up for sale for $120,000. Now, her daughter was in control of everything. She had her lawyer write me and demand that I never get in touch with her mother again. The daughter was obviously scared that I would call her mother and that Mrs. Murphy would ask me to save her and take her back to her home.

Unfortunately, there was nothing I could do. About six months later Mrs. Murphy died. She requested in her will that I celebrate her funeral mass. After the mass, her daughter warned me not to go to the cemetery. I went there anyway because that was according to the wishes of my friend, Mrs. Murphy. When I followed the hearse into the cemetery, her daughter confronted me and ordered me to stay away from the grave.

A local priest did the grave site ceremony. I looked on from a distance. After the ceremony was over, I witnessed something that nearly broke my heart. The daughter along with Mrs. Cain were returning to their car, arm in arm, laughing their heads off. After the funeral, I figured all contact with them would now be finished—at least that is what I thought.

As it turned out, for the two women, it was not over by a long shot. Soon afterwards these two women were busy hatching a plot to bring me down. Mrs. Cain knew of a family close to her home; the Snedo family. She was aware of a conflict this family had with St. Rose of Lima School and its principal.

In about May of 1980, Mrs. Snedo brought her daughters, Nora and Mary, to register them in the private school. The principal tested them and recommended that they go to a public school instead. Mrs. Snedo became furious and went around town complaining that the Church had rejected her kids because they were poor. To assuage her anger, I suggested to the principal that I would go the house and help Mrs. Snedo understand why the school refused to accept them.

I drove to the house, knocked at the door and Mrs. Snedo came out. When she saw me, she acted very erratic and excited, hugging and grabbing me profusely—probably expecting that I had good news. She invited me inside, and when I tried to explain to her why the children were *not* accepted in the school, she became physically aggressive and verbally irate. I literally ran out of that house, jumped into my car, and went home to the rectory office.

After that episode, Mrs. Snedo began calling Sister Mary, the principal, and me on the phone constantly. Now she was accusing her husband of molesting the two daughters. Sister Mary and I were concerned about the children and we called DYFS, the local child protection agency. The children's father asked to see me and after a long meeting with him, I became convinced that he was not a threat to his little girls. I felt badly for him and asked DYFS to "back off." The family appeared to be safe.

In 2002, somebody mentioned to me that Mr. Snedo had died. It was soon after Mr. Snedo's death that Mrs. Cain and the other woman moved to hatch the plot against me. They went to the prosecutor's office, met with Detective Reedy, and accused me of molesting Nora and Mary when they were between six and seven years old. Detective Reedy went to the home of the now adult girls and informed them that they had been "molested by Father McCarthy when they were children." The girls knew nothing about this. But Reedy was not to be denied. "You don't remember because it was so painful and horrific that you buried it, but he did molest you," Detective Reedy assured them. Finally the sisters, albeit grudgingly, went along with what he claimed had happened.

One morning, after the initial criminal investigation was over, I visited my friend Dr. Ferese, a psychologist. After I discussed my plight, he suggested that we visit the Snedo home. Dr. Ferese went to the door alone while I waited in the car. Mrs. Snedo opened the door and invited Dr. Ferese into the house.

About an hour later they both emerged from the house. Mrs. Snedo came over to my car window and said to me in the presence of Dr. Ferese: "We never accused you of anything. Somebody came around here and told me that my daughters were molested by Father McCarthy when they were children." Mrs. Snedo went on to say, "One of my daughters went along with it, but the other resisted."

Dr. Ferese and I went home. A short time later, the lawyer hired by one of the women conspirators heard about our visit. He wrote the diocese telling them that if they handed any information about the accusation to me, he would sue the diocese.

My first canon lawyer, Dr. Michael Riordan, requested the files from the diocese that were given to them by the detective. The diocese refused. My bishop then sent my files to the Vatican requesting that I be permanently removed from the priesthood because, as he stated: "Father McCarthy committed an egregious act. He was molesting two young sisters." He further stated that I was a danger to the people of God and should be removed immediately.

I believed that my bishop was intentionally misleading; he mentioned that the girls were nine and ten years old at the time of the alleged crime. The girls were between six and seven years old at the time of the alleged offense. He never mentioned that I was retired at my own request and living by myself in a one bedroom apartment almost an hour driving time from the parish. He also failed to mention that he had already censured me – forbidding me to dress as a priest, saying public mass, going to the parish, or contacting my former parishioners.

In response to the charges made by my bishop, and in an attempt to correct the misconceptions he tried to promote with the aid of the detective's report, I wrote him two long letters, on August 15th and September 6th, explaining in detail all of the events previously described, and exactly as I have related them in these pages. But he did not respond.

$*$ $*$ $*$

This entire horrible saga is having a devastating effect on my health. I cannot eat or sleep. I've lost more than fifteen pounds. At one stage I was rushed to St. Claire's hospital in Denville, NJ with what looked like a heart attack. I have chest pains as well as back pains. It all turns out to be due to severe stress. It is the darkest place I have ever been in; it is a living hell on earth for me. I would not have survived the onslaught without my wonderful friends who have circled around me, and the prayers of hundreds of people from inside the parish as well as from the outside—and from all social levels with smart and capable people like Jack Kraft, a municipal bond lawyer who is guiding me in a legal and personal way. Also, Mrs. Sil Newman, who no matter how difficult it gets, is prepared to defend my case and to go as far as humanly possible to prove me completely innocent of all charges made against me.

But even with this legion of friends and community support, it continues to be an incredibly taxing uphill battle, and an extreme test of my ability to maintain my sanity.

CHAPTER 3

IN MY DEFENSE

My bishop received a trumped up report from Detective Reedy. In this version, I had allegedly gone to the Snedo home not once, but *seven* times, and had perpetrated the molestations each time with the aid of hand puppets. Without due process I was immediately censured. At the time, I did not know about the charter I mentioned earlier (one accusation of abuse and the priest is removed). Nor did I know the contents of Detective Reedy's revised report (which was kept from my canon lawyer and me for over a year). Thus, I could not understand how I was subjected to such harsh punishment, especially with the accusation based on an anonymous letter. I was indeed overwhelmed when an incredible number of parishioners rallied to my support. As one example, I enclose the letter to my bishop, composed by my friend, Sil Newman, in her hopes of clearing my name and having the censure revoked.

[EXCERPTED]

September 9, 2003
Most Reverend Bishop,
I have been a resident of East Hanover for over twenty years. Therefore I have known Monsignor McCarthy since he was assigned as pastor to Saint Rose of Lima Church...

For the past one and a half years, I have been living in Denver, Colorado. I returned three months ago and I have begun to hear from other parishioners what I had already read in the Star Ledger, news articles mailed to me in Colorado regarding accusations raised against Monsignor

McCarthy of having molested twenty-two years ago, two girls, ages six and seven. This unfortunately sad news has kept me very perturbed, since from the moment I heard it, I knew, as I know today, that he is innocent of such bile accusations.

...Searching for other avenues to obtain a better picture of what had happened, the first thing that came to my mind was a local lady [NAME DELETED] whom I had met twenty-two plus years ago under peculiar circumstances. [She] came to my house about that time to tell me how much she loved Monsignor McCarthy, and that since he was not paying any attention to her, she had decided to go to the confessional box to tell him that, and to sit every Sunday in the front pew across from the pulpit to make sure that he would see her. I advised her to leave Monsignor alone and to dedicate more time to her husband and her family. At that time, Monsignor requested me to write a report regarding the above goings on, which I mailed to you and a copy of which is most likely still in your files. (Soon after this my husband's job required us to live in Spain for three years. I never heard from nor saw [her] again after our move.)

...now in my frustration to find out who are the women accusing Monsignor McCarthy, the first person I wanted to talk to face to face was [the mother]. I visited on September 5th in the evening. I bluntly told her, that I am very concerned about all the rumors going around about Monsignor McCarthy and that I would like to know if her daughters were the ones molested by him. She replied saying that he never molested her children.

...Bishop, it is indeed an injustice seeing how Monsignor McCarthy's reputation has been tarnished and how badly he has been treated. I, a devout Catholic layperson, cannot believe that on the diocesan level no close look was given to these false accusations.

Sincerely,
Sil Newman

$*$ $*$ $*$

ADDITIONAL SUPPORT:

My close friend, Dr. Frank Ferese, a psychologist, stretches his profession to reach beyond the pale. Dr. Arthur Hoagland, my medical doctor and close friend and powerful advisor helps me to survive medically. Sister Mary, the former principal of the St. Rose of Lima Academy has been honest and forceful in my defense. Doris and Dennis, friends of mine, gave me a quiet place by the ocean to find solace and peace. Doris often cooked my favorite food, particularly her specialty, cream of broccoli soup. Barbara Kelly, my beloved sister in Christ, kept in constant contact and often revived my drooping spirit.

In a deep spiritual way this torturous time was a blessing. It is one thing to preach the lessons of the Bible on Sundays from a pulpit. But now, more than any time in my life, and in every daily moment of my life, I was able to identify with the suffering of Jesus. After the Last Supper, Jesus went into the Garden of Gethsemane where he fell on his knees and sweated blood and pleaded with the Father to remove this chalice of suffering from him. God the Father, in his infinite wisdom, chose not to grant this request; instead He sent angels to comfort Jesus. God has sent many angels into my life to comfort me in my hours of suffering. Some of them were lead by my friend, Connie Menza, who collected hundreds of signatures on petitions from around the parish and sent them to my bishop in an effort to exonerate me.

One such petition follows. It is important to note, as you will read in the petition, *that while the civil case against me was dismissed for both lack of evidence and expiration of the statute of limitations*, I still had to face a grueling canonical trial that was to be held months later to determine my guilt or innocence in the eyes of the Church. (NOTE: the "months" turned into years.) The verbatim transcript of my canonical trial, held by the diocese, and the verdict will be discussed in a later chapter.

To Whom It May Concern:

Monsignor William McCarthy was accused of a crime with one solitary anonymous letter, written by a person unrelated to the supposedly hurt individuals. The person used this devious method with the intent to destroy the reputation of Monsignor William McCarthy of whom she had an intense "hatred." The truth or non-truth of what happened to these two little children, now nearly thirty-year-old adults,

12

is irrelevant to her, so long as her goal was accomplished.

The prosecutor's office made a thorough investigation of the accusation and found no credible evidence of a crime and the case was dismissed. That statute of limitations was not relevant since he was not charged with a crime. Consequently the Church had no right to impose restrictions on Monsignor McCarthy and invade his privacy in a cruel manner especially in the Beacon. For his entire priesthood of forty years as an active, holy, productive priest he was never accused of even the slightest crime against a minor. Surely, a pure history of that nature should have satisfied the requirement of the Church. That anonymous letter should have been thrown in the garbage. An anonymous letter has no credibility. Monsignor McCarthy should not have to suffer for this frivolous "self interest" false accusation. Monsignor McCarthy is totally innocent.

Signed by the Committee to Restore Justice to Monsignor William McCarthy:

Ron DeSena   John Ullianiello

Doris O'Dea   Connie Menza

Dr. Frank Ferese   James F. Tunny

Delores Ullianiello

*   *   *

Jesus looked down from the cross and said, "Father forgive them for they know not what they do." I have to look down from my crucifixion at two accusers and also say, "Father forgive them for they know not what they do." They are blinded by hate and revenge. No one throws stones at an empty apple tree. It is the apple tree laden with the most fruit that gets targeted. These women are throwing stones of false accusations at me in their determination to bring me down; and so far they have succeeded. They have crucified me to a cross of unbelievable sufferings of stress and anxiety. I've gone through stages of psychological meltdown, feeling all alone and abandoned, even by

God. I often have fallen on my knees and cried out like Jesus: "My God, my God, why have you abandoned me?" I have my own personal Good Friday, but I firmly believe I will somehow at some time have a resurrection—total exoneration. I intended to expose—and if necessary to sue—the perpetrators of the plot. To bring them to light and make them confess before the world their guilt and their evil scheme. But in the end I've resolved to leave their fate to the hands of God. For He does not need my help to mete out justice; as always, God will do what is right in His own time, in His own way.

CHAPTER 4

COUNSELING INTERVENTION

Soon after I was censured by my bishop, the diocese called an emergency meeting of the parish to inform the congregation of Saint Rose of Lima, that I, their former pastor, had been accused of molesting two sisters, over twenty-three years prior, in their home. I was not present, of course, but I was informed of the meeting by several parishioners the next day. This is a summary of their accounts of what happened:

Over 600 people showed up angry and upset at the audacity of the diocese to accuse their beloved pastor of such an outrageous crime. The diocesan press reporter and the Vicar General of the diocese went before the people. Their attitude of arrogance and insensitivity further inflamed the anger of the parishioners. Several people stormed the stage, grabbed the microphones, and lambasted the bishop's emissaries. These so-called experts were unable to answer even rudimentary questions about the case.

My friend, Dr. Arthur Hoagland, tried to give an opening statement, but could not finish as the intensity of the emotions present at that moment were overwhelming.

Sister Ann grabbed the microphone and severely scolded the diocesan officials for their outrageous claims, and told them in no uncertain terms what she thought of them. She let them know they were a disgrace to the Church for accusing an innocent man without any concrete evidence. "I've known Father McCarthy for twenty-three years," Sister Ann said, "and there is no way he would do anything of this nature. How dare you try to destroy a good, decent man's life."

George Metola, a long time parishioner, yelled out, "If Father McCarthy allegedly committed such an act twenty-three years ago, how come there was no accusation ever—either before or after this allegation? There is no such person with this so-called compulsion who would only do this once. Even the ordinary person on the street is aware of the nature of this phenomenon. And yet, you stand before us and act as if you know nothing of this—how dare you?"

In response, the Vicar General then stuck his finger in George's face, and stated with a smirk, "He is guilty!"

Several other parishioners politely stood up and asked intelligent questions, but were answered with ignorant replies. Obviously, these diocesan representatives were uneducated with the subject matter and unacquainted with the facts of the case. They were just there to parrot what they had been told to say.

Eventually, noticing that many of the hundreds of people present in the hall were getting more and more agitated, the two diocesan officials quickly excused themselves and made a fast getaway, barely escaping without being hurt. On their way out they promised to have a follow-up meeting in the near future. But the two of them never again showed their faces at St. Rose of Lima Church...they knew better! They had come with an authoritarian attitude, but they left defeated and downtrodden. They did more harm than good and totally traumatized the parish, especially many of the young people.

*   *   *

I was told that for weeks later, several of the children walked around the school feeling scared that someone might jump out from behind a corner and attack them. We have to ask ourselves, who were the real offenders of children? The answer is obvious.

But here's the saddest thing of all: the one who respected children the most was the one falsely accused, and is now going through hell on earth. This is what we call justice in a free democratic society? I don't think so. Worse still is that this travesty of justice was inflicted by the Church—the very institution that supposedly is the epitome of justice.

One parishioner later commented: "The entire atmosphere of the meeting was as if Father McCarthy had been *convicted* of the crime of assaulting children, when in fact he was never charged with a crime. He was never brought up before the diocesan board set up to deal with cases of this nature—never even spoken to by any of the diocesan officials, including the bishop. Yet, at the meeting we were assured that this in fact did happen."

This parishioner also stated that she went up to the Vicar General and asked, "How could this happen?"

He responded, "What could we do? These two sisters, now adults, came to us and made this accusation."

This was a fabricated lie. These sisters, never up to this time, had gone to the bishop or any other diocesan official and made this accusation. It was months later when the original promoter of justice brought them and their brother to the diocesan center, got them in a room and said, "Now, we have to get our act together and make sure you don't contradict one another." He literally rehearsed their accusations with them, telling them, "Don't be afraid. All you have to do is write out your statement and read it, and have your lawyer with you." — all of which was not allowed. It was because of misconduct like this that he was removed from his position, and a new promoter of justice was appointed. The former so-called "promoter of justice" was being pressured to do everything he could to convict me, even if it meant breaking the law. How tragic!

∗   ∗   ∗

Winston Churchill said, "If you are going through hell, keep going or the ultimate victory is virtually preordained. Of all the possible alternatives, only complete exoneration is the true outcome. Otherwise you will continue living under a cloud."

CHAPTER 5

AN AVALANCHE OF LETTERS

Many letters of support with evidence of and belief in my innocence were sent to Bishop Serratelli, who had replaced my former bishop, some of which were also sent to me personally. They kept coming in during this nightmare almost every day; they helped me to survive. I feel moved to share with my readers a small sampling of these amazing letters [ALL EXCERPTED]:

March 18, 2005

Dear Bishop Serratelli,
    On behalf of Monsignor McCarthy, I am writing this letter regarding the unsubstantiated charges waged against him and for which he has wrongly been relieved of his duties as priest.
    ...Without a fair hearing, he has been deemed "guilty as charged." The handling of this matter [is]unjust and undemocratic, and cruel; not what one would expect as justice fairly adjudicated by the Catholic Church.
    In a previous letter to Msgr. McCarthy's bishop, I described a visit I made to the alleged victims' home.
    ...as the visit ended the mother walked me [to] the car and stated clearly in the presence of Msgr. McCarthy and myself: "Father McCarthy, we didn't accuse you of anything--a detective came around here and tried to convince my daughters that

18

you molested them 23 years ago--they objected and refused to go along with him."

...this detective tried to attribute the writing of the anonymous letter to Shana M., which is now proven false.

I believe it is possible that [the]detective had some personal motive having nothing to do with the alleged incident with the children. After the anonymous letter was sent to the prosecutor's office and the author of the letter could not be found, the prosecutor's office ended its investigation ...However, why it restarted four months later, is uncertain...

As a practicing clinical psychologist for 37 years, I can say without hesitation, Msgr. McCarthy is innocent. He does not possess the characteristics of an individual who would commit the horrible and horrendous act of child abuse.

Why did Msgr. McCarthy's bishop believe the report of that detective, as if he was infallible? It appears he never made the slightest effort to investigate this accusation himself... God forgive him for trying to ruin a life with no evidence, no due process, no trial and conviction. The ramifications of this haphazard dismissal after years of service have rippled across every facet of Msgr. McCarthy's life. It seems reprehensible to me that he has been cast aside with no true effort and support to promote his innocence.

...Please help to right the wrong that has been done to this innocent man and to remove the cloud that has cast darkness and suspicion on a good and wholesome life of service as a priest, in the image of Christ and his ministry.

Cordially,
Frank R. Ferese, Psy.D.
NJ Licensed Clinical Psychologist

* * *

March 29, 2003

Dear Bishop Serratelli,

...In a follow up visit to [the mother] a month after my first visit, I again asked her if she or [her daughters] are accusing Father McCarthy of molesting them. She said and I quote: "He never molested my girls, for if he had done so, I would have killed him."

This is confirmation of my second encounter with [the mother]. Why didn't the bishop investigate more closely this case? He obviously made a rush to judgment that must be immediately corrected.

...I beg you, please look into Mgr. McCarthy's impeccable record covering his forty years of service in the priesthood. It is painful to see how these false accusations have destroyed his life. In my opinion the bishop should have brought this case to a satisfactory closure by means of exonerating Mgr. McCarthy, just as any church authority would have done in this situation.

Sincerely yours,
Sil Newman

* * *

LETTERS OF SUPPORT TO MY CANON LAWYER:

June 21, 2004

Reverend John J. Farley
[ADDRESS DELETED]

Dear Father Farley:

I am enclosing an article that I received concerning the rights of accused priests, and I wanted to send it to you for your review.

...I hope you are making progress in the case of Msgr. McCarthy. From his description of the file of

20

the Diocese and the investigation of the Prosecutor's office, I conclude that the charges against him have no merit and that he should be exonerated. I hope you are of the same mind.

Very truly yours,
Jack L. Kraft, Esq.
Fellow of the American College of Bond Counsel

*   *   *

October 15, 2004

Dear Fr. Farley,
    ...I have been a friend of Msgr. McCarthy for over forty years, since we were assigned at neighboring parishes. I have traveled to Ireland with him and have visited his home there on two occasions. I have met a number of his family on various occasions. Over the years we have vacationed together traveling in the USA and to Mexico.
    I have visited him in all of his assignments over the years. I have never heard any complaints about his priesthood nor about any dubious relationships. On the other hand I have heard compliments about him, the way he lives his priesthood, his concern for souls and his obvious interest in the welfare and care of the parishes in which he has been assigned.
    ...A reconcilliation is long overdue if the good name of Msgr. McCarthy is to be publicly cleared. There has been more than a year of publicity in the press that has harmed his reputation and hurt him emotionally.

In Christ,
Msgr. Paul F. Knauer

*   *   *

21

October 29, 2004

Dear Father Farley,

I have known Monsignor William McCarthy for over 35 years and I am happy to call him my friend as well as a brother priest.

...I am appalled by the accusations leveled against him, I am convinced they have no foundation whatsoever and that an innocent priest has been falsely accused. This is the work of an evil person who has a personal vendetta against Monsignor McCarthy.

...Our two parishes are contiguous and in the past 22 years that I have been serving at Saint Ann's I have never heard a single complaint about the character of Monsignor McCarthy.

I urge you to work as diligently as possible to clear the name of this innocent man...

In Christ,
Rev. Msgr. Martin McDonnell
Pastor / Saint Anne Church

* * *

November 11, 2004

Dear Father Farley,

...I have had the privilege of knowing Father McCarthy for many years. He is a prayerful industrious priest loved and revered by the people in ALL the parishes he has ministered in. He has been faithful to his ministry for forty years and a loyal successful pastor for twenty-three years.

...For a person of such excellent character to be accused of such a heinous crime is ludicrous. He would never do such a thing. I trust that you will do everything possible to ensure that he is exonerated as soon as possible.

Yours sincerely in Christ,
Rev. Jeremiah C. O'Riordan

*   *   *

November 9, 2004

Dear Father Farley,
   ...I have known Msgr. William McCarthy for many years. I was the pastor of St. Nicholas Church, Passaic, NJ when I met Fr. McCarthy. I never witnessed any of the activities or symptoms of which he is now being accused. His assignments at the time were Director of the CYO Youth Group and Coordinator of the Altar Servers. During that time no complaints were filed and no accusations made.
   ...Msgr. William McCarthy is a good man and a hard working priest. He was well liked by all members of the parish. I was a guest of his family in Ireland for two weeks and saw firsthand that he comes from a good family...He would never do anything to bring shame to them.
   I pray that his situation can be resolved in an amicable manor...

I remain sincerely yours in Christ,
Msgr. Charles C. Cassidy

*   *   *

November 17, 2004

Dear Father Farley:
   It is with deep concern that I write to you regarding Monsignor William McCarthy who I am convinced is wrongly accused of child molestation. I cannot even imagine this good man being in such a predicament and I wholeheartedly defend him in every way possible.
   I have known Father Bill for close to fifty years. In September of 1957 he and I entered St. Patrick's College in Carlow, Ireland to begin studies for the priesthood. Toward the beginning of 1958 both he and I decided to apply to Bishop McNulty...to become seminarians for his

diocese. Through the following six years Bill was an exemplary student, a man of deep devotion, with an excellent academic record and an adherent to every aspect of seminary discipline.

...As in our seminary days, I continued to be amazed at his enthusiasm, his strong faith and his disciplined work ethic.

A man of prayer and a priest of deep devotion, he surely was an example to his parishioners in every way. Constantly seeking new ways to bring Christ's message to others, he was frequently cited for his inspiring methods of conveying the Gospel. His great desire to be the best that he could be won the admiration of many for his enthusiasm and his spirituality...

I am appalled to even think that he has been accused of such behavior. In my mind Father Bill has been wrongfully accused and I stand by that statement with absolute certainty...

Sincerely yours,
Rev. Monsignor Eugene M. Boland,
Pastor / Saint James R.C. Church

*   *   *

LETTERS OF SUPPORT SENT TO ME:

April 30, 2002

Dear Father McCarthy,

Although I am not really a member of St. Rose's, I do attend Mass a few Sundays a month at the church. I do so because of your excellent and well prepared sermons. You are always upbeat, the message is pertinent and your jokes not bad at all. I leave Mass with an excellent feeling and know the reasons I am there.

...I feel terrible as do so many others that at times all priests are lumped together for the actions of a few. Results of recent polls show that the vast majority of people love the Church, and realize that

99% of priests are outstanding and anxiously await changes that need to be initiated.

...Keep your chin up. We both know Prayer is the answer.

Cordially,
Ronald J. Bushwell, CLU, ChFc

*   *   *

5-15-2003
Fr. McCarthy:

...What does one say to a friend whom I have always respected, greatly admired and still do? Our society is a great one, but regrettably some of those in power, the "weak ones", find it much easier to align themselves with those who are quick to make decisions, reach conclusions without facts. Sorry to say, some of our leaders are weak in character, don't have the strength to yell out "Before we reach any decision, we afford the defendant, the opportunity to be heard." They are the ones who follow the route to afford them the most notoriety.

This picture is before us in everyday life, some of our state governors and state senators in too many cases, turn their backs on God to follow the largest number of votes. However, God will not permit injustices to flourish ad infinitum...

Sincerely,
Neil

*   *   *

May 23, 2003

Dear Father McCarthy,

...You may not remember us. But I felt I had to write and let you know that we have faith in you and know that you will be completely exonerated of all allegations. We knew you when you were at

St. Michael's... All four of our boys went [there].
Bill our oldest and Frank were altar boys. Dan and
Raymond are the youngest. And at no time were you
ever not respected and loved by the parishioners.
...Please know that you are in our prayers and are
confident all will work out for you.

Fondly,
Pat & Henry Rafferty

P.S. God bless you and give you the strength needed
to face this tragic situation.

$$* \quad * \quad *$$

August 22, 2003

Dear Fr. McCarthy,
   ...I want you to know that we think of you often
and pray that you are doing well.
   ...We miss you very much. We will never forget
your compassion and thoughtfulness all the time
that Chad Eden, our grandson, was dying.
   ...Take care of yourself and maybe someday we
will see you again.

Sincerely,
Mary Bertolo and Family

$$* \quad * \quad *$$

Date: [NONE]

Dear Fr. McCarthy,
   ...We have never doubted your innocence and want
to thank you for your service and dedication. Your
sermons were always inspirational and "right on".
We will miss them and your humor too.
   ...We hope your illness will be resolved soon.
However you choose to spend your retirement, know
that we at St. Rose will always remember you.

26

Best wishes,
Sara & Salvatore Sorce

* * *

April 19, 2003

Dear Msgr. McCarthy:
...I want to take this opportunity to tell you again, I believe you and know that you would not say you didn't do something if you did.
...In my eyes, you have always been a very holy man and you brought Jesus to your congregation as much as you could, whenever you could. While I was a member of your parish, I was strengthened constantly with all you did in bringing the Holy Spirit to my life and the lives of all your community.
...Your story is like Cardinal Bernadin's. I am hoping your name will be cleared of all wrong doing just like his was.
We will never know why these things happen but for some unknown reason it has and I pray God will give you His peace thru this trial. I will also pray for your accusers that they will tell the truth and let you have back the privileges due you as a Roman Catholic Priest...

Love and peace,
Rita DeRiancho

* * *

Date: [NONE]

Dear Father McCarthy,
...I was devastated at all that went on at St. Rose. I am unable to understand why anyone would want to hurt you.
You have been a wonderful pastor and served at Saint Rose so well all these years. I was so disappointed at the bishop's letter to keep you off

the property of St. Rose and to say that you could not represent yourself as a priest. That hurt. They don't even wait for your innocence to be proven.

...May God protect you and take care of you. We thank you so much for your great help to us when we needed it. We miss your homilies...

We pray that your illness is being arrested.

Sincerely,
John and Ann Buckelew

*   *   *

May 18, 2004

Dear Father McCarthy:

I am taking this moment to let you know that I, as well as others, are praying for you, that we do not believe any lies written about you in the papers, and that should you ever need anyone to vouch for you, you most certainly can depend on my entire family.

...Father McCarthy, we have all known you for many, many years, both my husband and myself, as well as our three children who are all adults now. You even married my daughter, Tracey. You've seen them through grammar school, high school and college, and we will never forget your kindness, integrity, and high moral standing.

...If ever there is anything any of us can do for you, you have but to ask and we will be there for you.

After I finish mailing this letter, I am writing a letter of recommendation to your bishop, attesting to your high moral values, as well as your utmost compassion.

Most Sincerely,
Marion Nugent

*   *   *

May 18, 2004
Ref: Father William McCarthy

Dear Bishop ...
    I wish to take this moment to write to you regarding Father William McCarthy.
    ...My husband and I, as well as our three children (two of whom are married with families of their own) have known Father McCarthy for many, many years...
    ...There is no way that any of us believe the vicious lies written about Father McCarthy, who has always proven himself to be of the highest moral integrity, as well as an extremely kind, compassionate man. We cannot say enough about this man.

Most Sincerely,
Mrs. Marion Nugent
Mr. Robert Nugent

*   *   *

I also want to thank all of the gracious people whose letters to me were not included. I wish I could have printed them all, but space limitations would not allow that. However, please know that all of you hold a special place in my heart. I don't know how I could have made it through my ordeal without your kind thoughts and strong belief in my innocence to keep me company. May God bless you in all ways and forever.

CHAPTER 6

COWARDICE

According to the gospel of St. Mark 6: 14-29, Herrod himself had ordered John the Baptist's arrest, and had him tied up and put in prison. Herrod did this because of Herrodias whom he had married; even though she was the wife of his bother, Philip. John the Baptist kept telling Herrod, "It isn't right for you to marry your brother's wife."

So Herrodias held a deep grudge against John and wanted to kill him, but she could not because of Herrod. Herrod was afraid of John because he knew that John was a good and holy man, and so he kept him safe. He liked to listen to John, even though he became greatly disturbed almost every time he heard John speak.

Finally Herrodias got her chance; it was on Herrod's birthday when he gave a feast for all the top government officials, the military chiefs, and the leading citizens of Galilee.

The daughter of Herrodias came in and danced, which immensely pleased Herrod and his guests; so the king said to the girl, "What would you like to have?" With many vows he said to her: "I swear that I will give you anything you ask for, even as much as half my kingdom!"

So the girl went out and said to her mother, "What shall I ask for?"

"The head of John the Baptist," Herrodias answered.

The girl hurried back at once to the king and demanded: "I want you to give me here and now the head of John the Baptist on a plate!"

This made the king very sad, but he could not refuse her because of the vows he had made in front of all his guests. So he sent off a guard at once with orders to "Bring John's head to me." The guard left; went to the prison and cut off John's head. Then he brought it on a plate and gave it to the girl, who gave it to her mother.

When John's disciples heard about this, they came and retrieved his body and buried it. (Mark 6: 14-29)

*   *   *

As the saying goes, "There is no fury like a woman scorned." Herrodias was scorned by John the Baptist and she was furious, and subsequently had a vendetta against John and was out to get him. In my case, as I mentioned earlier, two women, as Detective Reedy eventually admitted, had a vendetta against me. They went to the prosecutor's office and accused me of having molested two little sisters between six and seven years old, well over 20 years prior. And while I have no definite proof, it is my firm *belief* that it was these same two women who also concocted the anonymous letter with the same accusation that was mailed to my bishop.

The detective's files on the case were also sent to my bishop, who censured me and in effect executed my soul. The bishop as it were gave my head to these women. And they achieved their goal, leaving me an emotional basket case. These women protected themselves from a lawsuit by hiring a lawyer to stranglehold these girls and prevent them from revealing the plot against me. That lawyer threatened the diocese with a lawsuit if the diocese turned over the files against me. Now I was in a "Catch 22" dilemma: an innocent man, but no matter which way I turned, I was without any means at my disposal to get myself out of the situation.

It is one foot forward and two feet backward. My two civil lawyers are frustrated in their efforts to exonerate me: the diocese is constantly stonewalling.

In the gospel of John 7:51, Nicodemus spoke up to say, "Since when does our law condemn anyone without first hearing him and knowing the facts?"

Why was I not brought before the diocese board; the very board set up for this purpose? My bishop did not question my accusers. He took the word of a detective bent on destroying me, even without probable cause or a reliable witness. I was not formally accused by the civil authorities, I was never charged with, let alone convicted of a crime; and yet the very institution that claims to be the ultimate defender of justice, unjustly condemned me, an innocent man, denying me my basic human rights. My bishop did a despicable thing that is extraordinarily damaging to me. The bishop acts as if he is above the law. Like Herrod, my bishop doesn't want to "lose face" with his advisors, and against his own convictions he set out to make himself look good at my horrific expense. Just get me out of the way so he will have one less problem in an atmosphere of panic within the Church hierarchy, who are constantly under media scrutiny for failure in the past to remove guilty priests who did enormous damage to children under their care.

Shortly before my false accusation, all of the bishops of the USA had met in Dallas and drew up a charter as a guideline for bishops on how to proceed in the case of a priest accused. All that was necessary was a letter or a phone call to the diocese accusing a priest of wrongful behavior. The diocese was excused from investigating the accusation; the mere accusation was enough to destroy a priest. Priests, especially pastors, often get anonymous letters complaining about the most trivial things. In the past, most of these letters were not taken seriously and were quickly discarded. Now, at a time when sexual misconduct permeates the air waves and inundates the media, some people bent on revenge against a priest see the opportunity to really hurt that priest.

In my case, an anonymous letter was sent to the diocese signed with a fictitious name. After looking at yearbooks, the prosecutor's office determined that they believed the author of the letter was a former student of St. Rose of Lima Academy named Shana. When detectives interviewed Shana in her home, she vehemently denied writing the letter, and further said she had informed the prosecutor's office that she did not write the letter. She concluded that she "Gave no information about inappropriate activity by Father McCarthy." She also was of the opinion that the prosecutor's office had no basis for this allegation, and was on a fishing expedition. My attorney, Gerry Rooney, wrote to the diocesan attorney stating, "It would appear that the case against Father McCarthy has not been substantiated and may have begun with fictitious and inaccurate information."

My attorney went on to say, "Moreover, there is information that the Snedo's have also denied anything happened. If so, the entire case against Father McCarthy is false and of course extraordinarily damaging."

So I keep asking, "Who wrote the anonymous letter?" The big question is, was there ever an anonymous letter? If there was, it is my assumption that it was written by one of those women who were plotting against me.

CHAPTER 7

SILVER LINING?

This indescribably malicious attack on me, in a strange, unusual way was a blessing, and had a silver lining in the midst of dark clouds. In the early days of my priesthood, I began to be known as the "building pastor." To the surprise of the community, the parish and the school were growing rapidly. I was receiving a lot of praise and applause. I was further honored by being made Monsignor. Very often in ceremonies I was like the first robin of spring, walking around in my red robe, proud as a peacock. Without realizing it, I was becoming pompous and haughty. I was losing sight of the humble, suffering Jesus, and in a matter of a few weeks I was humbled beyond imagination. I became living proof that "Pride comes before a fall."

In one swift moment I was cast off my pedestal and trampled on, falsely accused of a despicable crime. My mind became my torture. Instead of my mind being the superb instrument of creativity and happiness it had always been, my mind became very distraught. It had taken me over and I became its slave. It was as if it was possessed by evil negative thoughts and I could not find the "off" button. I went into deep worry with feelings of anxiety and depression. I began to get a totally desolate view of life. I became a victim of my childhood wounds.

*   *   *

I was the second youngest of 11 children. My family was incredibly busy running a butcher business, a milk service, and a farm in Ireland. With so many older siblings successfully competing for our parents' attention, I felt I was invisible. And unconsciously I made a decision as a child: *In order to be loved, I would have to earn it.* I would have to accomplish something very special. I decided that I could not be loved for myself, but only for what I achieved.

I became extremely studious, studying day and night. I graduated from high school with honors, and I continued to push forward, day and night, to achieve my childhood dream of becoming a priest. In the seminary I excelled in grabbing most of the awards at my final exam. I was given the nickname "Tulet" (winning) McCarthy.

The most memorable day of my life was being ordained a priest of God on June 8, 1963. The ordination took place in St. Patrick's seminary in Ireland for the diocese of Paterson.

A month later, Monsignor John P. McHugh, welcomed me at Kennedy Airport and brought me directly to my first assignment as associate pastor of St. Patrick's Church in Chatham, New Jersey.

Monsignor William Looney was my first pastor. He welcomed me with open arms and immediately put me to work, telling me to put on my cassock and go into church and hear confessions. I had never heard confessions before and this was my first time. I walked into the church and at least 50 people were lined up along the wall waiting for this greenhorn to hear their sins and give them absolution.

I was not prepared for the experience. Many of my penitents were scrupulous and kept repeating and exaggerating their sins over and over again. At the end of the confessional period I was completely exhausted.

I went back to the rectory where the cook, the pastor's sister, all dressed in green, had prepared a huge Irish dinner of corned beef and cabbage. It was my first meal in America, and everything was done up in green: the tablecloth, the napkins, and the plate. I'll bet at the time I was literally turning green in the face; even my bed sheets and pillowcases were green. There was no doubt in my mind that a special effort had been made for my benefit, and this was all part of the "welcome wagon" for a newly arrived Irish priest.

My pastor, Monsignor Bill Looney, was a charmer, always praising me and telling me his wonderful jokes (and some not so wonderful). He had a quick, sharp sense of humor. I remember sitting at the dining room table one day for lunch, when the phone rang. The woman at the other end said: "Monsignor, would you be having lunch at this time?"

He swiftly replied: "No, we usually have a piano lesson at this time."

One time, the nuns of the parish where badgering him to buy a new car, their first. He resisted. But when a parishioner called the pastor and said, "Monsignor Looney, I hear you are buying something..." Monsignor's answer was: "Yes, we are buying a sightseeing bus for the home of the blind in Morristown."

Another day, a particularly bothersome lady came into the office and asked Monsignor Looney for an unusual favor. When he told her he could not oblige, she became belligerent, so he politely asked her to leave. On the way out, she turned and yelled at him, "If I was married to you, I would give you poison."

He shouted back, "If I was married to you, I would take it."

He told me the story of his first assignment at Assumption Church in Morristown, NJ. He knocked at the rectory door. The old, near-deaf housekeeper opened the door and said, "Who are you?"

"I am the new curate," he replied, "and I have been assigned here by the bishop."

"What did you say?" she yelled.

"I am Looney," he shouted back, realizing she was hard of hearing, "and I am the new curate."

To that she replied, "Sure, come right in, you will feel right at home with the other loonies we have here."

Another time, he was upset at a parishioner's rude behavior and said to him, "You know, I never forget a face, but in your case I'd be glad to make an exception."

It was always a joy to work alongside Monsignor Bill Looney, and after two years being his associate, when he died suddenly, I was brokenhearted.

A short while later Monsignor John Shanley was appointed pastor. He was also a lovable guy. We bonded like father and son. I used to call him "Cardinal Spellman." I thought he looked exactly like him. One day I received a letter from Bishop Casey telling me that I was going to be transferred to St. Nicholas in Passaic, New Jersey. I was shocked and when I was leaving St. Patrick's, Monsignor Shanley and I cried like babies.

I moved to the inner city and the pastor, Father Charles Cassidy, gave me a great welcome. All around the rectory were poor minorities living in humble conditions. It was the 1960s; and rioting, looting and burning were the norm in the cities; and so it was in Passaic. With great zeal I got involved in the inner-city programs to help the poor and disenfranchised. With the Council of Churches and Synagogues we started a "home vacation" program for the inner-city kids. We sought out well-to-do suburban families to take an inner-city minority kid into their home for the summer. It helped greatly and produced a lot of good will.

We also organized a food basket event. The gym at St. Nicholas was packed to the ceiling with canned food, turkeys, fruit and vegetables, etc. But during the night, kids from the projects came to the building, broke in, and it was a free for all. When I went to the hall in the morning, it was totally cleaned out. *Well,* I thought, *the stuff was for them anyhow. I guess it was just a form of "self service."*

Two years into my assignment at St. Nicholas, Bishop Casey felt that the pastor was not doing enough for the inner-city and the pastor was moved. I was not happy with this decision, so I requested to be moved also. Parishioners from the Third Ward objected to the moves and many heated demonstrations took place outside the church and in front of the chancery office.

In the end, the pastor, Father Cassidy, Father Murphy and I were sent to new assignments anyway. I was assigned to St. Michaels in Netcong. I joked that I was being sent to Hong Kong. It was way out in the country. I went there with the new pastor, Father Jim Doyle. We got along famously; he was a former chaplain of the Navy. One Halloween I donned his Navy uniform and went from door to door in the parish. People got a big kick out of it. But when Father Doyle heard of my caper, he wasn't so amused. But with time he finally saw the humor and came to forgive me.

Netcong is practically an Italian town, and I became more Italian than the Italians themselves. A little elderly Italian lady, Mary Stracco, adopted me as her son. She was a real blessing in my life. During my time at St. Michaels my birth mother died in Ireland—a little part of me died with her.

Many times I have a flashback to when I was eight years old. I came home from school one day and asked where Mom was. My older sister told me that she had been rushed to a hospital and was not expected to live. I almost died myself and felt incredibly abandoned. There was nothing I could do to help and I spent most of my time looking out the front window, wishing that my mom would come home. After a few weeks my family took me to the hospital. Seeing my mom again, breathing on her own, was life-giving for me. I might not have survived emotionally if my mom had died at that time. I honestly believe that my intense prayers to God helped to heal my mom.

Left to right: my sister Pam, Mom, and myself. Notice the curl in front of my brow. I hated it and my mom thought I looked cute with it. Pam was very shy, as you can see. At this stage I was an extrovert.

Giving my first blessing as a priest to my mother, immediately after my ordination.

Blessing my sister, Mona, immediately after my ordination.

NEWSPAPER ARTICLE [EXCERPTED]:

Thursday, August 3, 1972

A GIFT OF A ROSE

There is a quiet young man in our midst and he is quietly doing a marvelous thing for our young people. At least on Saturday night we know the St. Michael's coffeehouse represents the heart and spirit of Father McCarthy who serves us in a project that is so vital to our youth.

...Father McCarthy, you are one of God's chosen. As a young man you are sharing your own soul and the soul of God with these teenagers. And I know many parents of the same teenagers must be very happy you came to [our town]. It is a sad commentary that it is rare to find a grown-up who can understand and work with the coming generation. I do marvel at the simplicity with which you relate God to them, and the earnestness with which they receive.

I know your genuineness and trust in them rubs off in their minds, which are perhaps bewildered by the things they face today as young men and women.

...Would you, Father, with my deepest regards... accept from [our newspaper] "The Rose of the Week?"

...And maybe sometime, while hardened individuals such as I, who sees constantly all the inhumanities of man; that visits the courts and the police, and roams the town in the wee hours; who sees all the heartaches and hurts, and the beaten and the maimed, which in turn has its effect on me, maybe I could come to you sometime and learn more of what I thought I already knew.

The Editor

*   *   *

After five years of ministry at St. Michaels, I was transferred to St. Cecilia in Rockaway, New Jersey. The housekeeper, Mary, was the boss and she ruled everyone with an iron fist. But not to be denied his authority, the pastor,

Monsignor Dennis Hayes, was notorious for getting rid of curates after a very short time. He had a German Sheppard that chased everyone away, and parishioners would often show me bites on their hands and legs. Monsignor Hayes was a very depressed man. He refused to accept the changes in the Church after Vatican II, and some people were even afraid of him. But to me, he merely appeared to be depressed most of the time.

Surprisingly, when I arrived at the parish, I found him very accepting of me. I could feel his pain and I spent many long hours talking to him. I finally invited him to a charismatic meeting at St. Michaels in Netcong, my former parish. I almost had to drag him to the meeting. He sat down just inside of the door, as if plotting his quick escape, very suspicious of this new movement in the Church. But I could soon tell he liked the music. I noticed him tapping his toe to the beat. After the prayer meeting, Mary Stracco introduced herself to him and gave him a book on the charismatic movement.

Monsignor Hayes came home very excited. That very next Friday he went to the prayer meeting at Convent Station conducted by Father Jim Ferry. From that day on, Monsignor Hayes never missed a meeting. He was baptized in the spirit and it changed his life. He was happy again and began to "loosen up" in the Church. He shocked the people with the change in him. He began to celebrate Mass with exuberance and joy. He was truly "born again."

The housekeeper, Mary, on the other hand, was not pleased and reprimanded me for changing him. I never did learn what her problem was and no matter how hard I tried, I never was able to get through to her, even with all the love and acceptance I poured on.

At one stage, Monsignor Hayes got on the pulpit and apologized to the people for his past angry behavior. He asked that if anyone was offended by his mean actions, they should come to his office and he would personally apologize to them.

It was an amazing transformation: he continued to grow in his spirit, and he remains completely optimistic even as he lives in the Little Sisters of the Poor nursing home in the Paterson diocese, now close to 100 years old. I could not believe it when he called me on his cell phone one Sunday to say that he was in church and God inspired him to call and thank me for changing his life and giving him happiness. It was one of the most astonishing phone calls I've ever received.

* * *

It was only six months later, in February of 2003, that my life was turned upside down by the horribly false accusation. I was stripped of my dignity and thrown to the dogs. In 2002, I had applied to my bishop to get permission to retire after 40 years of service. The rule was: a priest could retire with full benefits at 40 years ordained. And you needed to apply a year before. The bishop had graciously granted my request; after 40 years I was looking forward to a happy and peaceful retirement. Little did I know that evil forces were at work to destroy me. The timing could not have been more mind-boggling. Almost simultaneously with the date of my long awaited retirement, the awful attack on me erupted, and my life was changed forever.

CHAPTER 8

THE TWILIGHT ZONE

For me, personally, the accusation is worse than it would be for most people. My life happiness depends on achievement and recognition. I identify my self-worth with my standing among life friends and loving acceptance. Now I am stripped of that, and I feel destroyed, as if all the good I did in my life has evaporated in a single instant. I feel overwhelmingly sad at the loss and am going through painful grief. The whole ordeal is a process of shock, anger, denial, and bargaining with God; but never acceptance. But I will fight till the very end, if I have to, to be exonerated. As Shakespeare said:

> He who steals my purse steals trash;
> T'was mine, t'is his, its gone;
> But he who steals my good name
> Takes something of great value which enriches him not at all
> And leaves me very poor indeed.

My thinking has become dysfunctional. The present moment hardly exists. Only the past and future seems important to me. I have an unconscious compulsion to keep the past alive, because without it, who am I? I look at the future through the eyes of the past, because my preoccupation with what happened to me I cannot find the present moment. My mind is grown into a monster. My life has been derailed. The plan is no longer mine and at this moment I've entered a profound moment of crisis. Why am I here? What am I meant to do? I've often told people in grief to "Let go, let God." I am now myself confronted with the deepest reality of life's loss. The awful feeling of loss has invited me to get closer to God. I keep repeating the Alcoholic Anonymous prayer, "Lord, grant me the strength to accept the things I can't change, to change the things I can, and the wisdom to know the difference." I feel numb, sad, angry and lonely. I keep asking myself: "Will I ever feel normal again?" I am anxious being alone. I need friends to be with me constantly. I need some distractions to keep me busy. I am far removed from my ordinary way of being.

I often think that I am losing my mind. Somebody once said: "Abnormal behavior in abnormal circumstances is normal." I go about my present life all the while storming through a wide range of emotions and constantly ask myself: "Will I ever return to normalcy?" Comforting passages of scripture keep coming to me, especially the passage that Jesus uttered: "Come to me all of you who find life weary and burdensome and I will refresh you." (Matthew: 11:28)

I am consumed by a pain greater than I could ever have imagined. I feel torn apart and am experiencing a terrible sense of isolation. My grief has hurled me into an unknown place, caught up in a time warp, in a twilight zone, in a place I have not been, and which I do not recognize.

As a priest who ministered to people for forty years, I was especially prone to fear of people being disappointed in me. I was, after all, accused of a heinous crime that must be very painful for people to hear. Sometimes I will hear through the "grapevine" about people who believed I was guilty and would angrily condemn me. Then of course, what was even more painful was when people began to expand the story and make it sound worse than it supposedly was. Sometimes people would mention names of gossipers and I would remember some of those people who I personally "stood up for" in the past. One case was especially hurtful to me. This particular woman (I am going to call her Jane) was sued by a family for abusing their child in the cafeteria of the school by slapping the little boy in the face. Jane was devastated and asked me to intercede for her. I went to the family that was suing Jane and pleaded with them to drop the charges, which they did. Now, a few years later, I am falsely accused and Jane has become my most vocal critic, even making up stories I never even heard of.

I find myself in a place which I do not understand. I am afraid, where am I? What has happened? Will I be lost here forever? What is going to happen to me? What's worse, I can still see into the normal world. People's lives swirl by in their routines of work, play, and prayer. There are colors and music out there, and laughter. The familiar is in the air; all right, all that was only a few days ago, I was a part of it, but no longer. Now I am here in this terrifying desolation and I just can't rejoin the other world, though it is tantalizingly close by, and all around me, but so far away. So I am frightened, hurting, and intolerably alone in the place of my pain. I seek refuge in a psalm:

PSALM 31:
Have pity on me, O Lord, for I am in distress;
With sorrow my eye is consumed;
My soul also, and my body.
For my life is spent with grief and my years with sighing;
My strength has failed through affliction,
And my bones are consumed.
For all my foes, I am an object of reproach,
A laughingstock to my neighbors,
And a dread to my friends;
They who see me abroad flee from me;
I am forgotten like the unremembered dead:
I am like a dish that is broken.
I hear whispers of the crowd
That frightened me from every side,
As they consult together against me...
But my trust is in you, O Lord;
I say, "You are my God."
In your hands is my destiny; rescue me from
The clutches of my enemies and my persecutors.
Let your face shine on your servant; save me in your kindness.

Though it seems a torment to see the other world and not to be able to be a part of it, there is grace there. It reminds me that the familiar and comfortable still exists. It gives me brief instances of pleasures to know that others have loved and suffered, and have recovered. That is the promise. Deep in the recesses of my heart I maintain the faith that the beauty I have known can be mine again—even though in some ways it will be different.

CHAPTER 9

DISORIENTATION

During this conflict, I feel I have lost my bearings. While experiencing this loss, I feel like I'm in the position of a sailor, in the middle of the ocean, whose compass has gone haywire on a cloudy night. I simply and frighteningly have lost my sense of direction. I've begun to experience brief memory loss and have an inability to concentrate or make simple decisions. I become dislocated and confused. I walk into a room and suddenly cannot recall why I am there. I may make a phone call and as I hear the ringing on the other end, I cannot remember who it is I am calling.

I am in mid ocean with a broken compass, and the clouds are covering the stars. I am still waiting for the sun to rise. I feel incompetent and unsure of myself. I realize that I am off-center and I've begun to wonder if I will ever be back on center again. Has something mendable been permanently broken within me? I doubt my ability to become a loving, giving, and functioning person again. I wonder if I have lost it for good. I find myself doubting others. How can they not see what I am going through? Have they just stopped caring? Did they really care at all?

*   *   *

This is difficult for me to admit, but I must be unwaveringly honest in all my journal entries: Sometimes I doubt God, after all, if God is such a loving parent, how can this be allowed to happen? Why is God letting me fall apart? Or is God even real? Why is my bishop so cruel and insensitive, more like a vicious wolf, than a loving shepherd of the flock of Christ? He trampled on my basic rights as a human being. He denied me the due process of Canon Law, and ignored my pleadings for a hearing. The whole situation seems like a freight train out of control and nobody can stop it. The bishop is determined to destroy me, and his associates egg him on and "hold his coat," while he psychologically stones me to death. The bishop and his associates are on a witch hunt to destroy as many priests as they can, guilty or innocent. This is a modern-day Inquisition. I am not certain if and when I will emerge from this attack and psychological stoning.

I pray: *God, I am confused. I am spinning out of control and I can't seem to help myself at all, why? Why am I acting this way? Help me please! I feel so helpless; I doubt myself in ways I have never doubted before. I am wondering if I'll ever be me again. Be with me in my confusion! Be my rock in this tumbling world! Be my strength! For I have none of my own.*

* * *

After the WWII, at Ravenstruck Concentration Camp, found inside the clothing of a dead child was this prayer: "O Lord, remember not only the men and women of good will, but also those of ill will. But do not remember all of the suffering they have inflicted upon me. Instead, remember the fruits I have borne because of my suffering; that got rid of my sins of superiority and of pride. When my persecutors come to be judged by you, let all of those fruits I have borne be their forgiveness."

* * *

In times of depression I fell to the ground. Tears poured down my face. I was weak and divided and I remembered everything that I couldn't forget. I remembered the accusation and the awfulness of it all; the destruction of my character, the lack of sleep, the shame of being accused of such a heinous crime, and my overwhelming sadness. I cried until I had no more tears. My eyes literally hurt and were red and swollen.

I am ashamed to say it now, but I wanted the agony of living to stop and to be relieved of this psychological pain—too deep for words. My heart was in a frantic search for God. How can I find Him in the midst of my confusion? I was anxious all the time; jumped out of my skin when the doorbell would ring. I became terrified when children were around. Would someone accuse me of even being near them? My future was hopeless having constant panic attacks while driving or just walking in the mall. I'd jump at every unfamiliar sound and found myself spiraling into a dark and life-altering abyss. Battling a false accusation of an unspeakable crime perpetuated by evil people in the highest positions of my diocese with impunity; relishing the thought of destroying me. All the time knowing without doubt that I was completely innocent. That in anyone's estimation should be considered an assault on the body of Christ—the Church; crucifying Christ all over again, just because they could.

I have heard it said that it matters little what happens to you, but it matters greatly how you respond to what happens to you. Hope not only springs eternal, but is available to everybody, no matter what may come their way. Personally, I am determined to stay hopeful; that somehow, sometime, some way, justice will come my way, I will be exonerated and free to live life to the fullest, never again to take life for granted.

CHAPTER 10

LOVE, ACCEPTANCE, FORGIVENESS

What is most mind-boggling to me is best summed up by the phrase, "How quickly we forget." I came out in full support of my bishop a year earlier when he was besieged with threats and accusations due to questionable steps he had taken. My former bishop had transferred out a priest from within his diocese who had been accused of molesting not one but several individuals. One of his accusers, an alleged victim, Mark Semano, was convinced that the bishop knew the priest was an abuser of children, but transferred him anyway.

In the year 2002, I wrote to the editor of the Star Ledger in defense of my bishop, who was constantly under attack by Mark Semano:

```
Dear Editor:
    Mark Semano's rightful unrelenting attack against
the priest that abused him has blinded him to his
abuse of my bishop. After all, pedophiles have no
conscience, no empathy for the pain caused to others.
Now it seems he has decided to show no empathy to
my bishop; he has no regard for how hurt he must
feel. You continue to re-wound him every chance you
get. Jesus said, "Has no one condemned you? Neither
will I; go and sin no more." A bishop is a shepherd,
schooled to heal and reconcile. When the Church
reassigns priests that have committed a pedophile
crime, they first send him away for counseling. In
the past, this compulsion was relatively unknown.
To claim that bishops willfully transferred these
sick individuals knowing that they would continue
```

this abuse is false. My bishop, and any bishop for that matter, never intentionally put the children under their care in danger. Mark Semano should have compassion for a compassionate man. I know of no more pastoral bishop than mine. He is the quintessential shepherd, with an untiring mission to constantly reach out to his people. This abuse by the priests under his jurisdiction has caused him indescribable pain and sadness. To add to this hurt is cruel and insensitive on Mark Semano's part, enough is enough.

Signed,
Monsignor William McCarthy, Pastor
St. Rose of Lima Church

* * *

A letter written by a close friend of mine, Father Jack Catoir, deserves printing in this book because it was a great comfort to me and hundreds of other people [EXCERPTED]:

CAUTION SUPERCEDES RUSH TO JUDGEMENT — by Father John Catoir
   ...I [have] campaigned for a "one strike and you're out" policy to rid the Church of priest pedophiles long before the bishop voted for it. Child abuse is a despicable crime. Pope John Paul said it well, "There is no room in the priesthood for those who abuse children."
   ...Part of my rage against this crime comes from a bad memory from childhood. I was once abused by a priest. It happened in the confessional, believe it or not. I resisted and went home crying in a state of shock. In my fear and confusion I buried the story, never telling a soul.
   So, when I read a letter to the editor criticizing me for trying to abolish the new policy designed to protect children, I had to laugh. I forgive those who might have misjudged me. I see in him the same rage felt myself many years ago.

50

Nevertheless, I believe that the time for healing must now begin. The bishops began cleaning up their act in 1990 when the first wave of scandal began. It is interesting to note that the lawyer who defended 185 victims in the Kentucky class action suit a few months ago said that of the 185 individuals he represented, only one case involved a crime that had happened since the year 1990. All others occurred many years before.

So the new policies are working. We simply have to keep refining the policy to protect the innocent against false accusations.

...We are called by God to presume innocence until all the facts are in. In our zeal to correct a horrible crime of child abuse we have to be on guard against destroying the reputation of any good priest who might be falsely accused...

...[this] happened to Cardinal Joseph Bernadin. Sometimes it takes a year or more to resolve the case. In the process the presumption of guilt continues to mount. We have to be extremely cautious in these matters so as not to judge too hastily. In order to eliminate one terrible evil, we should not allow another one to take its place. The presumption of innocence is a God-given right as well as a legal right in American law.

...Less than two percent of the priests have proven to be pedophiles. We pray for their victims. We also pray for the good priests who have had to suffer in a different way because of these few bad apples. All of us need to forgive our sick brothers because the Lord asks it of us. We also need to trust the good priests among us. They have chosen a life of service and altruism, and they deserve our respect and loyalty.

∗ ∗ ∗

Taxiing down the tarmac, the jetliner abruptly stopped and returned to the gate. After waiting more than an hour the plane finally took off. A concerned passenger asked what had happened. "The pilot was concerned about a noise he heard in the engine," the flight attendant calmly explained. "It took us all this time to find another pilot."

The truth can be terrifying, sobering and, if nothing else inconvenient. Facing the truth often demands change on our part, a change of perspective, attitude, lifestyle, approach. To be a person of authentic faith means to face and seek out the truth, regardless of the consequences, regardless of the cost to our egos or wallets, regardless of our doubts and cynicism and fear. To live our faith means to live the truth about love, justice, and forgiveness with integrity and conviction, no matter what the cost or consequences. Seeking and following the truth begins with embracing the spirit of truth, the wisdom, the wholeness, the love of God, who is the first, and the last and the constant reality.

CHAPTER 11

A WOUNDED CHURCH

Around the year 2001, the media was constantly reporting disturbing news of priests abusing children. I was very upset and outraged and I wrote a message for my parish bulletin:

A Wounded Church – by Father Wm. McCarthy

On September 11, 2001, our nation was severely wounded by the terrorists attack on America. It was a defining moment in all of our lives and we were changed forever. However, instead of dividing us, it brought us closer together as a people. Heroes surfaced and made us even more proud. We continue to rise from the ashes and rebuild our nation and our lives.

And now, unfortunately, our beloved Church is deeply wounded. Accusations of sexual abuse by priests are sweeping across the Church. Those shocking revelations are shaking the Church to its foundation. It is the greatest scandal ever to hit the Church. We are all wounded by those revelations. It is beyond our comprehension that a priest of God would commit such a heinous crime. Jesus said: "Anyone who scandalizes a little child, it would be better if a millstone would be tied around their neck and he drowned in the bottom of the sea."

Why then would a man of God stoop so low and

endanger his own salvation? Psychologists tell us that pedophiles have an uncontrollable compulsion to move toward committing this horrific act. As young men they were aware of this inordinate tendency and felt very uncomfortable and even frightened. They reasoned that if they became a priest, ordination would erase this sinful compulsion and they could live an upright life, free from pain and confusion. Unfortunately that was an illusion —ordination does not change a person's basic nature.

Consequently, now they find themselves in even greater jeopardy. They are in a tug of war between the world, flesh, and the Devil. For a pedophile the flesh always wins. It is an incurable mental condition, a danger to any child in their custody.

In the past, bishops believed that after the priests received psychological counseling, they would be cured, and could be reassigned to another parish. That was a terrible mistake, as the priest was now free to continue their sick behavior. The whole priesthood is now under a dark cloud and the Church itself is severely wounded like our nation. In order to rise from the ashes, we have to make a more concerted effort to remove pedophiles from the priesthood. The pedophiles are in a sense, terrorists disguised as men of God, ready to hit again at any moment the most innocent among us. The powers that be in the Church must be scrupulously vigilant in protecting innocent children at all costs.

Many Americans asked after the September 11 tragedy: "How come the CIA, FBI, and the best law enforcement agencies in the world could let these evil people slip through their fingers and commit the greatest crime in this nation's history?" Many people asked the same question of our shepherds: "How could they be so unaware of this dangerous threat to the people under their care? Putting in effect a 'fox in the chicken coop.'" It is my understanding that Rome has recognized that a man ordained with this mental condition has in fact

an impediment against receiving the sacrament of
ordination itself; and therefore are not priests at
all and the ordination is null and void.

* * *

How ironic that a year and a half later, I am accused of a similar crime. It
quickly occurred to me that innocent priests could also be victims of this
horrible crime. I now find myself embroiled in a never-ending battle trying to
prove my innocence. To my consternation, I have concluded that I may never
be exonerated inside the Church. The process is too impotent and incapable
of removing the accusation from anyone.

When I finally retained a civil lawyer, Gerry Rooney, he wrote a
condemnatory letter against my bishop and sent it to Rome. A copy was
sent to my canon lawyer, Dr. Michael Riordan, and I was dropped like a hot
potato. Dr. Riordan told me that I made him look like a fool in Rome and he
went on to berate me for going over his head.

I realize now that my canon lawyer was nothing more than a lackey of
my bishop, hired by him and paid by him to do nothing more than control
me for the bishop to do with me what he wishes, which is to evaporate my
life. I am being victimized over and over again. I am frightened to look at
the news on TV. I am unable to read newspapers. To pick up my mail is
tremendously unnerving. I still often shake with uncontrollable nervousness
when I open letters that appear to be threatening. Driving on the highways is
really difficult, I cannot focus on the road and often cars begin blowing their
horns to me as I unconsciously go over the lane on which I am driving.

* * *

On July 21, 2003, my canon lawyer received a copy of a letter from my bishop
that was sent to Rome demanding the removal of my priesthood.

CHAPTER 12

THE TEARING DOWN

It even further demoralized me when the new regime took over after my retirement. They became almost compulsive maniacs, driven by some mysterious force to tear down my reputation and everything that reminded them of me. They fired or demoted my most admired and treasured employees, humiliating them with crude and insensitive language. Almost immediately they demolished the setup of the administrative offices and removed my official portrait from the lobby. They tore down the recently constructed walls and statues of the sanctuary, and repainted the entire church a new color. They removed statues from outside the church and threw them in the garbage. They frequently talked about "poor Saint Rose" and claimed that the finances were dismal.

The truth was, before 9/11 and the 64% raise in salary of the teachers in the schools, the collapse of the stock market and the corporate scandals, the parish had a surplus of $700,000 invested. Our parish accountant of 23 years, Gene Gromaek, gave the new regime a clear explanation of why our healthy financial picture changed rapidly into a deficit, citing the reasons I already mentioned above.

The new regime ignored the explanation and told everyone that the old regime had run the finances poorly. They humiliated Ron DeSena, the head of the financial committee of the parish council. Ron DeSena is one of my most revered friends; he was truly Mr. Saint Rose. He recognized the importance of the parish council and made it operate like a corporate body, a well oiled machine. He ran a very elegant golf tournament that raised significant funds for St. Rose of Lima Academy. He was in effect my right-hand man in administrating the parish. He made untold sacrifices to be present at almost every function of the parish. The parish built a new addition to the school in the Early Childhood Center. It gave me great pleasure to dedicate the building to Ron DeSena, christened and named The Ron DeSena Annex.

MY PARISH HOME
ST. ROSE of LIMA CHURCH, EAST HANOVER, NJ

ATTITUDE
by
Charles Swindoll

"The longer I live, the more I realize the impact of attitude on life. Attitude, to me, is more important than facts. It is more important than the past, than education, and money, than circumstances, and failures, than success is, than what other people think or say or do. It is more important than appearance, giftedness or skill. It will make or break a company...a church...a home. The remarkable thing is we have a choice every day regarding the attitude we will embrace for that day. We cannot change our past...we cannot change the fact that people will act a certain way. We cannot change the inevitable. The only thing we can do is play on the one string we have, and that is our best attitude...I am convinced that life is 10% what happens to me and 90% how I react to it. And so it is with you...we are in charge of our attitudes."

The following poem was composed by the school staff on February 8, 1982. I cannot tell you how deeply it touched my heart when it was presented to me.

P.S. My given Celtic name is Liam. While I changed it to the anglicized version, William, when I came to America, many close friends preferred to address me by the original.

Father Liam is our pastor and friend,
He is always available, too
He cares about us one and all.
His love for us always shines through.
As a friend he helps where he is needed,
He does the very best he can do.
He shows a special love for his job,
He is loyal, hardworking and true.
As a pastor, he speaks the Word of God,
To the parish and students of all schools.
He preaches all the words of the Father
And he helps us obey the golden rules.
We thank God for sending
Father Liam to Saint Rose.
We'll love him while he is here,
And we'll pray he never goes.

—Your children at St. Rose School
Catholic Schools Week; February 8-12, 1982

CHAPTER 13

THE MAGIC OF PUPPETS

In 1976, when I was associate pastor of St. Cecilia is in Rockaway, New Jersey, I felt led by God to the puppet ministry. I purchased a home course on ventriloquism, and I quickly took to it, like a duck takes to water. For some reason it came easy to me. I found it helpful in bringing the Gospel message to children. One day a newspaper reporter slipped into the church during a mass in which I used puppets at the sermon time. Shortly afterward an extensive article appeared in the local newspaper. And after that publicity, people traveled miles to experience the puppet show. (Little did I know my reputation would later be used against me—when the two vindictive women told Detective Reedy that I used the puppets as a ruse to molest the two little sisters.)

[EXCERPTED]

"PRIEST SPREADS MESSAGE WITH PUPPETS"
by Laura Henning, Staff Writer; East Hanover Township, NJ
    It was not the usual puppet show when the Reverend William McCarthy, pastor of St. Rose of Lima church, approached the microphone with puppets in his hands. The setting was the sanctuary of the church, the event was a special children's Mass, and the students of Saint Rose of the parochial school were the audience.
    There was a certain spirit of levity but the message of love was serious. Later, talking about his

59

"puppet ministry," the priest in a voice reminiscent of his native County Cork, Ireland, explained that as far as he knew this was the only one in the Catholic Church.

...He finds the children relate well to his puppets. Rolly, his blond haired protagonist, is an imp who always contradicts his mentor. He is loath to act loving to his "sister" Connie a moppet-like puppet operated by Geralyn Candura, an eighth grader, and Patty Nostrame, a seventh grader. McCarthy noted that the students were on the shy side, but they have blossomed since taking in the shows.

...In the middle of McCarthy's talk with Rolly, up popped Molly from behind a marble lectern (operated by Susan Carroll, a sixth grader). Her recent performance was Carroll's first, and she admitted being "a little scared."

McCarthy proves to be an in-depth ventriloquist... He practiced alone in his room and "Neighbors would hear funny sounds coming from my room," he recalled with a smile...

...After the special mass at which the puppets gave the message, the students filed out on their way to class and several exclaimed: "Rolly is the best! He is number one!"

...Father McCarthy is indeed unique in the Catholic Church.

Puppet Ministry

Shown are many of the puppets I used in my ministry to the little ones of St. Rose, especially at the 9 o'clock children's Mass on Sundays. Rollie is the star and favorite of the puppets; Connie is his sister. The others are Grandma and Grandpa, Bird, Grouchy, and Doggie.

Jack Galvin's Speech to Fr. McCarthy

On behalf of the entire Search ministry here at St. Rose we would like to express our sincere thanks to Father McCarthy for sharing the vision of this program with our youth minister. this program could only have been possible by the support of our Pastor. When Search 1 was just a great vision but not yet a reality we had to approach Father in hopes to convince him that we needed a mansion and that mansion should be in Loveladies, and that mansion should be on a beautiful beach and it should be filled with many teenagers and those teenagers shall find God, many for the first time. Since Search had happened 8 times, reaching over 300 teenagers who's lives have been impacted by one beautiful weekend. Search has taught us all the important things that our high schools have left out. For one, it taught us that we need not worry if we don't find Jesus because you can be sure he will find you. It taught us that its not about how many friends we have but how many people we have been friends to and it doesn't matter how much money we earn but how much of it we may give. It taught us that today is temporary but what we accomplished today will last forever.

Search will never quite be the same without Father's speeches about reality, watching him walk on the beach with brother Frank and listening to us pouring out our hearts at confession. Father has been the rock on which this program began its building. Father always would say that when he was wrong everyone let him know but when he did something right no one said anything. Father, have we ever told you that you're our hero? Probably not but you truly are the wind beneath our wings.

–Search 1-8

Rev. Msgr. William McCarthy
*"The Wind
Beneath Our Wings"*

St. Rose of Lima
Search/Youth Ministry

One of several awards I received in recognition of my service to the youth community.

CHAPTER 14

DREADED DISEASE

At about seven years old, while I was being reared along with 10 siblings on a farm in Charlesville, County Cork, Ireland, my parents discovered an enlarged gland in my neck. They brought me to a doctor for tests and he diagnosed tuberculosis. My mom arranged for me to go to Mercy Hospital in Cork city for surgery to remove the gland. I spent a long time in the hospital. My most vivid memories of that time were twofold:

First, a beautiful nun, Sister Cecilia, a cousin by marriage "hovered" over me and gave me medical care and attention. Her glowing, beautiful face is as vivid to me now as back then, a lifetime ago.

Secondly, I remember looking out the window of my room at the River Lee meandering through Cork city. There, just below me, were a dozen or so swans swimming peacefully in the river. I was captivated by these beautiful creatures with their pure white feathers and regal long necks. For the rest of my life the swan remained my favorite bird, which I later discovered is recognized as the "Prince of Birds."

A short time after the TB gland was removed I felt this continuous throbbing in my shoulder. Even at my tender age of about eight years old, I knew instinctively that it was a flare-up of my tuberculosis. I was determined to fight it all by myself, and basically ignored it. One day a mobile X-ray unit came to my school. I was terrified: I hid so I would not be examined for TB. I thought, if I am diagnosed with TB, I will be sent to a sanitarium and isolated from society and then I could never achieve my dreams of becoming a priest. Fortunately, I was able to continue with my education and finally graduated from high school.

Thirty years later while getting a chest X-ray in the USA, the doctor informed me that my lungs were scarred like a plowed field—but it had calcified and I would be all right. Later I fell on my knees and thanked God for protecting me and helping me to stay on course to becoming a priest.

Reminiscent of my six-month stay, as a child, in Mercy Hospital, Cork City, Ireland; which was the first time I ever saw swans.

CHAPTER 15

THE SEMINARY

Through my mother's efforts and her contacts with the Ray family in Charlesville, Ireland, I was accepted into St. Patrick's College in Ireland. My family put me on a train and after several long hours, I finally arrived at the seminary. I remember distinctly walking through these huge gates and approaching that impressive building and campus. I gathered with forty other freshmen and was interviewed and registered with the president, Dr. Lennon.

Among the crowd was a student from County Kerry. He was exceptionally small with dark hair and a gleaming white complexion; probably a descendent of the Spanish Armada. His name was Michael Flynn. I befriended him and became his class companion. Michael had a photographic memory but could not apply his knowledge to paper. At the end of the first year he failed the exam and was held back. Unfortunately at the end of the second year he failed again. He was called to the president's office and informed that he was being dismissed from the seminary. Poor Michael cried hysterically for days.

We all finally left for vacation and went to our individual homes. I paid a visit to Michael at his home in Kerry. I met his widowed mother and his brother. They were living in a little thatched farmhouse near one of the most picturesque places by the ocean I'd ever seen. I discovered that Michael as a young boy had to milk the cows before he went to school. He then had to ride his bicycle three miles to school over a pothole-laden road, and traveled the same road back home after school. Then he had to help milk the cows again and finally do his homework and go to bed, only to repeat the same thing the next day.

Now Michael was home from the seminary, never able to return. He was ashamed to tell his poor widowed mother, so he hid his suitcase in the barn. But at the end of vacation time, he had no choice but to tell his mom. They both cried for days. Michael tried to apply to other seminaries, but he was turned down time after time. Finally he was accepted to a seminary in Scotland. At the end of the year he failed the test and was dismissed once again. He was heartbroken. After countless more applications he was accepted into a seminary in California, USA. After one year he failed again and was asked to leave.

Someone found him a job as a superintendent of an apartment complex. It was there he met a beautiful Spanish girl, fell in love and got married. They eventually had five wonderful children. He now has many grandchildren and is rich in many things money can't buy.

* * *

As a young priest I was assigned by my pastor as the youth minister in Chatham, NJ. Consequently I had to learn to perform many sports. In my late 20s I had to learn roller skating, ice skating, and skiing. My friend, Father Paul Kramer, taught me how to ski. At first, just to learn the basic snowplow maneuver was extremely difficult, but I finally became an avid skier.

I started a ski youth group in Rockaway, New Jersey and went skiing faithfully every week. After being appointed pastor of St. Rose of Lima, the church in East Hanover, shortly thereafter I organized a ski group. The very first night of skiing, a young girl from the parish hit a tree on the ski slope. She was severely hurt and stayed in a coma for several weeks. I was devastated. Finally she came out of the coma and was eventually rehabilitated back to good health. But that was the end of my skiing career. I put my skis in the basement of the rectory and never skied again to this day.

* * *

My parish, St. Rose of Lima Church, organized a trip to Rome. Marge Yatchison, a faithful and successful parish tour director, enlisted 50 people, including myself, for the trip to Florence, Venice, and Rome. Florence and Venice had memorable sights, but it was my arrival in St. Peter's Square that was the most awesome: I went to my knees and kissed the ground. This visit was the fulfillment of my childhood dream.

The Pope of Rome was the one who sustained the people of Ireland through difficult times. Because of the Rock of Peter they remained true to their faith in spite of enormous persecution and suffering. Now as an adult I was finally in the very heart of Rome; full of emotions I toured St. Peter's and it was breathtaking. I became convinced that Michelangelo was more than a mere man, but was sent by God to accomplish the impossible. That Pieta was indescribably beautiful.

The very next day I was scheduled to celebrate mass with my 50 pilgrims in St. Peter's. The attendant brought us downstairs to the Hungarian Chapel. As we followed him we passed right next to the tombs of Pope Paul VI and Pope John XXIII, my two heroes. It was almost beyond my emotional strength to continue. I celebrated mass in the chapel with my 50 parishioners. All of us were crying with joy, it was a mountaintop experience. I never felt closer to Christ and His Church.

The night before our departure for home, I got a telephone call at 2:30 in the morning. It was from Ann Mastro who was crying because her aunt was near death. I jumped out of bed and ran to her room. Fear gripped me when I saw the elderly woman was deathlike on her bed. Something inspired me to go back to my room and get an inhaler—for what I don't know. When I went to my room, my door was locked. I ran to the lobby to get another key, and after a long time one was found. I went back to my room, got the inhaler and returned to Ann Mastro and her aunt. I put the inhaler in her nose and squirted the liquid out. She immediately jumped up in the bed and seemed to come alive. A little later she got up, took a shower and was the first one in the bus and finally on the plane.

How and why did all this happen? I can only attribute it to my intense prayers that she would be all right. When at last we arrived back in the parking lot of St. Rose of Lima Church, I was thankful and grateful to be home. But shortly, my associate's father, Charles Waller, informed me that there was a major accident in the parking lot while I was away. A couple, Joan and Eddie had started their car after Mass. While pressing on the gas, the accelerator got stuck; the car took off on its own and ran into the school wall—but not before hitting Carol Smith and throwing her into the air. Nearly dead, she was rushed to the hospital in Morristown.

After hearing the news I went immediately to see her. She was critical but alive. Thank God she recovered completely and came home, but she had to use a cane to get around. It was comforting to see her come to church every Sunday. She was truly a woman of faith and good news. However, I'm sad to report that Ann Mastro's aunt died a few weeks after returning home. But thank God her dream to visit Rome before she died was accomplished.

CHAPTER 16

SAINT ROSE

Shortly after I announced my upcoming retirement to my parishioners, the following verse was composed. It was inspired by *Candle in the Wind*, a song with music by Elton John and lyrics by Bernie Taupin, originally written in 1973. In 1997, Elton performed a remake of the song as a tribute to Diana, Princess of Wales.

For a second time the lyrics have been transposed, this time to honor me, by a parishioner of Saint Rose who wishes to remain anonymous. I am forever grateful for these kind words:

Goodbye to Saint Rose's pastor; may you ever grow in our hearts.
You were the grace that placed itself where lives were torn apart.
You call out to our parish family and you whispered to those in pain.
Now you rest in retirement and the stars spell out your name;

And it seems to me you lived your life like a candle in the wind;
Never fading with the sunset when the rain set in.
And your footsteps will always fall here along the many corridors of Saint Rose.
Your candle's burned out long before your legend ever will;

Loveliness we've lost these empty days without your smile.
This torch we'll always carry for our wonderful parish family.
Even though we try, the truth brings us to tears;
And all our words cannot express the joy you brought us through the years.

It seems to me you lived your life like a candle in the wind;
Never fading with the sunset when the rain set in.

And your footsteps will always fall here,
Along the many corridors of Saint Rose.

Goodbye Monsignor McCarthy; may you ever grow in our hearts;
You were the grace that placed itself where lives were torn apart.
Goodbye our parish pastor from a parish lost without your soul;
Who will miss the wings of your compassion more than you'll ever know.
*Your candle's burned out long before **your legend ever will**.*

CHAPTER 17

REFLECTIONS

I am a victim of thinking that I will never feel happy again. The beginning of healing may be there, but I refuse to let it in because of my resistance.

One of my more powerful teaching stories I have ever read is told in Joyce Rupp's book, *The Cup of Our Life*. A father is away from home when robbers come and set fire to the house and take his young son away with them. The father returns to the ashes of his house and believes his son died there. He grieves uncontrollably for many months. The son manages to get free from his captors and finds his way home. He knocks on the door and cries, "Papa, Papa," but the father refuses to open the door thinking it is one of the neighborhood children taunting him. Eventually the son goes away, never to return. In this story, the father resists the truth that can bring him joy and freedom from his loss because he clings so much to what he thinks is the truth.

I am in a place of darkness, and being a pessimist by nature, I have the terrible feeling that I will never break loose. I pray incessantly that God will give me peace, and trust that I will eventually be exonerated, and that He will lead me to greater freedom and inner healing. I must remember as I ponder what is gone from my life that I am not alone, that I am not a poor helpless creature. There is always grace and I must trust the Lord; he is my hope and my strength.

*   *   *

I read another story in Joyce Rupp's book, *The Cup of Our Life*, which was personally revealing to me in my deep loneliness. Joyce tells the story: "One Thursday when I was visiting at Kavanaugh's House, a residence for terminally ill persons, I met a woman named Agnes. She was sitting by the bedside of her husband, named Al, who had a brain tumor. Next Thursday I again found Agnes faithfully sitting there by Al. This time she told me about Miriam, a woman whose husband had died at Kavanaugh House the week before. Agnes only knew Miriam from a few conversations they had before Miriam's husband died. This new widow understood what Agnes was going through and wanted to support her. She began calling Agnes each evening to see how she was coping. Agnes told me how much the phone calls helped get her through each day. As the weeks unfolded I saw how one woman in the midst of her own loss, reached out in compassion to another who was in pain. Miriam could not do much for Agnes by changing her situation, but she helped greatly with her caring presence."

Compassion is the quality of being able to get inside the skin of another in order to respond with loving care. There is no quality that identifies a Christian more than that of compassion. Jesus consistently loved this quality, and encouraged it in his disciples. He repeatedly insisted that offering compassion to another was the same as extending it to Him. Compassion can be very demanding; it is not easy to know the pain and to feel the trust of another. Sometimes compassion asks us to simply be with someone, to wait patiently, to experience their powerlessness with them. As Mary Joe Meadows points out: "You must get near enough to suffering to feel it, but not so close to get lost in it."

Scholar Marcus Borg notes that compassion is the central quality of God in both the Hebrew and the Christian scriptures. He emphasizes that God is compassionate, feels our pain, our loss, and our suffering. In my suffering, many people who have suffered themselves have been faithfully there for me. I am thinking especially of Hilton and B. Otero. They stood by their only daughter who was sick for many years, suffering from anorexia and then cancer, and finally died. I knew their loss must be unbearable. I ministered to them during their ordeal. I was there for them, but in hindsight, I didn't feel their pain.

Now I am suffering, and they have gotten inside my skin and feel my pain. Many other people who have had great pain in their lives are also there for me. I am thinking of Sylda and Peter Grassman, Edith and Jim Austen, Lois Pelecia, Jack and Joy Kraft, Sylvia Farro, Bill, Jim and Betty, Bill and Mary O'Brian, Gus and Marie Auermiller, Joann and John Lester, Patsy and Anita Montello, Barbara Keating, Doris O'Dea, Arthur Hoagland, Barry Halloran and Inge Pironti. When I think of these compassionate people, I see some common characteristics. Often they have a generous heart, a non-blaming and non-judging mind, a passionate spirit, a willingness to sacrifice their life, a keen empathy, and the love that embraces the oneness of all creation.

"And whoever gives even a cup of water to one of these little ones in My name, truly I tell you, none of these will lose their reward." (Matthew: 10:40-42)

* * *

Joyce Rupp also says in her book, *A Cup of Our Life*: "Some of our greatest blessings have been difficult situations, uncomfortable ones we want to throw out of our lives as quickly as possible. Sometimes our greatest pain holds a gift for us that is hidden for a long, long time. The blessing is disguised amid the turmoil for a long time. Sometimes we are unable to accept the blessing because we are still too hurt, too angry, too grieved, or too overwhelmed to receive it. It is only much later that we see the gift that has come from what we thought would destroy our happiness forever."

When the accusation hit me, I felt it was a curse; I could never say it was a blessing. A fellow priest, Monsignor Jack Derick, who was also falsely accused, told me over lunch that what happened to him was a blessing. I was shocked by his statement. *How could that possibly be?* I kept asking myself; but I can now say that the insight and spiritual growth that gradually came out of my experience were blessings disguised with the sorrow. Sometimes the pain of our life doesn't make much sense, but usually disguised blessings eventually come to light when we leave the fray behind and begin to let go of what has brought us so much misery. As I heal, I begin to see the blessings that are mine.

A PRAYER BY JOYCE RUPP:

Holy wisdom, come with your vast vision. Help me to sift through the rubble of my trying times; to find the teachings that can guide my life. You, who see far beyond the devastation, lead me to believe that there might be gifts in what I want to toss away. I offer you my gratitude for all the disguised blessings that are mine.

* * *

Jean Houston tells a story about herself as a youth, going to hear a presentation by Helen Keller, who was blind and deaf. Houston said that after Helen Keller finished speaking, she knew that she had to talk with her. She got up and presented her face to Helen Keller. Jean Houston described the experience this way: "She read my whole face and I blurted out: 'Ms. Keller, why are you so happy?' She laughed and laughed, saying, 'My child, it is because I live each day as if it was my last, and life with all its moments, is so full of glory.'"

During my carefree days of exciting moments of pastoral ministry, I realize now, I was unconscious of wonder and awe, I missed out on experiencing the daily gifts of life. As I awaken to what's within me and around me, I begin to relish and taste life afresh each day.

Andrew Harvey writes in *The Way of Passion*, that if we were really looking at this world, we would be moved a hundred times a day by the flowers at the side of the road, the people we meet, by all that brings us messages of our own goodness and the goodness of all things. To be grateful is to affirm goodness wherever we find it. The problem with being grateful is not the lack of countless blessings; the problem is with being inattentive and unaware of these blessings.

After the attack on me I didn't see the sunshine anymore. I failed to smell the roses. My state of gratitude grew lean. I now consciously try to alert myself to my daily gifts and begin again to see the universe as one huge blessing.

> *I thank you God, with my whole heart,*
> *I will tell of your wonderful deeds,*
> *I will be glad and exalt in you,*
> *I will sing to you, for you have dealt bountifully with me.*
> *Your steadfast love endures,*
> *I know I must make a concerted effort to live this day as if it was my last.*
> (Psalms 9:1-2, Psalms 13:6, Psalms 118:29)

*   *   *

Jessica Powers wrote a marvelous poem in which she addresses God as a "God of too much giving." She then describes herself as getting inebriated with God. She is filled with overwhelming joy because God has offered her too much of divine goodness.

God is above all else a being of immense beauty. The mysterious Beloved is forever wooing us. As I look at my life, I count as my greatest blessing my fascination with the universe: the dome of the sky, the decorations that God put in place, the stars and the chandelier of the sun, the moon, and the planets. On a dark night with a moon sitting out in space looking almost close enough to touch it, I experience God's awesome presence. It was just a week ago, November 14, 2003; there was a lunar eclipse. The sun, moon, and earth were all aligned in front of each other with the earth reflecting a bright yellow light over the moon. In the midst of my sadness, this site welled up in me the indescribable presence of God in my inner being. Feeling the essence of God's beauty reminded me of the underlying harmony beneath all the chaos. This moment of encounter with the divine beauty, I felt, was given with unconditional love. I recall once more, that I am in the embrace of a God of love, who calls me his beloved. Can I want for anything more?

CHAPTER 18

GOD WINKS

My good friend, Joe Larena, gave me a book entitled, *When God Winks (How the Power of Coincidence Guides Your Life)*. This book, by Squire Rushnell, explains that there is more to coincidence than meets the eye, and unveils a wondrous map that has quietly guided me along the path of my past. He defines the word "coincidence" as the sequence of events that although accidental, seem to have been planned or arranged. He describes "God's wink" as a personal signal or message directly from a Higher Power, usually, but not always, in the form of a coincidence. I asked myself: "Was I led to this moment to learn more about my life and its mysterious guideposts? What the author calls God's winks, did that project me in new directions and place me into situations I never anticipated?" Without these false accusations that hit me, I would never have written this book—nor would I have experienced a new relationship with the suffering of Jesus.

I am beginning to suspect that coincidences, or God's winks, are messages to me on my journey through life, nudging me on the ground path that has been designed especially for me. I find that Rushnell's book gives me a simple bridge to self-discovery. I am learning ways to open my eyes to see the amazing waves that Higher Power has been working in my life. I am consciously trying to discover the *winks* in my life that lead to possibilities I have never imagined, and to be prepared to take active steps toward goals and dreams that may now seem distant. Somewhere up above is a universal guidance system and I am on that radar screen.

As I sort through the turning points in my life, I can almost chronicle past *winks* —such as the timing of when I first realized what I wanted to be when I grew up. I remember glancing at a picture of my uncle Dan, a priest, in a painting all dressed up as a canon of the Church. I was probably seven

74

or eight years old. But it had a profound effect on me. I was suddenly filled with a knowing of what my life's calling was. I am aware of many more *winks* from God, too many to enumerate.

Was the accusation "a wink from God?" Only time will tell. Right now I feel it is the worst possible thing that could have happened to me. I am certain that a recent casual conversation I had with my friend, Father Paul Knauer, set me on a path that connected me to a lawyer, George D. Finding George was definitely a huge wink from God. He is a brilliant lawyer, who was from the beginning a committed advocate for my cause. Father John Farley assigned to me by the Head Canonist to be my canon lawyer was also, I believe, another wink from God.

I can honestly say that the Head Canonist of the diocese, was a man of the highest integrity, and one of my greatest blessings. His being a part of my life at this critical juncture was by no means mere coincidence, but a direct intervention by God.

*   *   *

And then… just when I was starting to feel good again… and in the midst of my ongoing struggle to free myself from the false accusation, my friend Monsignor Knauer suggested I visit Father K., who was well known as a firebrand against priests who were accused of pedophile behavior. I made an appointment to see him. I met him at his office and we sat down.

"I know and appreciate your mission to weed out guilty priests from the priesthood," I stated. "That's why I'm here. How would you deal with a priest who was accused, but who is completely innocent?"

He stood up from his desk, glared at me and yelled, "That's what they all say—but they are as guilty as hell!" He then walked out of his office, and left me all alone in my pain.

I got up, left the office, and went to my car, wounded all over again. I said to myself, "What a hypocrite! He has closed his mind to the possibility of an innocent priest." He was caught up in the witch hunt of the time and I became another one of his victim priests. No room in his mind for exception to his thinking.

This effort on my part only put me further into sadness over my never ending plight. I had to drive a long way home to my apartment, having been rejected by my fellow priest, who I thought would be a friend. Another indicator of the insanity that permeated the Church with priests turning against each other; all trust and respect gone. One more nail in my "coffin of despair."

The picture of my father's brother, Canon Dan McCarthy, hung on a wall in my parents' bedroom. Looking at that picture as a child, I believe, was "God's wink" to me to decide to become a priest.

YEAR TWO (2004)

CHAPTER 19

SURRENDER

After my own personal 9/11, I was psychologically brought down and essentially lost. I gave way to panic, acting merely out of some defense mechanism, and I didn't spare God from these reproaches. Why had He failed me at this crucial moment of my life? Why had He not shielded me by His grace from this attack now? I was totally broken and confounded. How could He have allowed evil people to conspire against me?

Little by little surely under His inspiration and his grace, I began to wonder about myself and my prayer. Why did I feel this way? Why did I have a sense of abandonment, a feeling of total anxiety; an internal meltdown? I was nearly out of my mind. Slowly and reluctantly, under the gentle prodding of grace, I began to realize that I had tried to do too much on my own and I had failed. I had asked for God's help, but had really believed in my own ability to meet every challenge. I had spent much time in prayer over the years. I had come to appreciate and thank God for His providence and care for me and for all people, but I had never really abandoned myself to it. In a way I had been thanking God all the while that I was not like the rest of men; that He had given me a good physique, steady nerves, and a strong will; and with these physical God-given graces, I would continue to do His will at all times and to the best of my ability. In short I felt guilty and ashamed because in the final analysis I had relied almost completely on myself in this most critical test and I had failed.

Had I not even set the terms upon which the Holy Spirit was to intervene in my behalf? I felt I had written down all the facts that should exonerate me. I felt He had abandoned me, and I proceeded to try to do on my own what I had already determined was a thing that must be done. I had not really left myself open to the spirit. I had in fact long ago decided what I expected to hear from the spirit, and when I didn't hear precisely that, I felt betrayed. Whatever else the spirit might have been telling me at that hour I could not hear. I was so intent on hearing only one message, the message I wanted to hear, that I was not really listening at all.

This tendency to set acceptable conditions upon God, to seek unconsciously to make His will for us coincide with our desires, is a very human trait and the more important the situation is, the more totally we are committed to it or the more completely our future depends on it, then the easier it becomes for us to blind ourselves into thinking that what we want is surely what God must also want. We can see but one solution only, and naturally we assume that God will help us reach it. In any case this tendency is strong in me. I had been strong willed as a boy, but the scriptures, actually the *Book of Wisdom*, says: "Like gold in the furnace, He tried them." Somehow by the trials and tribulations of this life our souls are purified and become more like God, and more easily obey His will. We must learn the truth of total dependence on Him; we can learn that all our actions are sustained by His grace and that without Him we can do nothing. God sustains me and instructs me by the light of His grace.

He who endures to the end will be saved. However, sometimes I feel so desolate that even prayer seems impossible. I often feel endangered and threatened anew, and I find no light or consolation in prayer. I find myself reproaching God for not sparing me this torture. Why does He permit it to go on day after day without finding some way to end it, or helping me to find a way to step back from the downward path I seem to be moving along? Sometimes the darkness closes in around me completely, perhaps brought on by exhaustion and I reach a point of despair. I feel overwhelmed by the hopelessness of it all and my powerlessness to cope. I sometimes cross over the brink into a fit of blackness I have never known before. This is despair; I have lost not only hope, but the last shred of my faith in God. I stand alone in a void. I have not even a thought of or recall the one thing that had been my constant guide, my only source of consolation, my ultimate resource; I have lost sight of God.

Recognizing that and coming to my senses, I turn immediately, pleading my helplessness to face the future without Him—again I am consoled by thoughts of our Lord and His agony in the Garden of Gethsemane. "Father," Jesus said, "if it be possible, let this chalice pass from me." In the Garden of Olives, He too knew the feeling of fear and weakness in His human nature as He faced suffering and death. Not once, but three times did He ask to have His ordeal removed or somehow modified, yet each time He concluded with an act of that abandonment and submission to the Father's will, "Not as I will, but as Thou wilt." It was not just conformity to the will of God, it was total self-surrender, a slipping away of all human fears, of all doubts about His own ability to withstand the passion of every shred of self, including self-doubt.

So with me it demanded absolute faith in God's existence, in His providence, in His concern for the minutest detail, in His power to sustain me, and in His love protecting me. It meant losing the last hidden doubt, the ultimate fear that God will not be there to bear me up. It was something like that awful eternity between anxiety and belief when a child in a swimming pool first leans back and lets go of all support whatever—only to find that the water timely holds him up and he can float motionless and totally relaxed.

In the hands of my lawyers I had moments of hope and doubt. My lawyer, George D., was always positive and determined, I would leave his office exuberated that finally something was being done; a lawsuit was being filed against the diocese, the bishop, and the prosecutor's office. A week would pass, and no news. Again I felt betrayed. "Why is this happening as I write this chapter in my life?" I keep asking myself. "Why is he stalling? Is it all hopeless?"

I thought of the scripture text: "The children of this world are wiser than the children of light." It seemed a peculiar thing to keep running through my mind, and yet a strange and exciting challenge for a priest fighting for his life. The challenge seemed plain. Could my sacrifice, could my total dedication, could my stamina in seeking God's guidance, be less than that of the children of this world? In order to survive I have to conquer one day at a time. The children of this world were dedicated to surviving this life by whatever method possible. I too must be totally dedicated using all the legal means available to exonerate myself, and with added dimension guided by the Holy Spirit, acting not as a child of this world but rather a child of light acting out of faith to accept each day, each moment as from God's hands. I would not merely, passively survive like the children of this world, but with His help and His grace would actually participate and I would survive. I never doubt because I do not fear non-survival. Death would simply be a call to return to the God I served each day. My life was to do the will of God, as the prayer our Savior taught us and put it quite simply: "On earth as it is in heaven."

Peace came as a renewed confidence not in my own ability to survive, but a total trust and confidence in God's ability to sustain me and provide me with whatever strength I needed to meet the challenges facing me. What greater peace and confidence could I require, I even looked forward to laboring again in his vineyard, ministering to God's people with renewed fervor and enthusiasm, never again taking for granted the treasure of the priesthood.

*   *   *

"The spirit is willing, but the flesh is weak"... especially in the agony of total mental exhaustion. To make matters worse, I tore a ligament in my knee and that eventually put stress on my back, so now I have severe back pain. Now I think of how much the body means to man, how essential it is to my well-being, how prominent a part in every activity of human existence is played by that clay into which God first breathed the breath of life. Men and women are creatures composed of body and soul. We have recited that truth from the day we first learned our catechism. But until the body fails us or pains us or forces itself upon our attention by some little twinge, we tend to take for granted this first and most precious of God's gifts to men and women. All of us are creatures composed of body and soul; and we work out our salvation in this veil of tears through the medium of the flesh. It's the first gift God and our parents fashion for us; it sustains and supports us through a long life. And when at last we are parted from it in death, it surely deserves whatever rest it can get when it rises to be glorified at the final resurrection.

"*The marvelous richness of human experience would lose something of rewarding joy, if there were not limitations to overcome. The hilltop hour would not be half so wonderful if there were no dark valleys to traverse.*" – Helen Keller

CHAPTER 20

MARITAL HAPPINESS

My training as a psychologist and marriage counselor has given me great insight into the process of how to make marriage work and help couples to have the relationship of their dreams. The key is education: being educated so you don't let your childhood wounds ruin your marriage. Not seeing each other as bad, but as wounded, and then healing each other's wounds. Your marriage must be a "conscious marriage"—conscious of each others' psychological wounds. If not you have an "unconscious marriage," your relationship will be a nightmare instead of the relationship of your dreams.

People believe they are free to marry who they wish, but that is generally untrue. Your subconscious mind leads you to pick a person with whom you can finish childhood. When you meet the person, you will have a feeling of fulfillment and familiarity. You will experience a feeling that you have known this person all your life. You will idealize the person as the most wonderful person you have ever met. What is really happening? It is that you have met and fallen in love with a person with whom you are incompatible. A person with the combined personality of your parents, especially their negative traits, you feel at home.

Romantic love is nature's anesthesia. It "numbs" you into not knowing all the things about your partner. If you did, you would spoil nature's plan to pair you with an incompatible person for the purpose of emotional healing. Romantic love is nature's trick by which it engages you, without your knowledge or consent, in the process of nature's own self-completion.

Marriage is not a fairy tale. It is a commitment, a decision. I teach a skill that helps couples discover their childhood wounds. Some marriage preparation courses give only a bunch of superficial advice—telling you that you should love your partner more, or kiss them three times a day, or ask them for what you want. Those things are nice, but you are already smart enough to know that you should be doing those things. You know how you should treat yourself and the people you love. The real question is, "Why don't you?" Why is it hard for you to talk about how you feel? Why is it hard for you to settle for less? We have given credence to the idea that when troubles come, you should change partners, while the truth is that the way you are living with that person must be changed.

It's all backwards. Rather than getting rid of the partner, and keeping the problem, you should get rid of the problem, so that you can keep the partner. So many people want to find the perfect partner, get married, and then worry about being happily married. Marriage is like a rafting trip, you have the choice about taking the journey, but you can't avoid the rapids along the way. You can learn what to expect, and if you practice on the smaller rapids, you won't capsize and drown in the big ones.

*   *   *

While it appears that we have the freedom to marry whom we like, the fact is that your unconscious mind chooses a person like your parents, with their negative traits to heal your childhood wounds and to help you discover your suppressed lost self. It is a time that you will find a person like your parents with their negative and positive traits. But usually you will unconsciously try to find a person like the parent you had the most difficulty with. In effect, what you are doing is trying to discover a lost part of you, lost in your relationship with the negative parent. For example, if a little girl failed to get the attention and affection from her alcoholic father, she will have a compulsion to find a man who is aloof and unaffectionate, unconsciously saying that, "I couldn't get it from my dad, I will make sure, that I will get it from this man who is similar to my dad." She is looking for love in all the wrong places.

All of us human beings are a walking encyclopedia of everything that happened to us in our childhood. Knowledge about childhood wounds is redemptive information; it's the map showing where the buried treasure lies.

Some marriages are in serious trouble and couples feel they cannot resolve it. The wall between them seems impenetrable. But I believe the wall will dissolve—like the Berlin Wall—as soon as the couples understand and get in touch with their childhood wounds, and look at each other not as bad, but wounded. Then they are in a position to help heal each other's psychological wounds. Romantic love is not at all what it appears to be. We are in love with a projection of our missing self, but our attempt to get through another "what is missing in ourselves" never works. Real love is something entirely different and better. But it only comes to couples who are willing to wrestle with their demons and stay the course during the difficult times.

*   *   *

In a relationship, when you have an emotional flashback, you are jumping to the wrong conclusion—you are assuming betrayal. Your partner then becomes the enemy because of your old unresolved feelings. Your relationship is like walking through an emotional minefield, with bombs waiting to go off. This starves love. The way you feed love is to become a love team, where you help your partner heal their emotional wounds and they help you to heal your emotional wounds. You can change your partner from the enemy into your greatest supporter by giving your partner a map of your wounds so that you can avoid them.

*   *   *

One of my favorite exercises that I taught the young couples about to get married is entitled "Caring Behavior." This exercise consists of one partner asking the other four questions:

1. What am I doing now that makes you feel loved, cared about and wanted?

2. What did I do when we were first together to make you feel loved cared about and wanted?

3. Is there anything I used to do that made you feel loved cared about and wanted, that you want to have reinstated?

4. What is there that you would like me to do, that you have never asked or hinted at, your most secret wishes that if I did them would make you feel loved, cared about, and wanted?

CHAPTER 21

MATCHMAKER

Prior to my decision to retire, and the subsequent conspiracy, this entire special ministry was extremely rewarding and fulfilling to me. One of my favorite duties was dealing with marriage in every aspect, such as: officiating at marriage ceremonies, giving marriage preparation courses, counseling troubled marriages, running a dating ministry, and even finding partners for people.

My first experience in getting potential partners for people began with finding a wife for my brother. After my dad died, my mom was now alone with my brother Dan in the homestead, called Shandrum House. I said to Dan one day: "Well now, all this beautiful farm is yours." He became very upset and yelled out: "What good is all this for me now—who is going to marry me at my age?"

He was about 40 years old. I went to visit a cousin of ours and said, "Denny, we have to find someone for my brother Dan."

"Don't worry Liam," Denny replied, "I already have someone in mind."

Two days later he called me and assured me that he had the right woman for my brother. A few nights later, we got Dan and Nora together. It was instant attraction. Three months later I married them at the altar.

The family was worried about the new woman going to live with mother. My mom convinced us that everything would be fine; as she said, "We will get along famously." I went back to America and resumed my work at the Parish of St. Michael in Netcong, N.J.

Two years later I went home. My brother Dan picked me up at the airport in Shannon, Ireland. On the way to the homestead, I asked him how everybody was at home.

He exploded: "That woman you found for me did not get along with Mom. She went back to her parents. It's all over."

I was horrified. I berated him for going against his wife in favor of his mother: "You committed one of the worst sins—your wife comes before your mother. Jesus said: 'You leave your father and your mother and cling to your wife, and the two shall become one flesh.'"

When we finally got to Shandrum House, I spoke to my mom, and told her the same words I had spoken to my brother earlier. I then convinced her to go and live with my sister Pam and her husband and kids. I rejoined Dan and his wife Nora and blessed them; went back to America and continued to pray for my family.

A couple of years later, I returned home to Shandrum House for another family visit. This time I found Dan and Nora happy and pregnant. After a few years, they had three wonderful children: Collette, John, and Ann. Nora and Dan were as happy as two bugs in a rug, and my mom was very content at my sister Pam's house.

*   *   *

A sidebar: John was Dan and Nora's only son. He went to college and graduated as a CPA. But his first love was sports. He became an avid hurler and went on to become the captain of the hurling team, and eventually went on to lead his team to become all-Ireland champions—winning their first ever all-Ireland title with the kids he grew up with. He has become a hero in his home town. And the whole 15 players on the team have become heroes to the people of Newtown, Shandrum, and surrounding areas. Nora and Dan were as proud as proud could be and of course so was I. After all, I was responsible for bringing them back together and I consider it one of my greatest achievements.

Great men have climbed the steps of the Hogan stand in the national stadium of Croke Park Dublin. Now my nephew, John McCarthy, deserves to stand alongside them. He will be the wind beneath the wings of youngsters who will now aspire to what he has achieved with every other member of his history-making team. Emotion filled the air in the great Croke Park theatre on St. Patrick's Day, March 17, 2004 as Capitan Fantastic, John McCarthy, lifted the Tommy O'Moore Cup high into the Dublin heavens, and how fitting it was that it should be he who had that great honor. One of the game's real great guys; he epitomized everything that Newtown Shandrum stands for. John McCarthy was his team's captain, their leader, and their inspiration and he is my nephew, in a way my greatest creation. God has a great sense of timing—bringing Nora and Dannie together as husband and wife and having a child born in December of 1972.

That changed the little village of Newtown, Shandrum forever and indeed an entire nation. He has even been compared to the most famous Irish hurler of all time, Christi Ring.

*   *   *

Now that I was bit by the "matchmaker bug," I felt a desire to bring people together. Let me introduce the reader to just a few of the twenty or so people I introduced to each other and ultimately married them at the altar. Eileen and her fiancé came to see me about marriage plans. Eileen was quiet and demure. Her fiancé was much older and rude to her. After they left I called Eileen and asked her to come and see me. I convinced her that her fiancé was not the right man for her. I called her parents and they arranged to have her go into hiding because he'd begun to threaten her with violence. About six months later she came to see me with another man about her own age. He was nastier and ruder than the first guy. I again called her in alone and convinced her that he was not the right guy either. She listened and called the engagement off. I prayed to the Holy Spirit to guide me in finding a nice guy for her.

One day I thought of Carmine, as his personality was very similar to Eileen's. I called them both to my office and introduced them to each other. I suggested they go to the local diner for a cup of coffee. A month later I saw them separately in church and I asked Carmine if he liked Eileen. He said that he did very much so. I questioned him as to why they hadn't seen each other in a month, and Carmine shyly shook his shoulders as if to say "I don't know." I got them back together again and this time it stuck. Six months later I married them. After a few years, they had two beautiful kids, Mary and Bobbie. They went on to be two of the smartest kids in Hanover Park High School. Eileen and Carmine after almost twenty years' are happier than ever, and still very compatible.

Anthony was anxious to find a girl that he could marry and have a family with. I must have introduced him to at least twelve young women, but none worked out—probably because Anthony was exceptionally shy. I was at the point of giving up, when out of nowhere walked this lady into the church hall. When I sensed her shyness, a feeling came over me that this was the one for Anthony. I introduced them to each other and in about a year's time I witnessed their marriage. Unfortunately, five years later they failed in their attempt to have children. However, they are very happy all the same; and it is my hope that they have since, as I suggested, considered adoption.

George's wife was dying of cancer for two years. I ministered to her throughout her sickness. Finally she passed away and I celebrated her Funeral Mass. John, a close friend, who was a surveyor by profession, helped me in building a number of buildings. One day while surveying on highway 206 in New Jersey, he was hit by a car and killed. I had the hard task of burying him. After a few months, I called George into my office and suggested that maybe he would like to be introduced to John's widow Rennil. George was not too happy about the idea. But I didn't give up; at our Parish Ball event in October, I managed for both of them to be at the dance. I introduced them, and suggested that they have one dance together. They did, and fell instantly in love. A short while later in the year they were married by me, and now, ten years later, they are still very much in love.

*   *   *

But, to be fair, not all of my matchmaking stories have a happy ending. One situation in particular stands out in my mind. Faye, a young, tall blonde woman ran into the parish office, came up to me and showed me a picture, asking, "Do you recognize this man?"

I told her that I did—that it was Joe, and he had been in my office on Saturday with his fiancé Janet making arrangements to get married.

"He better not," Faye stated emphatically, "he and I are engaged and planning to get married in March. My family is coming from California, and I have the hall booked, the band, etcetera."

I immediately called Janet's mother and said straight out, "Do you know that Joe is engaged to another woman?"

"Father McCarthy," she laughed uneasily, "you are a big kidder."

"I wish I were," I sighed deeply. "This is serious—Joe really is engaged to another woman."

To make a long story short, that night the two girls, Faye and Janet, got together. Neither one of them recognized the Joe the other knew. He had been living a double life and intended to marry both of them. Because he traveled for a living, it was easy for him to work out the details of the deception.

Sometime later I studied his psychological profile. As a child, his father was constantly unfaithful to his mother. The mother was always crying. Joe made a decision as a child. Women are bad, they take daddy away from mommy, so women should be used and abused. Consequently, he was engaged to two women at the same time, and dated several other women on the side.

Two of the brides whose marriages I celebrated over the many years.

Out of all fifteen hundred or so brides that I witnessed get married over forty years of my ministry as a priest, Joyce Alexander was my favorite.

CHAPTER 22

JOB

As I personally struggle with my thoughts, constantly obsessing and *awfulizing* my situation, asking, "Why did God allow this terrible thing to happen to me?" I am often led to read the *Book of Job*. Job was a pious man; he was so good, so perfect, it appeared that God had favored him and showered him with blessings. While Job was flourishing, all around him people were suffering.

One day, the story goes, Satan appears before God to tell him about all the sinful things people were doing on earth.

God says to Satan, "Did you notice my servant Job? There is no one on earth like him, a thoroughly good man who never sins."

Satan answers God, "Of course Job is pious and obedient—you make it worth his while, showering riches and blessings on him. Take away these blessings and see how long he remains your obedient servant."

God accepts Satan's challenge. Without in any way telling Job what is going on, God allows Satan to destroy Job's house and cattle and his children. He afflicts Job with boils all over his body, so that his every movement becomes physical torture. Job's wife urges him to curse God, even if that means God striking him dead. He can't do anything worse to Job than He already has done. Three friends come to console Job and they too urge him to give up his piety, if this is the reward it brings him. But Job remains steadfast in his faith. Nothing that happens to him can make him give up his devotion to God. Finally God appears, scolds the friends for their advice and rewards Job for his faithfulness. God gives him a new home, a new fortune, and new children.

The moral of the story is: when hard times befall you, don't be tempted to give up your faith in God. He has His reasons for what He is doing, and if you hold on to your faith in God long enough, He will compensate you for your suffering.

Over the generations many people must have been told that story. Some no doubt were comforted by it. Others were shamed into keeping their doubts and complaints to themselves after hearing Job's example.

The author of the *Book of Job* was confused by it. What kind of God would that story have us believe in who would kill innocent children in order to prove a point? And what kind of religion is the story urging on us, which delights in blind obedience and calls it sinful to protest against injustice. In an effort to console Job, whose children have died and who is suffering from boils, the three friends say all the traditional, pious things: "Don't lose faith despite these calamities. We have a loving Father in Heaven, and He will see to it that the good prosper and the wicked are punished."

Job had probably spoken the following words innumerable times to other mourners, as indeed I have heard several times at funerals and tragedies in my ministry as a priest. I recall a comical remark by a woman in Ireland when she said to the son of the diseased father: "I am sorry for all the trouble your father is causing in heaven." Job, in the remarks said to him by his friends who meant well, realized for the first time how hollow and offensive they are. "What do you mean, 'He will see to it that the good prosper and the wicked are punished?' Are you implying that my children were wicked and that is why they died? Are you saying that I am wicked, and that is why all this is happening to me? Where was I so terrible? What did I do that was so much worse than anything you did, that I should suffer so much worse fate?"

The friends were startled by this outburst. They responded by saying that a person can't expect God to tell him what he is being punished for. At one point one of the friends says, in effect, "What do you want from God, an itemized report about every time you told a lie or ignored a beggar? God is too busy running a world to write you, to go over His records with you. We can only assume that nobody is perfect and that God knows what He is doing. If we don't assume that, the world becomes chaotic and unlivable."

Job doesn't claim to be perfect, but says that he has tried more so than most people to live a good and decent life.

The friends asked: "How can God be a loving God if he is constantly spying on people, on any imperfection in an otherwise good record, and use that to justify punishment? And how can God be a just God if so many wicked people are not punished as horrible as Job is?"

The friends say, "Job you really had us fooled, you gave us the impression that you were as pious and religious as we are, but now we see how you throw religion overboard the first time something unpleasant happens to you. You are proud, arrogant and impatient. No wonder God is doing this to you. It just proves our point that human beings can be fooled as to who is a saint and who is a sinner, but you can't fool God."

The friends continue to voice complaints and Job continues to defend God. Finally Job states, "If a man is accused of wrongdoing without proof, he may take an oath, swearing to his innocence. At that point the accuser must either come up with evidence against him or drop the charges." Job swears to his innocence. He claims that he never neglected the poor, never took anything that didn't belong to him, never boasted of his wealth, or rejoiced in his enemy's misfortune. He challenged God to appear with evidence or to admit that he, Job, is right and has suffered wrongly. And God appears. There comes a terrible windstorm out of the desert, and God answers Job out of the whirlwind.

Job's case is so compelling; his challenge so forceful that God Himself comes down to earth to answer him. But God's answer is hard to understand. He does not talk about Job's case at all—neither to detail Job's sins, nor to explain his suffering.

Instead, He says to Job, in effect, "What do you know about how to run a world? Where were you when I planned the earth? Tell me, if you are wise, do you know who took its dimensions, measuring its length with a cord? Were you there when I stopped the sea and set its boundaries, saying here you may come, but no further? Have you seen where the snow is stored, or visited the storehouse of the hail? Do you tell the antelope when to calve? Do you give the horse his strength? Do you show the hawk how to fly?"

And now a different Job answers saying, "I put my hand to my mouth, I have said too much already; now I will speak no more."

I take Job's story to mean what I have said already in another part of this book: "God cannot do everything." God wants the righteous to live peaceful, happy lives, but sometimes even He cannot bring that about. It's too difficult even for God to keep cruelty and chaos from claiming their innocent victims. But could man without God do it better? God has a hard time keeping chaos and limiting the damage that we can do.

Innocent people do suffer misfortunes in this life. Things happen to them far worse than they deserve, they lose their jobs, they get sick, and their children suffer. But when this happens, it does not represent God punishing them for something they did wrong. Man's misfortunes do not come from God at all.

There may be a sense of loss in coming to this conclusion. In a way it is comforting to believe in an all-wise, all-powerful God, who guarantees fair treatment and happy endings, who reassures you that everything happens for a reason, even as life is easier for us when we could believe that our parents were wise enough to know what to do and strong enough to make everything turn out right. But it is comforting the way the religion of Job's friends is comforting. It works only as long as we do not take the problems of innocent victims seriously. When we have been like Job, as I in a way have been, I cannot believe in that sort of God any longer, without giving up my own right to feel angry, to feel that I have been treated badly by life.

From that perspective there ought to be a sense of relief in coming to the conclusion that God is not doing this to me. If God is a God of justice and not of power, then He can still be on our side when bad things happen to us. He can know that we are good and honest people who deserve better. Our misfortunes are none of His doing, and so we can turn to Him for help. Our question will not be Job's friends' question, "God, why are you doing this?"

Rather, "God, see what is happening to me: Can you help me?" We will turn to God not to be judged or forgiven, not to be rewarded or punished, but to be strengthened and comforted.

If we can bring ourselves to acknowledge that there are some things God does not control, or that He chooses not to control, many good things become possible. We will be able to turn to God for things He can do to help us, instead of holding on to unrealistic expectations of Him which will never come about. We can maintain our own self-respect and sense of goodness without having to feel that God has judged us and condemned us. We can be angry at what has happened to us, without feeling that we are angry at God. More than that, we can recognize our anger at life's unfairness, our instinctive complaint at seeing people suffer as coming from God who entreats us to be angry at injustice and to feel compassion for the afflicted. Instead of feeling that we are opposed to God, we can feel that our indignation is God's anger at unfairness working through us, that when we cry out, we are still on God's side and He is still on ours.

CHAPTER 23

IT DOESN'T MAKE SENSE

Does anything happen for no reason? Does everything have to be reasonable or happen for a specific reason? Is there a sensible explanation for why wind and weather combine to start a forest fire on a given day toward certain homes rather than others, trapping some people inside and sparing others, or is it just a matter of pure accident?

Some people will find the hand of God behind everything that happens; some will say, "Our prayer was answered." Does that mean their neighbors' prayers were neglected and their homes burnt down? Was it God's will that their home burnt down? As I said earlier, God by his very nature of pure goodness cannot will something negative. Murders, accidents, robberies are not the will of God, but represent that aspect of reality which stands independent of His will, and which angers and saddens us. God does not reach down to interrupt the laws of nature to protect the righteous from harm, otherwise he would be constantly interfering in His own creation, and it would appear that He made a mistake and He has to correct it. When something bad happens, God does not cause it and cannot stop it. Would this be a better world if certain people were immune to laws of nature because God favored them, while the rest of us had to fend for ourselves?

*   *   *

What did I do to deserve this? That's really the wrong question. Being sick or healthy is not a matter of what God decides we deserve. The better question is, "If this has happened to me, what do I do now, and who is there to help me do it?" I was wrongfully accused of a heinous crime and punished by my diocese for something I had absolutely nothing to do with. Do I blame God?

96

A better question is, "What do I do now?" Like Job, I need friends to tell me that what has happened to me is very unfair, and of course I have many who tell me just that. Also they tell me I must keep my mind and spirit strong so that I can continue to fight for justice.

I can't hold God responsible for the evil women who plotted against me and used an innocent family as their weapon of my destruction. One of the worst things that happens to a person who has been hurt by life, is that he tends to compound the damage by hurting himself a second time. Too often in our pain and confusion, we do the wrong thing; we let sadness, hopelessness and loneliness make a bad situation worse.

When things don't turn out as we would like them to, it is very tempting to assume that had we done things differently, the story would have had a happier ending. If I had not confronted those two women in the past for their bad behavior, maybe this would not have happened to me. Now I am regressing to, "It's my fault." This I think comes from the notion that we are the cause of what happens—especially the bad things that happen. It seems to be a short step from believing that every event has a cause to believing that every disaster is our fault. The roots of this feeling seem to be in our childhood. Psychologists speak of the infantile myth omnipotence. A baby comes to think that the world exists to meet his needs and that he makes everything happen in it. He wakes up in the morning and summons the rest of the world to its tasks. He cries and someone comes to attend to him. When he is hungry, people feed him, and when he is wet, people change him. Very often we do not completely outgrow that infantile notion that wishes cause things to happen.

What happened to me was not God's doing and God cannot make it vanish. Hundreds of people I know are praying for me. What exactly they are praying for I don't know. People who pray for miracles usually don't get miracles any more than children who pray for bicycles or good grades get them strictly as a result of praying.

There is an amusing story of a little boy who prayed that he would get a bicycle, but nothing happened. So he got a statue of Mary, put a blanket around it, and hid it under his bed. Then he got on his knees and prayed: "Jesus, if you don't give me a bicycle, you will never see your mother again."

I do believe that people who pray for courage, for strength to bear the unbearable, for the grace to remember what they have left instead of what they have lost, find their prayers answered. Rather, they discover that they have more strength, more courage than they ever knew themselves to have. Where did they get it? I would like to think that their prayers helped them find that strength. My prayers are mainly to Jesus for a peace to cleanse my mind of fear, anxiety, and stress: "Dear Jesus, give me your peace. You said to your apostles, 'My peace I give to you—my peace I leave with you.' Look not on my sins, but my faith in You and give me your peace."

The God I believe in does not send us the problem; He gives us the strength to cope with the problem. The conventional explanation, that God sends us the burden because He knows that we are strong enough to handle it, has it all wrong. The expression that God will never give you a cross you can't carry is false. God does not will burdens on His children. It is true that when we reach the limits of our own strength, something unexpected happens. We find reinforcement coming from a source outside of ourselves and in the knowledge that we are not alone. God is on our side, and we manage to go on.

As a priest I have seen people experience indescribable tragedy: the death of a child, the birth of an extremely retarded baby, being the victim of a terrible accident that left them paralyzed for life. Yet, they go on with their lives and learn to cope. They learn how to meet all disappointments with faith in themselves and the future; and how to respond to heartbreak with understanding rather than bitterness and despair. From the perspective of other people's response to human suffering, I learn to dream again and envision a better world than the one I live in, and I learn the human quality of resilience.

In my tragedy, I discovered people around me and God beside me, and strength within me to help me survive one day at a time. After all, I say to myself, no one ever promised us a life free from pain and disappointment. The most anyone promised us was that we would not be alone in our pain, and that we would be able to draw upon a source outside ourselves for the strength and courage we would need to survive life's tragedies and life's unfairness. I think of the conspiracy and all that the false accusation has taught me; and I realize how much I have lost and how much I have gained. Yesterday seems less painful and I am not afraid of tomorrow.

CHAPTER 24

LEARNING TO DIE

In all the years I have dealt with death, the more I am convinced that most people do not know "how to die." Having come to realize that we are more than the body and mind and more than their combined self-image, the ego, we can begin to view dying and death through quite different eyes. We are no longer quite so afraid of our own thoughts and feelings, however disturbing they may be. We know there are more than our thoughts and feelings and the mind that experienced them. We are also souls and as such we come to the mystery of dying and death without quite the same level of fear and dread.

I don't mean to sound simplistic, nor am I implying that I have arrived at a point where death holds no fear for me. Having worked with the dying since the 1960s, I can say without speculation that it is possible to approach our deaths without the degree of emotional suffering that we come to accept as a grey area in our culture. In places like India the approach to death is radically different than it is in the West. It is possible to prepare ourselves consciously for our own passing over, and to spend our last days with love in our hearts, and with the kind of support that will help us make this happen. It is possible to meet the moment of death with openness equipped with our expanded definition of what we human beings are, and to prepare ourselves for what—according to every mystical tradition—will follow after.

I try to free myself from worrying about the past and from anxiety about what is to come in the future by fully entering the present moment. When you deepen into a moment you disappear—at least the solid "you" that you are used to experiencing disappears. Exactly what will happen or what will be necessary when the time comes, we can let our preferences be known. This is not a simple issue. Although pain management has made enormous strides in the past twenty years, it still remains a slippery slope, since most doctors are concerned solely with the body and place little emphasis on the quality of the dying person's consciousness. We must try to determine how much of the suffering we see on the deathbed is due to the patient's struggle to remain conscious against the onslaught of marketing drugs. In their zeal to alleviate one kind of suffering, are doctors helping to create another by overlooking the importance of meeting our deaths with open eyes personally, physically, and philosophically as much as possible while living? How else would a materialistic culture view the death of our material being except as an abomination and a defeat?

* * *

Since that terrible attack on me in February of 2003 when I was falsely accused of a heinous crime, my world as I knew it came to an end. Consequently my entire attitude toward death has changed and implications of my life have been profound. I am not completely rid of fear. I can honestly say that from where I sit today, death does not terrify me as it did on a good day with my mind at peace; death and life seem almost equally appealing. Thanks in large part to the conspiracy which has brought death a great deal closer, I have learned to relax my hold on this body to rest in life—like a bird resting on a dry branch ready to fly away. Since my own personal 9/11, I sometimes go to bed praying that God will take me in my sleep. I pray myself to sleep saying over and over again: "Jesus into your hands I surrender my spirit, take me in your arms and lift me high—into your hands I commit my spirit—give me peace, remove the anxiety and pain from my life."

* * *

Whether people are facing death themselves, confronting the death of a loved one or working professionally with the dying, their concerns seem to center on the same questions. There are some who say that they can handle the dying part, but don't like the idea of being dead.

Others seem quite content to be dead—if only they didn't have to endure the dying. (This reminds me of a Woody Allen quip: "I don't mind dying, I just don't want to be there when it happens.") Finally there is fear of the death moment itself that we may find ourselves in the wrong place or the wrong state of mind to meet the end peacefully.

Examining death will not necessarily give us answers. By beginning to ask the important questions, however, we investigate a process of opening and deepening that can alter our life in miniscule ways by lingering the answers of dying and death into the present moment. Though I feel blessed for the years I've spent with the dying and better prepared to meet my own end, I haven't arrived at any conclusions knowing that each personal death is difficult and contains a mystery that can't be fathomed. "Be patient," Relke advised, "with all that is unresolved in your life and try to love the questions that can't be given, for you wouldn't be able with them, and the point is to live everything. Live the questions now and perhaps without knowing it you will live along someday into the answers."

*   *   *

In preparing for our own death it is fair to say that what worries us today, will worry us on our deathbed. Since dying is often not easy it will be helpful to have as much equanimity and clarity as possible to meet this challenge, and reduce our suffering. In his book, *How We Die*, Sherwin Nuland describes the physical and emotional distress that comes at the Moment of Death: The stoppage of circulation and slowing of the heart muscle upsetting its natural rhythm and forcing it into the chaotic squirming of ventricular fibrillation, the inadequate transport of oxygen to tissues, the failure of organs and the destruction of vital centers. With that can come the experiences of constriction of air—like gripping the chest, a cold sweat, shortness of breath, and sometimes excruciating pain. The question is, where can we hope to stand in our consciousness during such traumatic conditions in order to die with clarity and grace?

The answer is, in our soul consciousness to the degree that it is possible. We wish to be able to stand aside from the death of the body and view this transition from awareness. This is extremely difficult, but not impossible, as the testimonies of conscious beings prove. In any case we aspire in that direction, knowing that the degree to which we can enter soul consciousness will stabilize us through the tumult of dying. With this in mind our mindfulness practices take on new importance. Just as an athlete prepares for a contest by strengthening his or her muscles, we prepare for death by balancing our minds and easing our access to wellness consciousness.

The more we are helped in this process, the better. Just as we employ midwives to help an infant with its birth, we would be wise in this culture to employ individuals specially trained to help us to die. It is logical but true that most people die alone in our culture in hospital beds in the middle of the night. This is not unlike pushing a boat out to sea at night without a map or light or compass, and no word of advice for the lone sailor. How different this is from the way of traditional spiritual cultures. In Tibetan practice, for example, monks and nuns are instructed in ways to guide the dying through their transition. They are trained to deal with the dying person's thirst, coldness, heaviness and breathlessness; encouraging the one who is dying not to cling to these phenomena. They offer such instructions as these: "As the earth element leaves, your body will feel heavy; as the water element leaves, you will feel dryness; as the fire element leaves, you may feel cold; as the air element leaves, your out breath will be longer than your in breath. The signs are now here, don't get lost in the detail. Don't cling to any of these phenomena; they are part of a natural process. Let your awareness go free."

We can transform ourselves into beings capable of meeting these phenomena consciously and without resistance. Although this final life situation may differ in intensity from other experiences we have had, the preparation is the same; namely learning to meet each thought and sensation as it arises with an open, loving heart; not clinging to the experience through either attraction or aversion, and bringing ourselves back to clear awareness.

$*$ $*$ $*$

How do we prepare for death? Mindfulness and meditation are great ways to stabilize the mind and heart and for readying ourselves for this challenge. But the moment of death can be truly scary. Let us use the analogy of whitewater rafting to look more deeply at this question. In order to ride the most powerful white water rapids, professionals rigorously train themselves not to lose their cool in the midst of rocks and torrents and waterfalls. It is one thing to imagine dying and another to be faced with, "Hey, I am going right now!" and remain calm at that moment. To face such rapids with clarity, one must be acquainted with how water feels to "Keep death present on one shoulder always," as Carlos Castaneda's teacher, Don Juan, advised him to do.

The wisdom of remembering death and preparing for it in each moment may be figurative—as in the dropping of autumn leaves—or literal as on a gravestone I found in New England that read: "Dear friend, please know as you pass by us, you are now, so once was I; as I am now, so you will be. Prepare yourself to follow me."

There is a common misconception that preparing for death will diminish the quality of our lives. But this is not the case. In my work with the dying I've constantly found that the time I spend in the presence of people on their deathbed is the time when I feel most profoundly alive.

Keeping death at arm's length prevents us from embracing our lives as fully as we would with mortality closer in our consciousness. With both death and love it is dissolving of boundaries between us and the mystery that loosens the grip of the ego and allows the soul to be revealed. People's greatest fear of dying is "unfinished business." To me very few problems are worth carrying into the moment of our death.

Through a thorough inventory of where we remain stuck, we prepare the way for a peaceful passing. Besides completing our work with other people, it is also important that our affairs be in order, legally, medically, and financially. It is advisable to sign a living will releasing our medical caregivers from the responsibility for keeping your body alive at any cost if you don't want them to, and to donate your organs to medical research should they prove to be viable, if you would like to make that kind of contribution. Additionally we should specify in writing how we wish our bodies to be handled when we die. Where do we wish to be buried, or cremated? Making up a will is difficult for some people. There is a superstitious belief that as long as the will has not been done, they can't die—a kind of magical thinking that can lead to confusion and trouble for those we leave behind. This attention to our material affairs is part of our spiritual practice, symbolizing as it does the final relinquishing of worldly power.

Important too is our choice of where we wish to die. In preparing for our own passing this is one of the most crucial decisions we need to make—before the advent of a crisis, if possible. Do we wish to be in a hospital where access to medical intervention is the high priority, or would we prefer to be at home? How can we bring a spiritual atmosphere into the place where we die, to render our passing more soulful, and help us to remain conscious?

It sometimes pains me to hear people saying things to a dying person, such as, "Mike, you are looking better—and the doctor has a new medicine for you. You will be up and around in no time." Afterwards those same people will go out into the corridor and say, "He is looking terrible. He can't last much longer." All of them seem to be involved in this deception and denial. Nobody seems to want to share the truth with him.

Since Karen Ann Quinlan, the hospice movement has made its appearance in this country. Hospice offers a welcome alternative to dying in a hospital for people whose illness or lack of care makes it impossible for them to die at home. Underlying the hospice movement is a far more enlightened view of dying: As a natural process not to be artificially extended beyond a certain point. For those of us wishing to approach death consciously, hospice may be an excellent environment relieved of the medical imperative to keep the body alive at any cost. There are also many caregivers within the hospice program who are deeply appreciative and supportive of the significance of the dying process.

Death is our greatest spiritual opportunity. By cultivating mindfulness we can prepare ourselves for this final passage by allowing nature rather than the ego to guide us. In so doing we become teachers to others and our own best friends, looking beyond the body's death at the next stage in our soul's adventure.

CHAPTER 25

OUR LAST WORDS

What will be our last or our dying words?

St. Stephen's last words when he was being stoned to death: "Lord receive my spirit."

The last words of Emily Dickenson, the American poet, were: "The fog is rising."

The last words of Goethe, the German poet and playwright were: "More light."

The last words of former American president, Teddy Roosevelt: "Put out the light."

In my experience as a priest at the bedside of dying people, the last words of people were generally of the following nature:

"I love you."

"Thank you for everything."

"Please forgive me."

"I forgive you."

"I am sorry."

"Pray for me and I'll pray for you."

"Love one another."

"There is a box under my bed with $5000 that I have been saving for you. Enjoy it."

What will be our dying words? In a way isn't that vanity? In a deeper sense aren't our living words much more important than our dying words? What are our living words? What words are we dying to say to each other that we aren't saying? Why can't we speak to each other words of forgiveness and stop holding on to hurts from the past? Why don't we have the courage to call up an old friend and tell him or her, "Thank you, you have meant so much to me in my life? I always looked up to you. You have always been such a good example on how it is to live a good life. I love you. I've just wanted to call and leave you this message for the longest time."

Why don't we have the courage to tell a spouse or a parent or a brother or a sister how thankful we are for all that he or she has done for us? Why can't we surprise the other with a card with our own special love words on it? As Leo Buscaglia often said: "Why wait till we die to give the other flowers?"

Why wait till the end to say: "I love you"? Do it now; say it now. Then when we die, people won't be concentrating on our dying words as much as on telling the story of how good we were while we were living; how joyful we were; how honest we were; how caring we were; how much like Christ we were. Instead of concentrating on our dying words, why not concentrate on living a good life, so when we die people's words about us will be:

"She always made you feel so special."
"Never knew him to hold a grudge."
"She never wasted a minute of time."
"She knew how to enjoy life."
"Never could have had a better neighbor."
"Great friend."
"Wonderful dad/mom."
"Always made you feel at home."
"Always went out of his way to help people."
"Unique, one of a kind; after God made him, He threw away the mold."
"Never heard a peep of gossip out of her."
"Wasn't into possessions and stuff, lived very simple, not caught up in materialism."
"Great to her children and grandchildren."
"Would give you the shirt off his back."
"Showed us what is really important in life."
"Left a marvelous legacy of love everywhere she went."
"She was always there, but she never got in the way."
"Terrible card player, but a great friend."
"If they did an autopsy, I guarantee they wouldn't find a mean bone in his body."

I hope people say of me: "He was single minded." I hope my last words would be, "Father into your hands I commit my spirit; receive my soul O, Lord and present me to God the most high." I hope at the other side I will hear: "Come you blessed of my Father, inherit the kingdom prepared for you from the foundation of the world."

CHAPTER 26

LIFE'S TRANSITIONS

In 2004 I made a conscious choice to deal in a positive way with a life altering change—I decided to live. "The Conspiracy" brought me to my knees and sent my life into a tailspin out of control. Despite my deep outrage at the unfairness of it all, the simple reality was that I was psychologically paralyzed. A remarkable change had occurred in my life that required me to work harder and try more diligently than ever I thought I could to find peace of mind.

How did I find the will for such a test? I am often reminded of the adage "Fake it until you make it." Sometimes it seems that setting a goal and taking the first small step are all I needed to really get rolling toward significant change. Just doing that can help find inner resources to actually make a change that I needed.

I now believe we all have a choice in how we live out our lives every minute of the day. Even though I am devastated, I still have freedom of choice. I am still making the decisions that govern my life and I am as much in charge of me as I would be if life were normal. Even though I am fully functional physically, I became paralyzed in an emotional sense. Maybe because I always had a low self-esteem I am still influenced by my upbringing—believing that I could only be loved for what I could achieve. However, I was able to muster up enough energy to set myself free.

Accepting change and creating change have been at the heart of my life since I can remember. Because of the obstacles I have overcome in the past, I have the inner courage to make my dreams seem not impossible, but inevitable. Growing older and accomplishing a meaningful life in spite of what appeared as insurmountable obstacles were fresh in my mind.

* * *

Now this "horrific attack" is just another challenge to overcome and go forward with my life. Just at a time when I thought I could rest on my laurels toward the end of my life I have to start all over again to regain my accomplishments. Yet, I am very frightened. I feel like the solid earth beneath my feet, the planet that I have felt so firmly planted in, has disappeared. I am emotionally free falling, so I do not know where; tumbling down a deep black hole, spinning out of control. It is the most terrifying feeling and there is absolutely nothing I can hold on to. It is a physical anguish as well, and some days I am very depressed, weeping and hiding under the covers of my bed to delay going out to face the world. I am embarrassed being in public—people looking at me and wondering: "Did he or didn't he?" I try very hard not to show anguish in public, but it is not easy; suddenly I am thrust into a world in which I am not who I am supposed to be, someone to be looked up to and inviolate. I find myself desperately swimming just to stay afloat and I feel an enormous sense of failure.

* * *

Needless to say, the enormity of change that engulfed me in that year brought me straight down to bedrock, to examining the very roots of my emotional foundations. It brought me back to thinking who I really was in terms of the planet and the purpose of life, rather than who I was in terms of what I did not have anymore. I was retired, but I still wanted to function as a priest. I enjoyed celebration of the mass for a few people around my dining room table. It kept me going, but I missed the celebration of mass in church and greeting hundreds of people. I have suffered a great loss and it was like a form of death. I asked myself the old question, "What ruins the picnic, the rain, or your attitude about the rain?" It's both of course, but the only thing I can do something about is my attitude, my perception, my reaction to the solution.

My immediate family in Europe and other places around the world know nothing about what happened to me. I went home on vacation with a heavy heart and a cloud over my head. My family had a great celebration planned for me to commemorate my retirement and 40th anniversary in the priesthood. I had to act as normal as possible, although frequently one or another member of my family would ask me if there was something wrong. They would say, "You got so thin and your face looks drawn, you have lost your usual jovial outlook." It was torture—I pretended I was adjusting to my retirement and it was taking a toll on me. But I would tell them not to worry; I will adjust and be fine again. I dreaded the evening news and the newspapers in case my name would be mentioned as being accused of a heinous crime. My family would die of shame and I could not let that happen.

Consequently I "laid low" and kept quiet, and mostly out of the public eye. I hid my pain and kept busy. Being with my priest friends, Father Bob and Father Paul, mostly kept my spirits up and carried me through the rough days. Obviously they could see everything, right through to the fact that deep down I was about as sad as I could be, quite beaten up emotionally. I was able to tell them the whole truth about myself and about what I had been through. Each time I spent with them became a turning point in my life; a kind of cleansing. What I learned from them was that grieving and dealing with loss, whether it is a death, or the end of a ministry, it requires a process of completion. Without processing the loss, it is close to impossible to move on and start a new chapter in life.

Everything in our life is about changes and choices. Something changes and we have a choice to make. There are two things we can do, one is to give up and mourn the death of the previous existence—and that is all right, and necessary for a while. But the other choice is to process your feelings about the change that has happened, find a way to get comfortable with it and press on.

When I am in the middle of a crisis, as I am with the "conspiracy," my respite is taking a walk and going to the ocean. I found an apartment near Long Branch Beach in N.J.; every chance I get, I go there and walk on the beach listening to the water lapping the shore; it helps to clear my mind. It is the most soothing and calming force for me. I have to hear the water; when I go to bed, I put a tape in my recorder that plays the ocean sounds. I go to sleep almost immediately, in the midst of thunderstorms, waves crashing, and every sound that water makes. Water centers me. If I am doing something I have to concentrate on, I'll plug myself into this sound—have it playing in the background while I am working. Instead of scattered thought, I have a laser focus. I find comfort in that sound and in the focus that comes when I listen. It seems to me that you affect remarkable changes in your life if you do not allow your spirit to be paralyzed. It seems to me that right now, with all the horrible things at work in my "world" I have two choices. I can choose to go down in a kind of tunnel and live there, fearful of impending doom. Or I can make the most of life today. I can have an effect on the future with my creative energy by opening my soul to the endless possibilities surrounding me. To me that is a form of acceptance as well as a positive way of moving on.

My friend, Father Jerry O'Riordan, was diagnosed a few years ago with leukemia cancer. Watching his transformations as he was treated for the cancer was an inspiration. He managed to be at once accepting of his illness and at the same time, he fought it with all his might. His attitude toward his illness, and all it brought, said a lot to me a about acceptance as well as letting go. When all is said and done, I absolutely believe that we must forgive in order to let go— either forgive ourselves for the choices we have made, or forgive those who have wronged us.

*   *   *

Of course, in other circumstances, when people seriously hurt you, or do really bad things to you, and get away with it, I am the first to admit it is very hard to forgive them. But I also know that it is worth trying. These are all part of creating openings for change; cultivating a positive attitude, willingness to let go, acceptance of myself and any situation, forgiveness. They all help me to let go when I need to. When change is knocking on the door or even when it has already burst into my life, it's all part of moving on so that I can imagine myself as somehow new. I think when you reach the bottom, anything is possible. Somehow it is an amazing clearing deck, and as painful as it can be to reach the bottom, in a certain way it is the most useful part of a crisis. A lot of people are stuck in ruts they cannot get out of, and until things get bad enough they can't seem to clear the deck and say, "Okay, now who am I really, and what do I really want?"

What I did first was to look at my past, my present, and what the endless possibilities for my future might be. Should I choose them? Especially when it's about "who I am" I had to take a clearer look at who I was. So often it is not until the chips are down that we actually start to look at the very foundation of our life, to really see "who I am" and in that process I can reassess and re-imagine my life. Everything I have been talking about takes time to develop and patience to allow it to do so. It always takes patience to handle the ensuing turmoil. No one gets to know the end of their own story ahead of time, and in the interim we each have no choice but to be patient while we figure out the next step in our own story.

Losing my patience with people is a constant struggle for me, and it offers loads of opportunities for learning. But while I am not a particularly patient person, I do take lessons where I can find them. One terrific place is from friends like Monsignor Bob Carroll. Patience has been paramount to him in the smaller day to day skills his life requires.

Our imaginations are so powerful and can do so much good in our lives. However, there are times when our imaginations work overtime, and fear can be one of the unfortunate by-products. Fear is the great stop sign that can halt change, or make it far more painful than it needs to be. Change so often takes courage, and fear so often provides the sticking point that overpowers courage.

My belief is that we don't have to give fear that much power; fear can be viewed as just another trick of the mind. We should not honor fear so much, after all F-E-A-R is just False Evidence Appearing Real.

Now I can look back and see a lot of things I was afraid of that I didn't need to be afraid of. I like to think that as I get older, I can, and often do stop being so fearful of things like change. I think those who become more fearful are those are those who are not willing to change.

Whatever it is in life, I just want that experience. Sometimes it is painful, but it is what makes you grow. I guess what makes me able to carry on in spite of my own personal 9/11 is the satisfaction and joy that I get when I succeed in finishing something after a long hard struggle. But when fear is at its worst, as when I read my former bishop's letter to Rome to laicize me, it truly numbed and paralyzed me.

Sometimes we only break the logjam of fear when someone else pulls us through it, and that is where my friends come in, Father Paul, Father Bob, and Father Martin, and hundreds of lay people. Fear has been a major issue for me in my life. How to get past that abject fear? To this day if I go to give a sermon, I'll do the talk and then when it is over, I'll realize that I have no idea what I have just said. I know I spoke from my heart, but I can never repeat whatever it was I have said. My way of coping with the fear is to call on the Holy Spirit and speak from my heart. Obviously I prepare ahead of time researching the subject and knowing how I feel about it. Then the information gestates and when I speak, it is not something that's been learned, something that's been written and performed, it is simply what's in my heart. I confess, I am in a state of total panic when I go to the pulpit, but then I get going and I forget about fear. The Holy Spirit takes me over and I have no idea where the thoughts come from, it is like I have been doing it forever and the fear is gone.

*   *   *

Monsignor Jack Dericks was accused of a similar crime as I was. I asked him, "How do you deal with it on a daily basis?"

He said, "Let me tell you, I am so glad I'm here. Every day is a gift to me. And everything is doable. If it is not a severe medical problem; any problem can be solved. Losing other things, material things, can be heartbreaking, but other than medical problems or death, it does not matter. My life has become calm. What I've been through puts everything into perspective. It seems that if you don't have a particular spiritual connection before you face great change in your life you are primed to develop one when you do. Facing something as frightening as a false accusation as I was did that for me. It awakened the spiritual side of my nature which I realize now was dormant. The 'attack' gave me an opportunity to reexamine my spirituality and it gave me a deep sense of a connection with God, as Father, Son, and Holy Spirit; and an ability to trust in God like never before in my life. It was the beginning of a new spiritual journey that led me to read the scriptures and say the Rosary and let go of fear with a capital 'F'."

As I mentioned earlier, while I was going through that really difficult time in my life, I used to take walks and listen to tapes, and try to understand what was happening to me, and why it was happening this way. One day I fell down on my knees in the middle of my walk and I just sobbed. I realized I'd given up everything and I didn't have anything else to give up, except my own life. In a flash I thought that this must be a teaching lesson from God about letting go in life. I had to let go of everything that was left in me. During this epiphany, I thought, "Oh no, I am going to die and God is preparing me." In that moment I deeply believed I was going to go, and soon. It seemed that my entire life had been an experience of letting go of everything that came to me even down to the moment, to this minute. I'd let go of parents and friends and family and children and work and the body and the whole thing. I was intensely trying to figure out how we learn what it takes to let go.

What I came to was the idea that part of what allows us to live with letting go is being in touch with what you do not let go of, the one thing that's forever is the spiritual basis of our lives, which in my belief is call soul—my consciousness—created by the faculties of my soul, my intellect, my will. My soul (consciousness) has an existence independent of my body and when my body dies, my soul and all our souls will continue to live. As my father used to ask, "How many souls could sit on the head of a pin?"

The pain of the accusation got me in touch with what is real in my life. My soul—and I know that if we can gracefully let go of what we must, we have got it made—then it is just about moving through life. But what we do not let go of is the spiritual reality.

I am now convinced that sometimes God puts a ring in our nose and leads us where we need to be. I would describe myself as very spiritually focused. But looking back beyond the "conspiracy," I wonder how many years God had been tapping me on the forehead before I woke up and heard it. It is almost as if I was led to it because of a personal tragedy. It does seem that if you are not spiritually aware, you may actually miss the whole idea about these moments that can be so difficult, and fail to see that they are actually gifts in disguise. Once you have visited this signpost and you can see the need for spiritual guidance in the midst of turmoil, it is wonderful to think of what can happen next.

* * *

I am determined that something good will come out of all of it, that my suffering will not be in vain. I hope I can help other innocent priests by getting on the "talk show" circuit, like Larry King, or writing a book to get my story out. All of this heartache has made me stronger because it made me see the value in having faith in God, and in having others around me who have walked this experience ahead of me. We all share what we know, and that makes me feel good.

Sometimes when you are walking up that mountain by yourself, you can say, "I can do it, I can do it" and if you realize you are not really walking alone; if you believe in a personal God "something" greater than yourself, it gets better. Like the little train that could: "I think I can, I think I can."

I believe it is all part of living in the moment. I would never have had so much love shown to me if I hadn't had to go through "the attack." Just the other night I was having dinner in Long Branch, NJ, sitting at a table with three priest friends, when in walked seven or eight other priests. When they saw me, they immediately came over to me and each of them hugged me like I was a lost long friend, I had never felt such support from so many priests all at once. Now whenever I think anything is tough, unfair, painful or even insurmountable, I think of somebody I know who is suffering a lot more than me.

At this moment as I look at my TV, I see all those poor people in Florida who lost everything during the many hurricanes that hit Florida this month of September 2004. I see Martha Stewart being made a public spectacle of and taken off to spend five months in jail. All of these individuals carry on and their families are full of love and support for them. Whereas many people would give up if they were faced with similar circumstances of daily life, they do not give up. In fact they go far beyond simply making do; they each found a way to excel in their own lives. Of course there are thousands of people whom you and I don't know who are this courageous, and what lessons there are for us all in their lives! Spiritual guidance comes in a variety of packages, and is delivered to us under many guises. Looking to one another, in the presence of God in one another and to the inspiration we can find in one another, is the way to begin seeing the gifts that even the darkest days can bring.

CHAPTER 27

A GOOD SHEPHERD

I've stated that I was losing faith and trust in the leadership of the Church, but God had a surprise for me. Along came an encounter that would redeem me from the pit of despair, into my life came a Good Shepherd named Bishop Serratelli, installed as bishop of my diocese on July 6, 2004—roughly one and a half years after my former bishop censured me.

He was everything I could possibly imagine a shepherd of souls could be. He could have misjudged me and cast me aside, having wanted nothing to do with me, not even wanting to be associated with me. I was, after all, considered by my former bishop to be a danger to the people of God; committing as he said in his letter to Rome, "an egregious crime" deserving the death sentence of my priestly life. Now my new bishop threw me a lifeline and saved me from a feeling of total despair and hopelessness. He had the grace to share with me as a historian, his knowledge of many saints of the Church who had been falsely accused of sexual misconduct.

Bishop Serratelli brought me into his home and sat in a simple chair close to mine. He was totally relaxed and unbelievingly open and humble, admitting his own fear and inadequacies. He began gently encouraging me to protect myself with good civil and canon lawyers. He told me not to be overly anxious, but at the same time don't give up fighting for my rights. I felt for the first time in my life that I was in the presence of a man like Jesus. I believe he was doing what Jesus would do; he was not lording it over me, but being humble and totally unassuming. No hidden agenda; "What you saw is what you got." He was patient and listened carefully to my story for more than two hours.

Afterwards, touched by his tenderness and warmth, I began to think back to my days as pastor and assistant shepherd of my bishop of the local church of Saint Rose. I began to mull over how "high and mighty" I had treated at times some wounded sheep of my parish, when I showed no compassion, only raw justice. Abraham Lincoln once said, "If you want to know the true character of a man, give him power."

I recall one time in the parish when the poor box was constantly being broken into and robbed. I installed a silent alarm in the inside of the box so that without knowing it, if an intruder forced the door open, the alarm would ring quietly in the parish office. A week or so later the alarm went off. I ran to the church while the secretary called the police. As I entered the church, I saw a well-dressed man walking out. I asked him if he saw anybody breaking into the poor box. He acted offended that I should ask such a question. Just then the police arrived and began to question him. In the meantime I looked closely at the poor box and noticed scotch tape slightly keeping the door closed. I went to the police as the man was being questioned and said to them, "If he has scotch tape and a screwdriver in his pocket, he is guilty."

The police searched him and found a screwdriver and scotch tape, so they arrested him. He pleaded for me to forgive him and said that he was very sorry, but I callously walked away, proud of myself that I had helped capture the culprit. The police threw him in the holding pen of the police station across the street from my church. Now I realize how rudely I behaved, and surely not what Jesus would have done. Why did I not forgive him, and tell the police to let him go? Why did I not visit him in the police station and give him some comfort. I failed miserably in being a shepherd of souls.

At another time I read in the diocesan bulletin an article about a man going around to parishes with a sad story that his daughter was hit by a car while riding her bicycle in South Carolina. She was killed and he had no money to get to the funeral, and he asked for money from the priest. It was a con, so the diocese was alerting the parishes to be on the lookout for a man with this story. It must not have been more than a week later when a man walked into my office relating this exact story. I told him to sit down, I would see what I could do, and that I would be back in a little while. I hurried to the rectory and called the police, and then I calmly went back to the office and continued the conversation with the man. Very soon the police arrived and arrested the man. The man asked me for forgiveness, but I dismissed his pleas and the police took him away. As before, I did not visit this man in jail. Now I realize that I again failed as a shepherd. What would Jesus have done?

In scripture, a woman accused of adultery was taken before Jesus, and He was asked if she should be stoned to death. Jesus turned to her accusers and said, "Let he, who is without sin, cast the first stone." Jesus then forgave her, saying, "Go and sin no more."

After I was falsely accused and my former bishop ignored my pleas for a hearing, my attitude has dramatically changed, sensitized to the pain and suffering of others. My new bishop, Bishop Serratelli, has inspired me to always do what Jesus would do. I was the recipient of a "new way," the way of Jesus. Jesus said, "I am the way, the truth and the life." He is the only way and any other way is not the right way, especially for a shepherd of souls; an alter Christi.

Myself (left) and Bishop Serratelli (right).

YEAR THREE (2005)

CHAPTER 28

DARK NIGHT OF MY SOUL

At one time or another, most people go through a period of sadness, loss, frustration or failure that is so disturbing, and long-lasting that it can be called a "dark night of the soul." For some people these situations are problems to be solved, however, for me it is the source of deep despair, not a surface challenge, but development that takes you away from the joy of ordinary life; an external event or an internal mood that strikes at the core of my existence. This is not just a feeling, but a rupture in my very being and it will take a long while to get through to the other end of it. Some people may call it depression, but for me it is a much more meaningful event. Depression is a psychological sickness, but a "dark night" I would describe as a spiritual test. A dark night pares life down to its essentials and helps you get a new start. I don't want to romanticize a dark night of the soul. In fact it seems like you won't always get through it. But in hindsight I see it as an opportunity to be transformed from within, in ways you could never imagine. I, for sure, would not *choose* a dark night of the soul for myself. I feel it is given to a person, or God allows it to come to you. I guess my job is to get close to it and sift it for its gold.

They say you probably know more about the depth of your soul from periods of pain and confusion than from times of comfort. Darkness and turmoil stimulate the imagination in a certain way; they allow you to see things you may ordinarily overlook. You become sensitive to a different spectrum of emotion and meaning. Personally I perceive the extremes of my feelings and thoughts and learn things I wouldn't notice in times of normalcy.

A dark night of the soul is not extraordinary or rare. It is a natural part of life and you can gain as much and more from it as you can from times of normalcy. Just look around at your friends and acquaintances. One is going through a divorce, another's mother is seriously ill, a young child has been hurt in an accident; and then there is war and fear of terrorism.

They say that if you give all your energy to getting rid of your dark night, you may not learn its lessons or go through the important changes it can make for you.

As I struggle through the dark night of my personal soul, I feel exhausted and in total darkness; feeling I will never see the light of day again, see the sunshine or smell the roses. My dark nights seem to come at me like a tornado, getting more and more intense as time goes on. I was enjoying the last months of my 40 years of ministry, looking forward to many more years of life in retirement, when suddenly out of nowhere came the awful accusation by a detective from the prosecutor's office. I was devastated and was plunged into the darkest place imaginable. The dark night of my soul had just begun, and it got darker and darker as the time went on.

I had just received a very glowing letter of retirement from my bishop that pleased me immensely. However, a few days later I received a letter from this same bishop, ordering me to leave the parish immediately and never return or contact any of my former parishioners.

I was not allowed to dress as a priest or say mass publicly, since I was "a danger to the people of God."

My successor as pastor of St. Rose of Lima ordered the staff not to ever get in touch with me; that my name was never to be mentioned. I was to be treated as a persona non-grata. Not allowed to be prayed for from the altar. Any symbol of my name was removed.

Even though I had developed a severe prostate problem, and had a bad back, I was refused entrance to the priests' retirement home in Chester N.J. I found it very difficult to live alone. I felt isolated and lost, having been deemed not worthy to live in the retirement home.

At the 40th anniversary celebration for priests' jubilarians, my name was missing; as if I never existed, even though I served 40 years of faithful service in the diocese of Paterson, rarely taking a day off. My other accomplishments include:

- Five years as associate at St. Patrick's in Chatham.
- Two years as associate at St. Nicholas in Passaic.
- Five years as associate at St. Michael's in Netcong.
- Six years as associate at St. Cecilia, Rockaway.
- Twenty-three years as pastor at St. Rose of Lima in E. Hanover.

In 2002, I applied for retirement after 40 years of service. The bishop gracefully granted my request. However, on March 21, 2003, the world as I knew it came to an end. I had my personal "9/11." The ultimate dark night of my soul had begun. I found myself in the darkest place I had ever been in.

*   *   *

John of the Cross (1541 – 1597) was a member of the Carmelites and along with St. Theresa of Avila, they tried to reform that order. Many in the order were so against John that they imprisoned him for eight months, during which he wrote a series of remarkable poems. His better writing is chiefly commentary on those poems, one of them entitled *Dark Night of the Soul* as a period of transformation. It is not always obvious how you benefit from the darkness. Sometimes a dark night makes sense because of what it contributes, not what it does for you. Mystics tell us that during the dark night there is no choice but to surrender control, give in to the unknowing, and stop and listen to whatever signals of wisdom might come along. It is a time of enforced retreat—and perhaps unwilling withdrawal. The dark night is more than a learning experience, it is a profound invitation into a realm that nothing in the culture so preoccupied with external success prepares you for.

The real dark night cannot be dismissed so easily. It leaves a lasting effect, in fact it alters you for good; it is nothing to brag about.

The author Thomas More says, "The dark night may be profoundly unsettling, offering no conceivable way out, except perhaps to rely on pure faith and resources far beyond our understanding and capacity."

The dark night calls for a spiritual response, not only a therapeutic one. It pushes you to the edge of what is familiar and reliable, stretching your imagination about how life works. A dying parishioner of mine once said she would never want to return to this life after years of pain and struggle. Personally I wouldn't want to live again and have to go through the darkest night of my soul of 2003 when I was falsely and unjustly accused of a heinous crime that changed my life forever.

The author Thomas More continues: "The best way to deal with a dark night of the soul is to be made luminous by it. You are not the owl seeing in the dark. You are the candle being burnt for its luminosity. It is not your luminosity that issues from a dark night, but the dim light of substance itself. Your dark night tells you that life is never as bright and successful and meaningful as you might imagine. If you never learn this lesson, the essential moonlight will forever be hidden from you. Nothing could be more precious than a dark night of the soul, the very darkness of which allows your lunar light to shine. It may be painful, discouraging and challenging, but it is nevertheless an important revelation of what your life is about. In the darkness you see things you couldn't see in the daylight. Skills and powers of soul emerge from frustration and ignorance. The seeds of spiritual faith, perhaps your only recourse, but certainly a valuable power are found in your darkness. The other half of who you are comes into view and though the dark night you are compelled. Your darkness has given you character and color and capacity. Now you are free to make a real contribution. It is a gift of your dark night of the soul."

The Irish writer, John Moriarty, dissenting a moment of intense transformation in his own life writes, "If nature can handle the destruction and reconstruction of a caterpillar into a butterfly, why shouldn't I surrender and trust that it can handle what is happening to me?"

*   *   *

I too must stand back and look at myself from a distance. See myself as part of the same world that changes a caterpillar into a butterfly, a storm into the increase of life, and a forest fire into an opportunity for new growth. I don't have to be sentimental about it, but I can have enough distance from my intensely personal thoughts and sensations to allow myself the experience. The distance doesn't take away any confusion or pain, but it does make the experience tolerable. Meaning allows me to go through almost any form of change, no matter what the cost.

The black of the dark night might come from ignorance, not knowing what is happening and where life is taking me. This is as true of a divorce as it is of a terminal illness. The only choice, as Igor Stravinsky said: "If the artist is to remain in the present, not bound or deluded by the past and not imprisoned in a fixed and defensive idea about the future. The worm has to let the transmutation take place. It would do no good for him to plan his wingspan and colors or to wish to remain in the snug safety of the tiny world he has known. The most difficult challenge is to let the process take place, and yet that is the only release from the pressure of the dark night."

For the first time I understood St. John of the Cross' dark night of the soul.

Mark Galasso grew up during my pastorate at St. Rose and is now an art teacher. His rendering of "my life in shambles" after the conspiracy is in a Picasso-like abstract. Some of the symbolism: spear = the attack of the false accusation / words coming out of my mouth = yelling and screaming up at God in disbelief / huddled figures = the people of the Church who turned against me / cockroaches = the creatures that invaded my apartment after the attack / fire = my priesthood going up in flames / head with big nose = the authority of the Church making judgment against me / light coming down = God's love and the people who supported me.

CHAPTER 29

THE "EIGHTH" DAY

Today, June 8, 2005, the 42nd Anniversary of my ordination which took place in St. Patrick's Cathedral, Carlow, Ireland, on June 8, 1963. On that great day, along with thirty other candidates, Bishop Lawrence Keogh placed his hands on my head and declared me a priest forever according to the order of Melchisedich. Today, June 8, 2005, is a day in which I still try to survive an attempt on my priestly life, a day I still wait for the ecclesiastical trial that will decide the fate of my priesthood, reminiscent of the day that St. Joan of Arc waited her ecclesiastical trial, the Inquisition that would sentence her to death in a fierce fire that consumed her body and ultimately killed her. The day the Church went down in euphony, an unholy day. Like the day called Good Friday, "good" because her death would forever be the course of strength for those falsely accused. It took the Church 500 years to admit their mistake and canonize her as a saint. (Let me make it clear that in no way do I even remotely compare myself to Joan of Arc. It is merely didactic.)

Today, June 8, 2005, I sit by myself on the beach in Long Branch, New Jersey and reminisce on the years of my active priesthood, holy days and happy days. Our calendars, once full of feasts of virgins, martyrs, confessors, now are crowded with unholy days. The day in Feb. 2003 when I was accused of a horrific crime, a day the detective told me I didn't remember because it was so painful and awful I buried it; a day on September 11, 2001 when terrorists struck our national financial center, the day they killed our innocent. Yesterday was the day the Church put Galileo on trial for claiming the earth revolved around the sun. "You can think it," the Pope told him, "just don't say so out loud."

Today, as I sit on Long Branch beach, I realize it was once known as Summer Capital beach where seven United States Presidents spent their summers at different rented houses. They got on a train in Washington, DC and came all the way to Long Branch, New Jersey. Across the street from where I sit is a shrine to these seven Presidents.

(1) Ulysses Grant – 18th President (1869-1877)
(2) Rutherford Hayes – 19th President (1877-1881)
(3) Chester Arthur – 21st President (1881-1885)
(4) James Garfield – 22nd President (died in Long Branch in 1881)
(5) Benjamin Harrison – 23rd President (1889-1893)
(6) William McKinley – 25th President (1897-1901)
(7) Woodrow Wilson – 28th President (1913-1921)

On this day, as I think about all of these Presidents, I think of the weight of the presidency on their shoulders as they vacationed on this very beach. As Woodrow Wilson once said, "If you want a friend in Washington, get a dog." I meditate on the deaths they have all died and think of the words spoken to the Pope on his enthronement: "Thus passes the glory of the world." (Transit Mundi Gloria) Dust thou art and into dust you shall return.

On this day, June 8, 1968, my hero Robert Kennedy was buried. My dreams for him as President were shattered. A very sad day indeed; an unholy day. His assassination came only two months after civil rights leader Martin Luther King Jr. was shot and killed in Memphis, Tennessee. Like King, Robert Kennedy had advocated social reform, defended the rights of minorities, and called for an end of the Vietnam War. The loss was devastating to many Americans and was made only more tragic by memories of his older brother's assassination five years earlier. On this day, June 8, 1968, he was brought to St. Patrick's Cathedral in New York City. I attended that funeral myself on the day of the 5th anniversary of my ordination. I remember Andy Williams singing Bobbie's favorite anthem, *The Battle Hymn of the Republic*. His brother, Edward Kennedy, delivered a eulogy, some of which I remember to this day: "My brother need not be idolized or enlarged in death beyond what he was in life. He should be remembered simply as a good and decent man who saw wrong and tried to right it, saw war and tried to stop it. As he said many times, to those he touched and who sought to touch him, 'Some men see things as they are and say 'why?' I dream of things that never were and say 'why not?'"

Another significant day was June 8, 1941 - the day the allies invaded Syria and Lebanon during World War II. The day of June 8, 1963 was for me a day of ecstasy, but on this day of June 8, 2005, on the beach filled with sad memories, it is a day of agony, but as they say in Ireland, "What doesn't kill you makes you stronger."

In the Easter Exsultet of the church it says, "O happy fault, O necessary sin of Adam, which gained for us so great a Redeemer." If the first man had not committed a sin of disobedience against God, it would not be necessary for the Son of God to empty Himself of His Godhead and come among us as a human being and through His death and resurrection dispel the darkness of sin. In a way, Adam's sin was a blessing. In a way, the false accusation of me was a blessing. It immediately brought me to my knees and brought me closer to the passion, death, and resurrection of Christ. Like Him, I was falsely accused, but like Him, I will eventually, like the Phoenix, rise from the ashes to a new life, a new birth, a deeper and fuller relationship with my redeemer Jesus Christ. I now more than ever identify with the Easter Exsultet—a hymn that I proudly sang in Gregorian chant every Easter day, which finally ends with the magnificent words:

May the morning star,
which never sets find this flame still burning,
Christ, that morning star,
who came back from the dead,
and shed his peaceful light,
on all Mankind.

I pray on my knees in my apartment night and morning before a picture of the sacred heart of Jesus: "Dear Jesus my Lord and Savior, let the truth shine brightly and dispel the darkness of a false accusation that surrounds me."

Eventually when that day arrives and the whole truth comes out, I will be able to sing the psalm, "This is the day the Lord has made, let us rejoice and be glad."

Because of that day, I will never take for granted my priesthood. As the saying goes, "You will never miss the water until the well runs dry." Again, I cry out, "O Happy Fault; O Happy False Accusation." It gives birth to the truth and the truth finally makes me free. Free to appreciate my priesthood and to realize how special I am, that God choose me to receive a gift: the power on earth to forgive sins and to make Jesus present on the altar in the littleness of a piece of bread and wine. The powers to renew the passion and death and resurrection of Christ. "O Happy Fault" again.

On the day of June 8, 2005, the 42nd Anniversary of my ordination, I went to see the movie *Cinderella Man*, a movie produced and directed by Ron Howard, and featuring Russell Crowe and Renee Zellwegger. It reenacted the true story of boxer James J. Braddock. It was especially poignant for me, a story that imaged my priestly life, a time of triumph and defeat and finally a great victory. Braddock's core story played out in a few concentrated months at the lowest point of the great American Depression. For some mystical reason, his life mirrored the nation's. He rose to the top of the bubble during the Roaring Twenties. When the bubble burst, his life deflated too, along with the lives of most Americans. As he made his comeback, it was clear that he was not an "individual" working alone. He was a member of a family—his own, his professions, and the American family. And so it was that a nation turned its eyes to a prizefighter's life as I personally make my comeback and fight the biggest fight of my life. Like Braddock I will not do it alone but with the help of my close priest friends and many supporters. And I hope, like in Braddock's fight, the entire American Church will turn its eyes to this falsely accused priest and realize that not all accused priests are guilty; and that my exoneration will encourage other accused priests to fight the good fight and never, never give up; and they too can have their day of triumph over evil.

During my fight to get my good name back and indeed my very life, I saw the best and the worst of humanity as portrayed in the movie *Cinderella Man*. When he was down and out some helped him financially and others turned their backs on him. In my case, some embraced me and some betrayed me. Some embraced me as it were at a distance, but many embraced me, closely, circulating tightly around me, with prayers, letters, visits and phone calls keeping me alive, sometimes barely hanging on to life with my fingernails and sometimes encouraged by some positive random acts of heroic kindness; people making great sacrifices letting go of pressing personal responsibilities and even sometimes traveling great distances to be with me at my most desperate moments, assuring me I can do all things through Christ who strengthens me, and live to see another day.

Many people wrote or called me on the phone telling me they had dreams about me; most of them dreaming I returned to St. Rose and that they received communion from me at the altar. One woman's dream was especially revealing. Her name was Meli. She said she dreamt that she was sitting on a bench in Lurker Park; Jesus came and sat next to her; suddenly she looked ahead and she saw me walking past her. Jesus turned to her and said, "That Father McCarthy...tell him not to worry so much." Then Jesus disappeared. This phone call was unusually inspiring for me. I felt special; who was I that Jesus was speaking to me through other people, even through people I barely knew.

There is a story about a man who once dreamed that he was walking along the beach with God. When he turned his head to glance behind him, he saw two sets of footprints in the sand, one his, the other God's. But when he gazed back farther to look over his whole life's journey, he saw there were stretches with only one set of prints and that these coincided with the saddest times of his life.

The man called up to God with a note of reproach in his voice, "Lord, you pledged that you'd walk with me all the way once I decided to follow you. But now it seems that you left me when I needed you most."

"My precious child," God replied, "I would never leave you. When you suffered most, in those times that you see but a single set of footprints, it was then that I carried you."

I understand that right now in the midst of my suffering I am being carried.

At times when I feel all alone, I close my eyes and fall into a dream-like state and realize that I am not alone after all, that I have more friends than I can count. I prayed and I wasn't alone, I had joined a huge chorus, I could hear prayers for me from throughout the diocese especially from people in the many parishes that I served. There was a rising tide of caring and belief.

$$* \quad * \quad *$$

My former pastor, Monsignor Dennis Hayes, as I mentioned earlier, had a dramatic change in his life after being baptized in the Spirit. Before his conversion, he was angry and depressed, his parishioners avoided him and many left the parish. After his conversion he became a different man: warm, loving and kind, reaching out to people with hugs and kisses. One morning at the breakfast table he looked sad.

I said, "What's the matter Monsignor? You look down and out?"

"Well," he said, "I had a terrible nightmare last night. I dreamt I was walking down Main Street in Rockaway, New Jersey, totally naked and people were mocking me and laughing. I was terrified, I was sweating and restless. Eventually I fell out of the bed and onto the floor. I then woke up shaken and exhausted. It was the worst dream of my life."

I said, "Would you like me to interpret that dream for you?"

He was surprised but agreed.

I explained to him that what happened was perfectly clear. "Before your conversion you kept at a distance from people, you never let them close enough to get to know the real you. Now you are friendly and relaxed and you have made yourself vulnerable. The nightmare was your mental unconscious expression of that vulnerability. You had stripped yourself of all protective defensive mechanisms, and in your dream you felt naked before the people, and that obviously was awfully traumatic, and consequently your nightmare left you drained. But I believe it was the final cleansing of the residue of your former life. Now you are free, free at last to live a full and happy life."

Now at 93 years old he is at the Little Sisters of the Poor Nursing Home in Totowa, NJ. I went to visit him a few months ago and he was bright, cheerful and happy. In fact, he said to me, "I am so happy, so very happy. I have Jesus right here with me."

Personally, I have my own nightmares to cope with the trauma of a conspiracy of a despicable nature, which includes post-traumatic stress disorder such as flashbacks and general anxiety. I've always known that I have a harsh inner critic that I can never please. This critic led me to feelings of inadequacy I saw how my critic had created a competition I could never win: me against me. Being a priest and exercising my priestly ministry opposed my inner critic. Here I had feelings of accomplishment. It compensated for my poor self-image. My priestly life helped me quiet my inner critic, which took over with a vengeance when my priesthood was under attack. My inner demons of shyness, fear, and inadequacy resurfaced and caused me indescribable mental pain.

For me personally in spite of everything, the day of June 8, 1963 was still the best day for the rest of my life; the dream of being a priest fulfilled. If I had to do it again, I would do it exactly the same, I didn't have a choice, it was God's call; it was my vocation.

CHAPTER 30

CANONICAL TRIAL: THE DECISION

As I struggle with the injustice inflicted against me, I must learn to be patient; even though patience is the least of my virtues. As my custodian, John Supka, used to say to me often: "If you are not patient, you will end up a patient." I have learned the hard way; because of my impatience I ended up on the brink of a nervous breakdown. I must become more like Jesus: "Like a lamb before his shearers he opened not his mouth."

I have discovered that impatience in pursuit of a quick fix can turn temporary setbacks into major setbacks. Being confronted with adversity can happen more often than most people will admit. It tested me in ways that others have never contemplated. But the truth is my life was pretty bad on the inside for five long years. I constantly experienced the darkness of doubt. My fragile self-esteem cracked and I beat myself up about it.

At one stage, my canonist, Father John, told me I had reached a crossroad. The new promoter of justice had stated, "The case is inconclusive and not provable, and it is up to me to make a decision." I decided on a trial and nothing less. Bishop Serratelli told me he was glad I didn't take the easy way out. He felt I was wise to go all the way to a trial; it was the wise thing to do.

I was determined not to let myself be paralyzed with negatives. I had to convince myself that tough times are the best times to get back to basics. I had to believe I was strong enough, although barely, to make a turnaround. To believe the bad ending with the conspiracy was not a recurring "thing." I confronted the darkness of doubt and thrust forward toward exoneration.

The last four letters of being an American are "I-CAN" — yes I can and I will not give up until I prove my innocence. I forgive those who tried to destroy me, but I can't forget...I want to lash out, but revenge is an unproductive emotion. I let my hard earned new perspective be the catalyst to a more humble charitable me. I have hit enough potholes in my life that I know I don't have all the answers. My first inclination was to beat myself up, putting myself into depression. But ultimately I turned my lost self-esteem into a newfound modesty. The older I get, the wiser I get and see opportunities to use it the right way in order to change lives with it. I can truly appreciate where I am right now and get up each morning invigorated and content because I have the opportunity to make every day a special day.

The key to achieving greatness is not so much what I accomplish, but what others accomplish with my assistance. Enhancing someone else's life through my experience is a major motivation in my life. I intend to leave this universe a little bit better than I entered it. But before I exit, I intend to make my final act memorable. But I must slow down and not rush to reach the future and in the meantime fail to enjoy life as it happens. I know I have been given a gift to enjoy life in a positive and constructive way and change others with it. I can truly appreciate where I am right now, and make every day a special day.

The above inspiration was motivated by Rich Pitino's book, *Rebound Rules*, which I highly recommend for others to read.

CHAPTER 31

SHYNESS

As a child in first grade, I was, they tell me, very cute looking with curly rusty hair. I was outgoing and to get people's acceptance and praise, I loved to tell funny stories in front of the class at the teacher's request. My classmates loved my jokes and laughed heartily at them.

In the second grade I was taken out of class and put in the hospital to have a TB gland removed from my neck. I was in the hospital for a long time and consequently had to repeat the second grade. I remember being very upset that I could not advance to the third grade with my classmates. I felt that I was being punished and that year was the longest in my life. Each day felt like a thousand years.

I finally advanced to the sixth grade. Brother Mullery was my teacher, I was his favorite student; in his eyes I could not do anything bad. Brother Mullery either liked you or disliked you. If he disliked you, he could be cruel and abusive. One day he mercilessly beat a child, slapping him in the face and even kicking him. I was horrified. When the child's father, who was a policeman, came to the school to speak to Brother Mullery about why he had beaten his son, he asked me what had happened. I told him the whole story, giving him all the details.

A few days later I was sitting in class and suddenly Brother Mullaney stared at me with a fierce, angry look and wouldn't take his eyes off of me. He traumatized me with that look, which to this day I have never forgotten. He then pulled me out of my seat by my hair, slapped me, beat me, kicked me and said he hated me. At that moment my life was changed forever; after that I felt like a different person, I became extremely shy and serious, and very studious. In a strange way it was a blessing. It grounded me and thereafter my greatest desire was to please my teachers and to strive for academic excellence.

All of which I achieved. However, that painful episode was never erased; it was recorded for ever in the tape recorder of my brain.

* * *

When this terrible "accusation" hit me, I had a flashback to that moment in the sixth grade. The recording was reactivated, and I was especially vulnerable to the attack. It became an obsession of my brain and now I don't know if I will be able to fully recover emotionally. I have regressed to an emotional belief that I have to succeed in order to be a worthwhile person. I irrationally feel I have to start all over again to rebuild my emotional health. I have to ask myself again: "Where is the evidence that my worth as a person depends on my succeeding? In what way would I be a rotten human if I failed at an upstart task?"

With my psychological training as part of my priesthood, I have to force myself to dispute my sad feelings whenever I see I am letting them creep back into my mind. I know I must vigorously dispute them. I keep taking on tasks and doing things that I emotionally fear. I do what I am afraid to do and very often I won't allow myself to cop out. Somehow I must become relaxed and comfortable again.

I must learn to clearly see the difference between appropriate bad feelings—such as those of sorrow, regret and frustration when I don't get some of the important things I want—and inappropriate bad feelings such as those of depression, anxiety and self-pity, when I am deprived. Whenever I feel over-concerned and miserable, I must admit that I am bringing it on myself. I strive now to make the removal of my misery one of the most important things in my life—something I am utterly determined to achieve. My psychological training taught me to fully acknowledge that I always have some choices about how to think, feel and behave, and to actively strive to make those choices for myself. There is no magical way to change my personality and my strong tendencies to upset myself. I keep looking for enjoyable things to do, such as reading, or visiting or entertaining my friends.

My major life goal is to again achieve emotional happiness, giving myself something to live for. Finding things to distract myself from serious woes and negative thoughts and help preserve my mental health. I noticed I have become addicted to negative thinking; constantly thinking the worst. When friends are traveling a distance to my apartment or traveling a distance back to their home, I worry until they have reached their destination. If they don't arrive in a reasonable amount of time, I imagine the worst, and make myself miserable with irrational thoughts, as someone called it appropriately "awfulizing." Since the "conspiracy" I do not read newspapers or look at the

TV news. I have an unconscious or ever-conscious fear of seeing my name on the TV news or in the newspapers. My irrational compulsion is to run somewhere far away from the "world."

I try hard to give up my negative thinking, no matter how hard it is to give them up, give them up, and give them up. Unfortunately I constantly backslide into negative feelings, thinking the worst. They tell me that is part of being a normal human being.

I have to be vigilant not to entertain the past traumas. I know I can't handle them entirely by myself and I seek help from others, and I fall on my knees and plead for my good Lord Jesus to give me strength.

No matter how badly I fall back and make myself upset, I can always accept myself with this poor thinking and then keep trying to change this behavior and see what I did to fall back to my anxiety and depression. Upon acknowledging negative events of my life I again experience sadness. I then revert back to irrational beliefs such as "I must not fail," or "I have to be accepted, because if I'm not, that makes me an unlovable person." And then I am once again into self-doubting, and again disturbing myself. I've got to surrender these thoughts, shut the door tight on these negative thoughts, seal the door and prevent them from "sneaking in."

I sometimes use an imaginary blackboard and write these negative thoughts and then erase them with a vengeance. I don't want them, I don't need them, and I hate them. Where is it written that I have to be accepted? I can answer: "I never have to be accepted, I am OK no matter what. I prefer to succeed and be approved; unfortunately underneath I still believe 'I really have to do well and truly must be loved.'"

I was taught early that winning and being right are necessary in all circumstances. Losing is like peer disapproval, a kind of death. I learned that I must depend on others for love, approval, and validation in order to find any degree of worth and happiness. I believe that—and if you think about it, it is some kind of slavery.

Every day I encounter evidence of my preprogrammed thought patterns and beliefs that remain unexamined and therefore continue to obstruct my openhearted love of life. All the indoctrinations of my youth still linger in the corners of my mind. My job now is to embrace these learned and often arbitrary patterns, fears, and prejudices with awareness and inquiry to dissolve them in the light of love and understanding. The examined life is the only life worth living, and the reality of what is only place worth living in.

Some time ago I stumbled on a photo of my school class and teacher Brother Mullery. He was standing immediately behind me with his fingers touching my shoulders. I began to reminisce about how he had traumatized me and changed my life. I gazed at this distant image of myself and immediately felt I could love this kid with all my heart. How I would love to take him in my arms and spend time with him, getting to know who he was, shy and scared and always blushing when anybody looked at him. His parents and siblings had almost forgotten him; he was on his own in a threatening world. He was a survivor, and with a squint of restrictiveness succeeded at achieving his goal. He dreamt the impossible dream no matter how hopeless, no matter how far. To reach the unreachable star, the star of the priesthood.

I ask, "Why did I have to go through the valley of death?" And I am led to the story of the Thornbird for the answer. There was a particular kind of bird that throughout his life was unable to sing until at the end it encountered a thorn tree. The bird then impaled itself on one of the thorns and in its mortal pain sang a song so beautiful that it stopped God in His tracks. He and all the angels stopped to listen. In short, only through our suffering can we discover the extravagant beauties of life.

Obviously there is validity in this premise, but I have always had to struggle in order to understand why God, who is love, seems to require so much hardship along our paths toward our wholehearted experience of compassion and truth.

The above sketch, drawn by a boyhood friend, depicts myself (Liam) and my sixth grade teacher, Brother Mullery, a strict and brutal disciplinarian who adversely affected my life.

CHAPTER 32

THE McCARTHYS & MY "SISTERS"

In speaking of "Sisters" in the following section, I am referring to those who are nuns or at least those women who especially today are recognized as nuns on the street.

My dad was the youngest of eleven children. He had seven blood sisters and six became religious Sisters (nuns). Since I was the second youngest of eleven, I only had the privilege of personally knowing two of them, Sister Finbar and Sister Paul Frances. They were two of the finest and holiest human beings I have ever known. Sister Finbar was the Mother Superior of a large convent/orphanage in Limerick City. She was looking forward to my ordination to the priesthood and died just a month before the event. I was devastated. It would have been a moment of immense joy for her.

My other aunt, Sister Paul Frances, was in a convent in England and at almost 100 years old I had the privilege of giving her my first priestly blessing. All six of my aunts who were nuns were powerful, successful women who made a major impact on the world. Because I had six aunts who were nuns, I have always had great love and respect for the nuns I worked with during my ministry.

I must admit that when some nuns discarded the "habit" and went in lay clothes, I was not happy. When I was appointed pastor of St. Rose, the principal of the school, Sister Mary, dressed in lay clothes. I asked her if she would at least wear a veil on her head, to distinguish her from laypersons. A little while later she showed up at the parish picnic wearing a veil. Now, 23 years later, she still wears a veil.

In my second year as pastor, I hired Sister Ann, Sister Dolores, and Sister Connie. I kindly informed each of them that if they got rid of their religious habits, they would have to leave St. Rose. Again, to this day, all three of them still wear the religious uniform.

Before I retired as pastor of St. Rose of Lima I had the unusual pleasure of having five religious sisters in the parish: Sr. Ann, Sr. Joan, Sr. Dolores, Sr. Connie, and the new principal of the school, Sr. Rita. All five of them were unique and special. Sister Ann was tough and feisty. She ruled the classroom, the sacristy, and the altar servers with an iron fist; but she was a great nun who achieved great things for the honor and glory of God. Sister Dolores will no doubt be canonized a saint of the Church. In her quiet unassuming way she does Mother Theresa type work among the poor and aged of the parish. Sister Connie is the "socialite" at every event and party of the community and in her unique way is a great religious presence in the parish. Sister Joan teaches first grade and is a very popular teacher. And Sister Rita is the quintessential principal, leading the academy to great heights of excellence.

Back row L to R: Kitty, Mona, David, Vera, Evelyn, Moss, Therese, Pam, Dannie.
Front row L to R: Mom, Father Liam (myself), Papa.
Brother James is not in the picture. His wife was giving birth to a daughter that day.

*   *   *

I have six blood sisters and each one of them is extremely special: Mona, Kitty, Vera, Therese, Evelyn, and Pam.

138

Mona was like a mother to me; she left home when I was a child and went to England to study to be a nurse, but came home every summer on vacation for two weeks. Those two weeks were usually the happiest two weeks of the year. She babied and protected me and gave me a lot of attention. She then married an Englishman named Harry. I despised him because he was mean and controlling. Poor Mona had a miserable life with him, he was always rude to her; she was a classical case of a battered woman. Every year before she would leave home after that two week vacation, she would cry hysterically for several days. It was heartbreaking. Mona was the most loved of all the family. She was humble and sweet and everything nice. She called herself "the ugly duckling of the family." To me she was the prettiest woman in the whole world.

My second oldest sister was Kitty, a tall beautiful redhead. She too became a nurse in England and was pursued by many eligible doctors and English gentlemen. She always came home on vacation and many of the local rich eligible farmers tried to get her attention. Finally Ben O'Dwyer, known as a rich landowner, got her attention. He wooed her relentlessly. Ben was fifteen years older than Kitty, but he was tall and handsome. They finally got married and Kitty settled down on a farm in Colemanswell County Limerick, and had seven children; three boys and four girls. All four girls became nurses like their mother. Two of the oldest boys, Tom and Jack did not get along with their father and left home. Tom went to England and became a policeman, and Jack went to Australia and became a successful builder. Gerrard, the youngest, took over the farm; and Kitty, still beautiful and fresh, is also active and involved in running the farm.

Ben died relatively young and I had the sad task of celebrating his funeral mass. I really loved him as a young boy. I practically lived at his place. He treated me like an equal and we had fun together for hours. My times spent at the O'Dwyer's were truly significant and helped me to develop a good sense of self-worth. A few years ago, my sister Kitty celebrated her 80th birthday and the following is a tribute I gave her.

A LOVING TRIBUTE
TO MY BEAUTIFUL SISTER, KITTY, ON HER BIRTHDAY
DECEMBER 20, 2000

The day you were born, a star was born. There is no better. I can still remember looking at you as a child and seeing the most beautiful woman on earth—that magnificent red hair and an awesome face and body. Without you in my childhood, it would have been impoverished. Going to your place in Colemanswell was the most memorable and happiest moments of my life. You and Ben treated me with the utmost love and respect. Your patience and acceptance of me as a young boy has never been matched in all these years. Ben was a "gentle giant" to me, spending hours discussing the news of the day, particularly political news, treating me like an adult. I can honestly say, I am what I am today because of you and Ben. You contributed in no small way to making my childhood happy and my life a success. You are without doubt the quintessential wife, mother, and sister.

Today, December 20th, I will remember you at the altar at Holy Mass. May the good Lord bless and protect you always.

Signed: Your loving brother,
Liam

Mom, myself, and Papa shortly after my ordination.

Front row L to R: my sister Evelyn and Dad.
Back row L to R: my brothers Moss, David, and myself. I am about 15 years old here.

My third oldest sister is Vera. She loved life to the nth degree. She loved to dance, sing, and tell jokes. She studied the hotel business and was very successful. She became the manager of several hotels. She met her Prince Charming, Edward Rosencrantz, and they raised five wonderful children. They purchased two large hotels in Westport and Dublin. They are now retired and live comfortably in a villa in Malaga Spain.

My fourth delightful sister is Evelyn. She married a neighboring farmer, Ed Clifford. They raised four great children, two boys and two girls. Evelyn loves to talk and walk, and loves people.

Theresa is my fifth sister. She was a great traveler. She came to visit me once in East Hanover's St. Rose of Lima's. She stayed in the convent and one day Sister Delores and Sister Connie dressed her up as a nun. She came to the rectory and I didn't recognize her. She was full of fun and a great dresser. She married John Joe Fitzgerald and had six beautiful children.

Pam is my youngest sister. We grew up together, just one year between us in age. We walked to school together and played together. We had all kind of pets: dogs, goats, songbirds and pigeons. We frequently rode our bicycles on a three mile journey to visit Jim Kenney, where we bought goldfinches and pigeons—they were homing pigeons. Pam and I would take the pigeons several miles away, release them, and then the pigeons would be home before us.

Pam married Maurice McCarthy and has two boys, Liam and John. Her husband Maurice developed Alzheimer's disease and died in a nursing home. Now she is all alone with her son Liam and runs a liquor bar and a farm. However, I have no worries about her; she is extremely capable and competent, and is greatly loved by her community.

Her son, a college student, came to live with me at the rectory for one summer. I got him a job at the local Gate of Heaven cemetery, for a while, cutting grass; but it was too hot for him in the blazing sun, which he wasn't used to in Ireland where the usual temperature is about 60 degrees. Eventually I got a job for him at Home Depot in East Hanover. I put a note in the Parish bulletin, asking if anyone had a bicycle to donate, and within a week about a dozen bicycles were offered. So John rode his bicycle every morning, a mile or so, to Home Depot. He got along famously with all the staff and made a little money which he put in the bank for a rainy day. While living with me, he got to know many parishioners. On Tuesday night he helped out at bingo. The bingo people loved him; they called him "Paul McCartney the Beatle," and he even looked like him a little bit. John eventually went back to the university in Ireland and qualified to be an engineer.

My oldest brother is James, he was a butcher for his profession and set up business in Galway City. He was a great success and made a lot of money. His wife, Delia, was a nurse who worked in the local hospital. They had three children, two boys and a girl. The two boys, Jim and Andrew, went on to become PhD's in science and are now working in France doing cancer research. Mary Ann, their daughter, is a sweetheart and has a great sense of humor. She is a computer genius and has a great job.

My brothers Moss and David are landowners and have more money than "God." They are fine fellows and I always enjoy their company. My family is very close and we have many family reunions. I never once witnessed a disagreement between any of them.

$$* \quad * \quad *$$

A TRIBUTE TO MY SISTER VERA
AND HER BELOVED HUSBAND EDMUND ROSENKRANZ

My sister Vera was the sixth child in a family of

eleven. She was my mother's favorite daughter. She was always positive and happy, constantly dancing and joking and the center of everyone's attention. She was physically pretty and beautiful inside and out. My mother encouraged her to study hotel management and after graduation, she got a job as a manageress in the Victoria Hotel in Cork City, and a few years later in a top hotel in Dublin, Ireland. Soon thereafter, she became a member of the social elite of Dublin, dating many rich and well-known bachelors. Finally, one night, she met a handsome, intelligent gentleman, a kind of James Bond / Pierce Bronson type. She fell madly in love and a short time later was married in a high society wedding in Adare Cathedral with a reception in Adare Manor.

They lived in a beautiful house in Dundrum, Dublin and went on to have three sons and two daughters; all bright and successful children. Vera and Edmund were a great team and worked together to eventually acquire great wealth, mainly from purchasing hotels. They made them successful and resold them for a great profit. Finally, they retired to a gated mansion in Malaga, Spain on the Mediterranean.

CHAPTER 33

OUR MISSION

Today, August 30, 2005, a hurricane devastates the southern states from Louisiana to Mississippi—all made unlivable—abandoned. I am thinking of my classmates, my fellow seminaries ordained with me—and who were assigned to the diocese of Natchoz- Jackson: Father Martin Ruane, and Father Noel Foley. Noel, a pastor in Biloxi, died of cancer two years prior to this hurricane. Father Ruane has lost his parish to nature's upheavals in the hurricane Katrina of August 2005. At this moment I think back to the lives of my fellow ordinandi of June 8, 1963. Fathers:

Bernard Dolan (Clifton, England)
Muiris Foley (Tucson, USA)
Philip O'Shea (Kildare, Ireland)
Patrick O'Neill (Southwark, England)
Martin Ruane (Natchez-Jackson, USA)
P.J. Clarke (Leeds, England)
Pat McMahon (Lancaster, England)
Joe Bredin (Clifton, England)
Eugene Boland (Paterson, NJ, USA)
Gerry Brennan (Los Angeles, USA)
Tom Cairns (Mobile-Birmingham, USA)
Noel Foley (Natchez-Jackson, USA)
Tom Cahalane (Tucson, USA)
Harry Doyle (Lancaster, USA)
Joe Hennessy (Tuscon, USA)
Bill McCarthy (Paterson, NJ, USA)
Patrick Mulvany (Lancaster, England)

Kerry Murphy O'Connor (Cork, Ireland)
Richard Hegarty (Cloyne, Ireland)
Henry Brady (Killaloe, Ireland)
Gerry Ferguson (Camden, NJ, USA)
Michael Mooney (Mobile-Birmingham, USA)
Philip Smith (Lancaster, England)
Billy Burke (Tuscon, USA)
John Carrigy (Sacremento, USA)
James Corbally (Alexishafen, New Guinea, Australia)
Michael Dyer (Mobile-Birmingham, USA)
Chris Concannon (Jefferson City, USA)
Daniel Logan (St. Augustine, USA)
Thomas Greaney (Jefferson City, USA)

At the bottom of the official picture of my ordination class is the mandate, "Euntes Docete Omnes Gentes" (Go and teach all nations). All thirty of us were scattered over a large area of the globe. We were sent into a chaotic world. The second Vatican Council was ending. The Church was being turned upside down and would never be the same again. The quiet unchanging days of our youth were over; we were not prepared for a turbulent hostile period in the Church. We were sent like innocent lambs into an angry world. It was as if a hurricane and earthquake simultaneously hit the Church. "Change" was the battle cry of the times; priests were at the headlines of the battle. Many of my class were hurt and confused, some abandoned the priesthood altogether. However, most of my classmates were heroic and attained magnificent achievements for the honor and glory of God.

The one who stands out in my mind as the saint of my class is James Corbally. His mother died when he was a child. He volunteered to be a priest in New Guinea, near Australia, and one of the most remote countries in the world. He had a mind of steel and worked like a slave in the country; spreading the good news of the gospel with joy and enthusiasm. Now over forty years later, he is slowly dying of Parkinson's disease, but still undaunted and never complaining—outwardly bent over but standing tall on the inside. Now in the year 2005, five have died, two of natural causes and three in an accident. Seven resigned from the priesthood and got married. The president of our seminary, Dr. Lennon, became a bishop and after retirement was killed in an accident.

The motto of our seminary proudly displayed on a crest in the building was "Rescissa Vecetior Assurgit" (The more you cut it down the more it grows). I vigorously follow that motto.

St. Patrick's College
Carlow
1963

EUNTES DOCETE OMNES GENTES

My ordination photo.

*   *   *

Growing up in the old homestead of Shandrum, my family constantly told the story of how one day Mom went into one of the fields to check on the cattle. The bull noticed her at a distance and galloped toward her groaning madly. Years before, her dad had indoctrinated her: "If a bull ever runs at you, stand still as a board and don't move a limb." Suddenly her dad's advice "kicked in," and she just froze where she was and didn't move a muscle. The mad bull galloped to within five feet of her, then halted. He just starred at her, tearing up the earth with his hooves and sniffing her. She stared him down and eventually he turned and walked away. This bull was not merely as big on the inside as he was on the outside.

The more one tries to pull me down, the more I will stand tall and like my mom, face the bull of a terrible attack, and by standing tall and unmovable, eventually the enemy will give up and go away and I will be free.

CHAPTER 34

HOLINESS

My great desire in life is to be holy, that is, to live a wholesome life; of course we all have different ideas of what it means to be holy. To be holy you don't have to be a priest in a monastery, or a nun in a convent. People do not need to be poor to be holy. Wealthy people can be holy. Married people can be holy. Sexual intimacy of marriage is not a barrier to holiness. God is love (St. John) and consequently "making love" is making God present. Our sexuality is pure and holy. To say that sex is dirty is an insult to the Creator, an indication that God made a mistake and created something unholy.

In Genesis 3:25 it says: "The man and his wife were both naked, yet they felt no shame." Once Adam and Eve ate of the forbidden fruit, they realized that they were naked, so they sewed leaves together and made loincloths for themselves. "God called to the man and asked him, 'Where are you?'" He answered: "I heard you in the garden, but I was afraid, because I was naked, so I hid myself." Then God asked Adam: "Who told you that you were naked?"

So the first sin was when Adam and Eve *believed* that sex was dirty. Something to be covered up. An insult to God the Creator. Ever since, the people of God, Jewish and Christian, have been plagued with the notion that sex is dirty.

Our sexuality is pure and holy and should be treated with the utmost respect and never used with aggression or abuse, but protected within the sacrament of marriage. Sexual intimacy is a profound gift of God, and it is an instrument of holiness.

Many people believe that if you want to be holy, you are not allowed to enjoy life. Some believe that to be holy you have to run away from the world. Others believe that to be holy you have to be in church on your knees praying all day. Others still believe that to be holy you have to walk around with a halo, and you are not allowed to smile or have any fun, or enjoy yourself at all. They think that to be holy you have to despise everything of this world and walk around with a long drawn-out, stoic look on your face. These are all very unnatural and unattractive ideals that the world proclaims about holiness. Holiness brings us to life. Holiness doesn't dampen our emotions, it elevates them. Those who possess holiness are the most joy filled people; holiness does not stifle us—it sets us free. The surest signs of holiness are an insatiable desire to improve oneself and an unquenchable concern for your happiness and the happiness of others.

CHAPTER 35

SURVIVAL

Concepts of survival, given by Laurence Gonzales, help me to apply them to my survival situation and help me through the dark moments, and to go out now and then to see the beauty, or to get a little adrenaline fix. I am trying to learn basic survival skills and a survivor's frame of mind.

Survival concepts: Perceive, believe, then act. I try to perceive what's really happening and adapt to it. Some survival techniques use the acronym STOP: Stop, Think, Observe, Plan. Survival is adaptation, and adaptation is change—change based on a true reading of the environment. If I reach a fork in the road, I carefully observe what the correct trail looks like, so I don't get lost.

The following is Gonzales' list of survival tactics, including how I try to practice them in my everyday life:

1. ***Avoid impulsive behavior***: In other words, don't hurry. By nature I am an impatient individual, I need results yesterday. I have to discipline my impulses and slow down, find emotional balance and control. What separates the living from the dead is an ability to see the error and adapt a determination to get back on the path.

2. ***Know your stuff***: I must know what and who I am up against. I must be aware of how evil my accusers are and to what extent they are prepared to go to destroy me.

3. ***Get the information***: I rely on my lawyers as to how I should proceed and follow their guidance even though I am frustrated by their tardiness. But they tell me that's how lawyers are.

4. ***Commune with the dead***: If I could collect the dead around me and listen to their tales, I might find myself in the best survival school of all. Since I can't, I pray to the saints, especially those who were wrongfully accused during their lives on earth. Like Joan of Arc, and of course Jesus, Himself, who was wrongfully accused, scourged at the pillar and crucified. No one can understand me better than Jesus.

5. ***Be humble***: Those who gain experience while retaining firm hold on a beginner's state of mind become long-term survivors. I never become so crazy that I have no doubt that I will be victorious. There is a saying in aviation: "There are old pilots and bold pilots, but there are no old bold pilots." However, I do not want to gobble like a turkey—I want to fly like an eagle. As the Man of La Mancha said, "I will follow that star, no matter how hopeless, no matter how far." And as Boon Brocket used to say: "I would much rather be on the ground wishing I were in the air, than in the air wishing I were on the ground." I must be realistic about my goals and my time frame. I must move through denial, anger, bargaining, and depression to acceptance as soon as possible. I hate this feeling of anxiety and depression. I know I will have to struggle for a time before I get there.

6. ***Stay calm***: Many times I am obsessed with fear, but I try not to be led by it. My fear often feels like and turns into anger and that motivates me and makes me sharper. I remain on guard against too much emotion. I try to keep my sense of humor so as to keep calm.

7. ***Think / Analyze / Plan***: I push away thoughts that my situation is hopeless, consciously taking control of the situation. I perceive that my situation is split into two people and I strive to obey the rational one. How hopeless it must seem to any outside observer, but I am acting with the expectation of success.

8. ***Decisive action***: I am willing to take risks to save myself. I break down a large job into small manageable tasks. I set an attainable goal and develop short term plans to reach it. I deal with what is within my power from moment to moment, hour to hour, day to day; then leave the rest to God. God helps those who help themselves.

9. ***Celebrate my successes***: I take hope even in my smallest successes; they provide some relief from unspeakable stress.

10. ***Count my blessings***: I am grateful I am alive; that I am a survivor instead of a victim. I keep focusing on my awesome friends, their unwavering support, and their patient endurance.

11. ***Play***: I use activities such as singing, or counting mathematical problems in my head, to stimulate, calm, and entertain my frantic mind. These activities sometimes lead to a new technique or strategy that could save me.

12. ***See the beauty***: I tune my mind to the wonders of the world; the appreciation of beauty; the feeling of awe. This appreciation of beauty relieves my stress. Just yesterday, my priest friend, Father Bob and I went for a walk by Highland Lake. We both sat down for a moment, and suddenly a mother duck and her single duckling appeared on the water. It was a sight to behold: mother and child. As we quietly looked on, the mother duck was teaching her baby many activities: cleaning herself, diving into the water for food, resting on a stone with her head under her wing. All of this helped me focus on something outside myself and helped me relax.

13. ***Believe that I will succeed***: Developing a deep conviction that I will overcome this ordeal and at least to do my very best.

14. ***Surrender***: I practice a kind of resignation without giving up—survival by surrender is God's power.

15. ***Do whatever is necessary***: I do not over or under estimate my determination, I must believe that anything is possible and act accordingly.

16. ***Never give up***: I must not be discouraged by attacks. I keep my spirit up by developing an alternate world made up of rich memories, to which I can escape. I search my memory for whatever will keep me occupied. I embrace the world in which I find myself, and see opportunity in adversity. I hope someday I will be grateful for the experiences I now am going through.

CHAPTER 36

TENTACLES

I am very proud of E.W.T.N. (Eternal Word Television Network). In 1982, Sean Flanagan and Brian Gail came to my office asking for my help. Brian had been to Alabama on business when he struck up a relationship with a nun, Mother Angelica, who was struggling to set up a television network. Brian discussed with me how we could help her.

We invited her to meet with me and a few men from Florham Park, NJ, including Sean Flanagan. She came to my rectory living room and shared her dream with us. We were very inspired. Brian, Sean, and I met several times thereafter to develop a strategy of how we could promote her TV network. We spoke with Samon's Cable Network in Dover, NJ and drew up a contract. The agreement was that Brian, Sean, and I would get 3000 homes to sign up for Samon's cable. Brian became the front man for the mission. He and Sean went to all the pastors of the Catholic parishes in Morris County, NJ, asking their permission to speak at all the masses encouraging parishioners to sign-up for Samon's Cable.

After about six months, we had over 3000 homes on board and Samon's agreed to install the cable for free, so that was an extra incentive. Once the homes were wired for cable, Mother Angelica's programs were immediately operative. That was the first "footprint" on the eastern seaboard. Then I went to my bishop and convinced him to write a pastoral letter to every pastor in the diocese encouraging them to install the cable. At the same time, people in general were cautious of cable television since it was a new phenomenon. My bishop also included in his letter a statement: "If any pastor wants more information, call Father McCarthy, pastor of St. Rose of Lima Church in East Hanover, NJ.

The campaign started by Brian Gail was a great success. He was a brilliant businessman and strategist. The bishop's letter of encouragement was also a great boost. So for the first time ever, EWTN began broadcasting... a small step for Morris County, but a huge step for the network of Mother Angelica.

Many pastors had called me for information. I remember in particular, Father Nick Bozza and Msgr. John Demkovich, who were eager to encourage their congregations to install the cable. They saw it as a great opportunity for evangelization, which the Catholic Church was sorely missing. I personally went to other bishops in the metropolitan area of New York and they likewise were excited to pick up the ball. I even went to Cardinal O'Connor of New York, and he was very positive and made a major contribution in terms of encouraging his pastors to go forward with promoting the network. Gradually, Mother Angelica's TV network spread rapidly throughout the East, eventually all over the United States, and finally the world.

In 1984, Dr. Arthur Hoagland and I flew to Alabama to meet with Mother Angelica. Unfortunately, sometime before she had a major stroke, was incapacitated, and only made occasional public appearances. Dr. Hoagland and I spent a week in Alabama and visited the network facilities every day. We became more and more inspired by what we can only describe as a *miracle* that a little-known nun in Baptist country could accomplish!

While at the facilities, I was given the privilege of celebrating mass with a few other priests. Many of my parishioners back home in East Hanover were watching with great excitement. Since I was close to retirement, my intention was to devote the twilight years of my life to promoting the network; especially in my native Ireland. But a major obstacle emerged...

I made an appointment to meet with the new director of the network and get his endorsement for my mission. Oddly, he was aloof and was not very enthusiastic to deal with me. I was baffled by his attitude, especially after I informed him of my role in getting the network started. He actually dismissed my role as insignificant and treated me badly. I was privately devastated. With Mother Angelica incapacitated and unable to support me, I left Alabama a defeated man.

I tried to understand the reason for the new CEO's behavior. Gradually, I figured out what had happened. At home in my parish, I'd proudly advertised what I planned to do after retirement: spend my time promoting EWTN. Little did I know that one of the "conspirators" in the destruction of my name and reputation had written to EWTN, saying that I was under censure by my bishop for a grave offense, and advising them not to have anything to do with me. Now I understood the rejection by the leadership at ETWN headquarters.

I've remain silent, until now, as to what exactly happened. It was another "nail in my coffin" and another wound to my already hurting mind, sending me further into a psychological tailspin. I never even talked to my friend, Dr. Hoagland, and bore the brunt of the rejection internally and privately pretending everything was fine. It became apparent to me that the false accusation was spreading its tentacles into every corner of my life, making it clear to me that I had to do everything possible to exonerate myself from this terrible accusation as soon as possible.

Thank God, Mother Angelica's network is healthy and well and doing amazing work on behalf of the Church. When I think back over the years I am amazed as to where I got the strength to accomplish as much as I did in the midst of the biggest crisis of my life. But when God is for you, who can be against you!? I believed God was still in control of my life. He was fighting my battles. He was directing my steps.

As the television evangelist, Joel Osteen, said in one of his talks: "When you go through a loss, when somebody does you wrong, when you seem like you have taken steps backwards, don't sit around, don't live like you are defeated. Rather, stay in the faith; you may not realize it now, but you're in a good position to go to a new level and discover new potential. You're going into new growth. You're going to blossom with a greater confidence. It may be uncomfortable. It may be difficult, but it is going to cause you to stretch and blossom in ways never imagined."

It is similar to a mother eagle teaching her babies to fly. When they are small they stay in the nest where it is warm and comfortable. The dad goes out, gets the food, brings it back all day long. The little eaglets just sing and play without a care in the world. But when they get little older, the mother eagle will grab one of the eaglets by her claws and take it way, way up in the air. The little eaglets sees all the beautiful sites below, not having to do one thing. But about that time, the mother eagle releases the baby. It starts falling toward the ground at ninety miles per hour. I'm sure that the baby eaglet must think, "Mother, have you lost your mind? Why have you abandoned me? Are you trying to kill me? Don't you love me anymore?"

But right before the eaglet hits the ground, the mother eagle swoops down and grabs the little one. The eaglet probably thinks, "Thank you so much! Now take me back to the nest where it is warm and comfy."

What does mother eagle do? She takes the eaglet right back up in the air and drops it again... and again... and again... until finally the little eaglet begins to flap its wings. The eaglet discovers it has something at its sides that he didn't know he had. He starts flapping and flapping and before long he knows how to fly. He is soaring through the air thinking to himself, "This is what I was created to be."

In the same way, sometimes in my life, it feels like God has dropped me.

It feels like I have been abandoned. Why did those people conspire against me? Why did I go through this loss? But God is not going to let me hit the ground. God has his eye on me. He is closely watching me. He knows that before long, like the little eaglet, I will step into a new confidence. I'm going to discover strengths I didn't know I had. I'm going to overcome obstacles that I felt were totally insurmountable. What I thought was my worst moment, will turn out to be my greatest opportunity. Without that attack on my character, I would never have stepped into my new destiny.

I heard a story about a man whose boat capsized in the middle of a huge storm and he ended up stranded on a deserted island. Just when he thought it couldn't get worse, while out getting food in the woods one day, he returned to find that the little hut he had built was on fire. Watching it burn was like pouring salt on his wounds. He was so upset he threw his food on the ground and said, "God, it is just not fair!" A couple of hours later he noticed a large boat coming toward the island. He couldn't believe it. It was the Coast Guard. He ran down to the shore, gave the captain a big hug, and said, "How in the world did you find me?" The captain replied, "We saw the smoke from your fire."

I thought my hut was on fire, but God has better plans for me. I realize now God is still in control. I was always in the palm of his hand. And God will open new doors for me. Now I know I can do all things through Christ.

The amazing growth of Mother Angelica's EWTN makes me very proud, and gives me another reason to believe my efforts, on more than one level, were not in vain.

CHAPTER 37

SAINTS

As a child I had great devotion to the saints, which really meant respecting them from a distance, not exactly following their example or applying their lessons to my life. My favorite was St. Theresa the Little Flower. I think I fell in love with her beauty as depicted in some holy cards. Later on as a priest I went through a period where I began to avoid devotion to the saints.

I now feel I was influenced by the Protestant Fundamentalists who constantly criticized Catholics for putting saints before Jesus. They quoted Scripture that Jesus was the only mediator between God and man. I began to question the doctrine of honoring saints. Were Catholics actually putting saints ahead of Jesus? For a number of years I struggled with that question. After some time of meditating, and a study of the matter, I finally found the answer.

Old Mother Church had not gone astray as the fundamentalists had claimed. It was some Catholics who had misunderstood and may in fact have fallen into heresy. The doctrine of honoring the saints is in fact authentic Christianity. There are many mediators between us humans and Jesus.

To ask a person or people gathered in church to pray for you, you are in effect making them mediators—between yourself and Jesus who is God. You can ask the entire court of heaven to be your prayer partners to go with you to Jesus to the Father. I find it very comforting to be supported by favorite saints before God. I have a great affinity for the statutes of the saints. They are physical manifestation of a spiritual reality.

After Vatican II many pastors removed statues of saints from their churches and put them in the basement or in a closet. Soon after I became pastor of St. Rose, I set up a shrine of statues in the old Baptismal Room, off the entrance of the church. I went to several neighboring churches and retrieved the statues hidden in their basements. My favorite one was a life-sized statue of Jesus, and before long it was everyone's favorite. These statues were to the people a great call to holiness and a challenge to grow holy. St. Rose is next to a busy road and there was a constant flow of people entering the church to pray before the statues and feel a call to holiness.

If we as Catholics were genuinely striving to become holy, the saints and our devotion to the saints would never suffer the criticism and blows that are endlessly leveled at them today. Unfortunately, sometimes veneration replaces imitation; the saints lose their genuine role in Christian spirituality.

St. John Vianney, Pastor of Ars, France, usually called Cure of Ars, is my idol as a pastor. Ars was a tiny place 22 miles from Lyons, with only 60 families. It was considered the Siberia of the diocese. The Cure preached boldly about the evils of his community. The people reacted violently at first, but in time the Cure's prayers and fasting began to reap a great harvest.

But the years between arrival in Ars and the Golden Years of Ars were a time filled with tremendous trials and suffering. Letters of false accusations flooded the bishop's office, and inquiries were made into his behavior in the small rural parish. In speaking out against the evils of the village, he pricked the conscience of many and their consciences often became hostile. Ignorance and sin confuse us, and in our confusion we cause suffering to those who are truly holy.

Late in his life, Vianney wrote: "If on my arrival in Ars, I had foreseen that I was to suffer there, I would have died on the spot." For his own prayer, Father Vianney spent long periods in front of the Blessed Sacrament, early in the morning and late at night. He encouraged his people to make regular visits to the church and sit before the Blessed Sacrament.

$$*\quad*\quad*$$

The good Cure knew that the Blessed Sacrament was the most powerful means of renewing the life of the parish. He was first a spiritual leader of his people and took seriously the responsibility of guiding their souls along the path of salvation. As his popularity soared, so did the criticism of him. His colleagues, the priests of France remembered well his lack of education. And as the people of France began to speak of him as a "Great Saint," great jealousy took hold of many.

I too was the victim of envy; of people who set out to destroy me. Fortunately the Cure would not allow any of this to interfere with his work. The more he was assaulted, the more he humbled himself. With his own life he showed us all that there is another way.

YEAR FOUR (2006)

CHAPTER 38

DEPRESSION

When my former bishop requested that John Paul II, the Supreme Pontiff, automatically laicize me—expel me from the priesthood, ex officio, an overwhelming sadness washed over me like an ocean and I was drowning. The pain was worse than physical pain. I have totally identified my existence, my self-worth, with my priesthood—now they have taken it away and they are taking me away with it. My priesthood was dying and so was I.

I was horrified—my whole life disappeared in front of my eyes; I could not stop screaming—it was like a nightmare that I could not wake up from.

I plunged into deep depression as my mind continued in its insidious meltdown. For days I could not eat or sleep, each day's pattern of distress exhibited fairly predictable alternating periods of intensity and relief. The evening's relief for me—an incomplete but noticeable let up, like the change from a torrential downpour to a steady shower—came in the hours after dinner time and before midnight, when the pain lifted a little and my mind would become lucid enough to focus on matters beyond the immediate upheaval convulsing my system. From time to time, I was rendered nearly helpless. I noticed my voice had the wheezy sound of very old age that I now realize was the voice of depression.

Depression is a disorder of mood, so mysteriously painful and elusive in the way it becomes known to the self—to the mediating intellect—as to very close to being beyond description. I was at a critical stage in the development of the disease of depression, although I realized I was close to a total ignoramus about depression, which can be as serious a medical affair as diabetes or cancer. The most honest authorities face up squarely to the fact that it is not readily treatable, unlike let's say diabetes. Serious depression does not disappear overnight. The disease of depression remains a great mystery.

In my reading, I have learned for example that in at least one interesting respect my own case was atypical. Most people who begin to suffer from the illness are laid low in the morning, with such malefic effect that they are unable to get out of bed. They feel better only as the day bears on. But my situation was just the reverse. While I was able to rise and function about normally during the earlier part of the day, I began to sense the onset of the symptoms at mid-afternoon, or a little later—gloom crowding in on me, a sense of dread and alienation and above all, stifling anxiety. I suspect that it is basically a matter of indifference whether one suffers the most in the morning or the evening; if these states of excruciating near-paralysis are similar as they probably are, the question of timing would seem to be academic. The reality was that my mind was dissolving. A lot of literature available concerning depression claims that nearly all depressive states will be subdued or reversed if only a suitable antidepressant can be found. The reader is of course easily swayed by promises of quick remedy.

For me the pain I was experiencing was most closely connected to drowning or suffocation; but even these images are off the mark.

Some people kill themselves, not because they are cowards, or feeble minded, but because they are afflicted with a depression that is so devastating that they can no longer endure the pain of it. The pain of severe depression is quite unimaginable to those who have not suffered it, and it kills in many instances because its anguish can no longer be borne. The prevention of many suicides will continue to be hindered until there is general awareness of the nature of this pain. Through the healing process of time and through medical intervention or hospitalization in many cases, most people survive depression, which may be its only blessing. But to the tragic legion that are compelled to destroy themselves there should be no more reproof attached than to the victims of terminal cancer.

For most people, unfortunately, suicide is a subject that is taboo, a matter of secrecy and shame. As I fell deeper and deeper into depression, the pain became unbearable. I spoke to my psychology friend, Dr Frank Ferese, and he sent me to his medical advisor, Brian Sullivan, who prescribed several antidepressant medications: Wellbutrin, Paxil, Effexor, and Lexapro. All of them only made me feel worse, made me edgy, disagreeably hyperactive, and when the dosage was increased, it blocked my bladder for hours. Many times I was rushed to the ER to have a catheter inserted into my bladder. I was told that ten more days must pass for the drug to clear my system before starting anew with a different pill. Ten days to someone stretched on such a torture rack, is like ten centuries, and this does not begin to take into account that when a new pill is inaugurated, several weeks must pass before it becomes effective. For reasons unknown to me, neither medications nor psychotherapy were able to arrest my plunge toward the depths. My face aged dramatically emulating my way of walking, which had slowed to the equivalent of a shuffle.

Loss in all of its manifestations is the touchstone of depression. I felt loss at every turn. The loss of my priesthood was devastating; causing the loss of my self-esteem and my own sense of self had all but disappeared, along with any self-reliance, and from dependence into infantile dread. One dreads the loss of all things and people, close and dear. There is an acute fear of abandonment. Being alone in my apartment, even for a moment, caused me panic and trepidation. Of the images recollected from that time, the most bizarre and discomforting remains one of me desperately clinging to a friend like Doris, Father Bob, Father Paul, Peter and Sil. This would hazard the opinion that many disastrous sequels to depression might be averted if the victim received support such as from those I have mentioned.

Meanwhile my losses mounted and proliferated. There is no doubt that when one nears the depths of depression, which is to say just before the stage when one begins to act out one's suicide instead of being a contemplator of it—the acute sense of loss is connected with knowledge of life slipping away at accelerated speed.

I had now reached that phase of the disorder where all sense of hope had vanished. I began to lose weight rapidly; was unable to sleep. In depression, faith in deliverance, in ultimate restoration is absent. The pain is unrelenting, and what makes the condition intolerable, is the foreknowledge that no remedy will come. If there is mild relief, one knows, that it is only temporary, and more pain will follow. It is the hopelessness even more than the pain that crushes the soul. One does not abandon—even briefly—one's bed of nails, but is attached to it, wherever one goes.

Suffering from depression you find yourself like a walking casualty of war, thrust into the most intolerable social and family situations. There he must stay despite the anguish devouring his brain. It is a fierce struggle to speak a few simple words. Sometimes I felt a feeling of "despair beyond despair." Most people in the grip of depression at its ghastliest are for whatever reason, in a state of unrealistic hopelessness torn by exaggerated ills and fatal threats that bear no resemblance to actuality. It may require on the part of friends, family, and admirers an almost religious devotion to persuade the sufferer's life's worth, which is so often in conflict with a sense of their own worthlessness, but such devotion has prevented countless suicides. During my depression I often thought of suicide as the only way out of my awful pain. My friends Father Bob, Father Paul, Peter and Sil, and Doris were in touch by phone nearly every day. Their support was priceless. It was Father Martin McDonald who kept admonishing me that suicide was unacceptable. I still look back on their concern with immense gratitude. If nothing else, the disease engenders lasting friendships.

After I began to recover and felt comfortable being on my own again, it occurred to me to wonder for the first time with any really serious concern, why I had been visited by such a calamity? The accusation was of course the triggering mechanism. Until the onslaught of my own depression, my psychological training on depression meant little; it was just "academic." I never gave much thought to my ministry of depressed people. Now I have greater empathy for depressed people and how vulnerable they are. As far as I know, depression was never part of my family history; in fact everyone in my family was mentally strong and healthy.

My momentary thoughts of suicide were always overcome by my deep faith in God and the afterlife. I always taught young people that you can't kill yourself, only your body. What do you do then? You are still alive and now you have to answer to Your Creator for what you did. Taking your life into your own hands is selfish when it belongs to God alone, and He alone decides our moment of death. To most of those who have experienced depression the horror of it is so overwhelming as to be quite beyond expression.

If depression had no termination, then suicide would indeed be the only remedy, but thank God it is conquerable.

William Styson in his book *Darkness Visible* states, "For those who have dwelled in depression's dark world and have known it's inexplicable agony, their return from the abyss is not unlike the ascent of the poet trudging upward and upward out of hell's black depths and at last emerging into what he saw as the shining world. Those, whoever have been restored to health, almost always have been restored to the capacity for serenity and joy. And this may be reason_enough for having endured the despair beyond despair."

Since my bout with depression I am no longer afraid of death, in fact I welcome it. Every night as I begin to sleep, I pray over and over again: "Dear God, I pray that this night I will be with you in paradise. Father into Your hands I surrender my spirit. Receive my soul, O Lord; look not on my sins, but my faith in You. Dispel the pain and confusion from my mind. Dear God, may I rest in Your peace."

CHAPTER 39

HEARTBROKEN

After the conspiracy my heart physically hurt, the psychological pain was indescribable. Depression set in during the months that followed and I did not know how to address it. I lost weight, I could not sleep. A huge weariness settled over me. Daily tasks took all the energy I could muster.

The psalmist expressed my desperation perfectly:

Save me O God
For the waters have threatened my life, I have come into deep mire
And there is no foothold
I am weary with crying
My eyes fail while I wait for God. (Psalm 69)

I knew that followers of Christ would follow Him not just in His victory over death, His resurrection, but also in the fellowship of His sufferings (Phil. 3: 10). If Jesus suffered, then so would those who followed Him.

I have asked at other times in my journal, why does a loving God allow us to suffer? It is a question without an easy answer. All we know is that suffering is part of the human condition. All of us have suffered, are suffering, or will suffer. Life involves joy and sorrow, as well as comfort and hardship. Knowing that we will suffer does not make our pain—when it comes—any less difficult to bear. Yet crippling with our suffering is not a useless activity. As I endeavor to gain clarity about my suffering, and I begin to better understand myself, I have learned to talk to God more specifically about the fallout from my experience. My relationship with God has deepened as a result and I open myself to an even greater understanding of His love and faithfulness.

How am I to understand God's heart toward me in my condition? As

I work through my emotions, I come to understand that for a Christian believer, heartbreak of any kind could qualify me as suffering for Christ. I may not be directly suffering for Christ. I may not be suffering for my faith in Christ, but I can turn my suffering over to Him. I firmly believe that God accepts all of my suffering, whatever its origin; He takes ownership of the pain I entrust to his keeping.

By placing my suffering in the Lord's hands, I am saying: "God I cannot fix this. I am helpless. I am totally dependent on you." In Hebrew, God says: "I will never desert you, nor will I ever forsake you." The psalmist wrote: "The lord is near to the brokenhearted." God loves us in our suffering; He is with us in our suffering. Our suffering becomes places of hope in the eyes of God, for He sees their potential.

As I pray and wait for God to restore me, it helps my morale to see evidence of His work in my life along the way. How He answered my prayers time after time. Instead of getting stuck thinking about what God had *not* done, I decided to go through my past life and remember what God *had* done. Way back to my first memory of psychological pain, which was at age seven, when I came home from school one day and my sister told me that Mom was rushed to the hospital with peritonitis, a deadly infection at that time. I prayed to God night and day that she would get better. Even to the doctors' surprise, she was totally cured and eventually came home and lived until she was almost 85 years old. If my mother had died when I was a child, I can't imagine ever being normal again. I believe she was healed because God answered my prayers.

As a teenager I was painfully shy. I would blush and be embarrassed at the slightest encounter with people. Here again, God answered my prayers and made my life tolerable. If I were to enumerate all the times God answered my prayers in a significant way, this book would not be large enough to contain all the stories. So I believe God had gotten me ready. He was involved in my life, He cared about me. I came away from these reflections assured of these foundational truths. God loves me, He would lead me, and He in fact would bring good out of my circumstances. These memories sustain me as my world fell apart, and help me survive the emotional pain. By focusing on what God has already done for me, I cultivate hope for the future and it helps me through my current situation and eases the hurt. I strongly feel the proof of God's participation in my life. When I can see His work, my faith increases. I start to believe that He really is helping me and that I just might make it to the other side of freedom and exoneration.

There are occasions when God does His work quickly. He does heal some people instantly. He can and does work in immediate ways. However, in my case, it seems to go on forever. It is long and arduous. I have to remind myself that God's timeline is eternal. He sees my end from the beginning. In His mercy He sticks with me for the long haul, for the length of the journey can be the hardest part. To paraphrase Charles Dickens in *A Tale of Two Cities*: "It has been the best of times; it has been the worst of times." The worst because of the accusation: the physical pain, anxiety and fear. The best because of all the times God answered my prayers, and the very best—the day I was ordained, June 8, 1963—God gave me my heart's desire. He gave to me what He didn't give to the angels; the power to make Him present in the Eucharist, and to forgive sins in the sacrament of Reconciliation.

CHAPTER 40

LONELINESS

As I look upon the cross, and recall the specific ways in which people share in its mystery, there are many perspectives to be considered. The mystery of the cross is that it gives rise to a certain kind of loneliness; an inability to see clearly how things are unfolding; an inability to see that ultimately all things will work for our good, and that indeed I am not alone. This sense of being abandoned, this extreme experience of loneliness, is evident in Jesus' cry: "My God, my God, why have You forsaken me?"

If the Lord experienced pain and suffering, can I as His disciple expect anything less? No! Like Jesus, I too must expect pain. However, in the suffering, death, and resurrection of Jesus, I find freedom: the freedom to let go, to surrender myself to the living God, to place myself completely in His hands, knowing that ultimately He will win out, giving me life. Peace and joy in the midst of physical, emotional and spiritual suffering. Jesus said: "Come to me all you who are weary and find life burdensome, and I will refresh you. Take my yoke upon your shoulders and learn from me, for I am gentle and humble of heart. Your souls will find rest, for my yoke is easy and my burden is light." (Matt. 11:28-30)

That is a favorite passage of mine. I find it so comforting, so soothing. Coming from a farming community, the yoke was put around the neck of an animal, and chains were connected to each side of the collar (yoke) and then at the end tied onto the "load" that had to be transported from one place to the other.

It appears at first glance that the invitation of Jesus is to find rest by pulling a heavy load. In my interpretation, Jesus is telling us, if we help others to carry their burden of suffering, pain or anxiety, we will forget our own suffering. If we think that we are suffering alone, go to a cancer hospital and soon we are not thinking of, or preoccupied with, our own suffering. Jesus also said: "Unless you die to yourself, you will never find yourself." I try to practice that teaching of Jesus; unfortunately most of the time I fail hopelessly—constantly falling back on self-pity and feeling miserable and all alone. I am so grateful for the hundreds of people who helped me carry my yoke of suffering and depression. Without their reaching out to me, I definitely would not survive. Simon from Cyrene helped Jesus carry His cross. Many, many people have helped me to carry my cross of psychological suffering.

Over my bed is a picture of Jesus with His outstretched arms; and looking down at me with a compassionate gesture. I put myself completely in His hands believing that He loves me and embraces me and will never abandon me, especially during this most difficult time of my life. It gives me hope in the midst of life's suffering and chaos. As I finish this passage, Fall is giving way to Winter. The trees are losing their vibrant colors and soon snow will cover the ground. The earth will shut down and people will race to and from their destinations bundled up for warmth. It is a time of dying.

I hope that by Spring my case will be resolved, my canonical trial will have come and gone, and I will spring forth into new life. I will be born again, I will be free. I expect to be exonerated and after exoneration I hope to be a poster priest for innocent priests. Otherwise my pain and suffering because of the false accusation will be in vain. I intend not to let that happen.

CHAPTER 41

TRUSTING GOD

As I have written, walking through the fallout of the false accusation is a demanding, often grueling process that continues much longer than I expected—well over three years already. I constantly feel overwhelmed. My occasional refrain is: "Lord you have picked the wrong person for this." So often I feel I can't handle the mounting challenges of my suffering. At times I feel I would have done just about anything to get relief.

In fact I've grown in strength and have learned a great deal about God and His promises by studying the life and character of the Old Testament prophets. I came away after reading Jeremiah more convinced that God loves me, and He would bring good out of my circumstances. Jeremiah experienced rejection in many distasteful and life-threatening forms throughout his life. His people publicly seized him and sought to kill him; priests and prophets called for his death. He was falsely accused of treachery. He was imprisoned, thrown into a well and left for dead. His life was not pleasant or comfortable; he was continually suffering.

When life becomes burdensome and all but impossible to bear, often the only question I have for God is: "Why?" I am in good company. Jeremiah also asked God, "Why?" I definitely wanted to know why God had allowed suffering like I experienced in my life. For all his distress Jeremiah remained determined to obey God, no matter what the cost. Jeremiah understood that a loving, compassionate God was in control. I believe that God is in control of my life too. "Before I was born, He knew me." Certainly He sees what I am suffering now. Nothing takes God by surprise. God told the apostle Paul: "My grace is sufficient for you, for power is perfected in weakness." (2 Cor. 12:9)

I realize now I was not as intimate with Him as I needed to be to understand the coming storm in my personal life. I must learn to trust Him first—only then can I venture to trust people, and it is to my great advantage to learn to do both. God knew what was coming, and He was faithful to get my heart ready to handle it. Of course I did not feel like I was ready to handle it. I felt like a mess, but I did not self-destruct, I was able to persevere. I fought to keep from sinking emotionally.

"Hadn't I prayed with everything in me asking God to do something extraordinary in my heart? Why has no miracle taken place? God seems not to be answering my prayers," I sometimes weep. Often exhaustion is my constant companion. I feel like I am dying a slow, excruciating death.

As the months drag on, I become overwhelmed by the futility of my position and have concluded that I cannot keep on living like this, just waiting for something to happen. I have said earlier that I desire the level of faith that enabled the biblical characters to survive, and was more often daunted by them. I became restless and overcome by anxiety.

Someone pictured my state of mind this way: "Behind me I could see the storm that had caused destruction in my life; up ahead I could see the beach I wanted to reach, but my feet were bogged down in the mud." The description could not have been more apt. I was living in the uncomfortable place of transition. Every life contains pivotal moments that alter one's course in significant ways. The conspiracy and my retirement stand out as two such moments in my life. From time to time I look back and reflect on how differently my life would have turned out if the "terrible false accusation" had never happened. God was my bridge over troubled waters, constantly calling on Him to drive out of me the demon of depression and anxiety—and the terrible urge to end my life, was the worst demon of all that haunted me.

CHAPTER 42

WAITING

As I write these pages, it is now April 1, 2006. The weather is warming up. The clocks jumped ahead one hour and spring has sprung. New life in nature is budding forth and at least unconsciously new hope, however faint, is motivating my life in a somewhat positive way thanks to a fax from my canon lawyer. It is a beautiful morning, the sun had just risen and I could hear the birds chirping. The fax was a copy of a letter from my new promoter of justice, stating that he doubts that the judges in the case would be able to reach moral certitude that I was guilty of the alleged offenses against the two alleged victims who were two little sisters. My canon lawyer stated that this means that the judges might decide that I am innocent (totally exonerated) or they might decide that the matter is "unproven" leaving it up to the bishop to decide whether or not to impose an administrative penalty in accordance with canon law. The promoter of Justice, Father Vincent G., A.F.M. was inclined to recommend that the idea of a trial be dropped due to what he perceived to be inconclusive (unconvincing) evidence. It was all mumbo jumbo to me and I insisted on a trial in the hope that the judges, once and for all, would decide that I was totally innocent and returned to the exercise of my full priesthood.

During this period in April of 2006, I feel like a yoyo, good news and bad news, back and forth. It feels like the authorities are playing cat and mouse with me. At night I crave a full night's sleep because it is the only way I can be sure to get any kind of relief. The medication usually keeps me asleep until about 5:00 a.m. and then I have to get up immediately and have a strong cup of high test coffee. Otherwise, my mind will regress back to negative thoughts and destroy my new day. That routine has become part of my life, especially during the winter dreariness. Easter is approaching. I begin to think, "Will I continue to stay on my cross of suffering or have a glorious resurrection?" Either way I have united my life with Christ's passion, death and resurrection.

*   *   *

It is almost Easter week, April 9 to April 16, 2006. Holy Thursday, April 13, 2006 is fast approaching, the commemoration of the institution of the priesthood, a very emotional day, considering that my former bishop bombarded Rome to have my priesthood removed. It was all so real all over again. Now a week before Holy Week, April 4, 2006, it looks like a breakthrough. A small amount of hope is finally surfacing after three years of hopelessness. I feel myself coming out of that funk mode (dejected state of mind). Finally, a light is shinning in the darkness. But I am optimistically cautious. I have to get out of my own way and finally stop feeling pity for myself. I've got a jump start, no matter how faintly. I am still fighting the good fight, even though I have a long way to go. I am down but not out. I have to pick myself up and continue the fight. I wanted a quick fix, but it has turned out to be a long upward battle.

My friends kept saying, "Hang in there, justice will be served sooner or later." I felt their words were mere jargon and meaningless. But still they were wise to continue to say these words, no matter how frustrating I felt them to be. Unconsciously, they were penetrating my brain and leaving an imprint that would sooner or later stick. You can do it, you can do it, so that finally I could do it—survive.

The Christmas and Easter celebrations of 2002 and 2003 were the most exciting of my whole priesthood. Remember, I had applied for permission to retire one year before as required by the diocese. So I knew that Christmas that the upcoming Easter would be my last as pastor. So I went all out in decorating the church and conducting uplifting ceremonies—my two favorite cantors, Lisa and Kim, lead the beautiful choir and they were magnificent. People were never so generous with their praise and exuberant compliments. Excitement filled the air.

Thank God I survived through these celebrations in spite of my pain. Now I had those events to look back on with great satisfaction because shortly after that, the conspiracy thing grew worse and worse until I could not take it anymore. So by March of 2003 I wrote to the bishop to move up my retirement by two months mainly because my prostate problems were getting worse and worse, and the doctor suggested immediate surgery to relieve the pressure; all caused I now believe by *emotional* unrelenting pressure. It was a nagging worry, but I had no choice but to keep on keeping on. A few times

I was rushed to the emergency ward of St. Clare's Hospital in Denville, NJ with what appeared to be a heart attack. But it was diagnosed as stress related. I had unbearable pain in my shoulders which turned out to be a flare up of my childhood TB.

Sometimes hearing about other people's sad stories and heroic struggles humbled me and made my problems fade in comparison. Notwithstanding my desperate mind, I felt that the hole I was in was far too deep for me to ever climb back out to the top. It reminds me of the fable I used to tell in church about the crow who tried but could not reach the bottom of a bottle with his beak where there was a little water. So he picked up little stones with his beak and dropped them into the bottle until the water reached the top and then he could quench his thirst and stay alive. I in my struggle to survive was able to see the water of exoneration at the bottom of the bottle of my life. Thank God I had good friends who dropped the stones of love into the bottle of my life, so I could taste the water of freedom and one day be able to live a full priestly life once more.

When with God's help I believe I will be exonerated, I hope I will be able to look back and contemplate what I've been through and be able to show the world that all priests who are accused are not necessarily guilty. I hope I will be able to reach out to other innocent priests who are falsely accused and help them in their struggle and give them hope.

If there is anything positive that I could possibly imagine came out of this horrible attack, it probably would be that I sure don't take my priesthood for granted anymore. I will treasurer every moment of being able to minister to the people of God—like it's been an education to me of the awesome calling of the priesthood. No doubt a very difficult learning experience that I surely would not have chosen freely. No one in his right mind would have taken this cruel journey by choice.

What made this journey especially painful for me was my psychological makeup, especially my impatience. It is the thing that troubles me the most about myself; it is what contributed to my depression. I studied depression in the Post Graduate Center for Mental Health in New York. Now I was studying depression not from a book, but from real life. Actually going through it myself in the arena of raw emotions makes me a student of the school of depression, and now I have firsthand knowledge of the subject. As I sit alone in my little apartment, I'm reminded of how uncertain life can be. It can be a beautiful sunny day like the first day of the week of 9/11; but there are always storms on the horizon. It reminds me how one minute everything can be okay and the next minute your world can be turned upside down.

During this lonely time I am all alone. My immediate family, brothers, sisters, nephews, nieces, relatives as far as I know, never knew about the attack on my character; and that is the way I wanted it. I tried with every ounce of energy I had to protect them from hearing about it. It would devastate them. God forbid that the people I love the most would be deeply wounded by a totally false accusation since they live in many parts of the world outside the USA. It would be impossible to get the whole truth out without causing confusion in my family. So instead of being able to lean on them and receive compassion and comfort from my own family, I had to keep them at a distance. I turned instead to my parish family who supported me unconditionally and never for a minute doubted my innocence.

As difficult as my life was during the years of an ongoing investigation, I can look back on that period as a blessing. I am now stronger for having climbed my way out and back to enjoying again the life that was taken away from me and slowly learning to forgive those people that put me through the ringer and squeezed the life out of me—an experience reminiscent of my childhood, when I observed my mother putting wet clothes through the ringer. I often thought what a horrible experience it would be to actually be put through a ringer. Now at this stage of my life, I feel like I have in fact had the experience, at least in a symbolic way of being put through the ringer; and let me tell you, it wasn't exactly soft and fuzzy.

Finally, may I dare say, if there is one message I want to leave from this journal, it is if there is a priest out there who is falsely accused, I want you to know, that you are not alone, and with perseverance and hopefully with patient endurance, you can make it to the other side of darkness.

CHAPTER 43

CRISIS

My passion during this dark period of my life is reading—especially biographies about people who have gone through personal difficulties in their lives, and have lived to tell their stories. Their stories of survival give me hope. My ordeal sometimes pales in comparison to their psychological or physical pain.

Just today I was touched by Senator Gordon Smith's *Remembering Garrett*, a story of one family's battle with a child's depression. Senator Smith's son Garrett battled learning disabilities and clinical depression for most of his life until, just before turning twenty-two, he took his own life. As parents, Smith and his wife Sharon, who had adopted Garrett as a newborn, were heartbroken; and as a United States Senator, Smith was forced to question whether he had the strength or even the desire to carry on in politics. In his book, Smith retraces his son's life leading up to his suicide, telling about the sadness he and his wife faced after the tragedy. But with the help of family and many friends, he not only returned to politics but became an unrelenting supporter of suicide prevention and in the process is now a crucial help to all parents fighting for a child struggling with depression.

The death of Smith's son could have destroyed him and plunged him into depression himself. But he picked himself up and not only saved his own life, but likely saved innumerable lives by writing his book. Definitely on this day, as I read his book, he substantially helped me to continue through my depression. If he could survive such an awful ordeal, so could I.

Just yesterday, April 2006, while browsing through Barnes & Noble, the cover of *People* magazine caught my eye with its bold cover headline: *Amazing Stories of Survival*; fifty tales of hope, heroism, and astounding luck. No doubt, most of us are quite willing to be satisfied with reading about other people who have been shot at, frozen on Mt. Everest, lost at sea for 144 days,

178

chased by a machete swinging madman, clamped in the jaws of a mountain lion, or hit by lightening and lived to tell the tale. We are happy that these calamities happened to someone else and not us.

Survival stories gives us hope that when you're caught in a crisis and you confront it with determination and courage, and you survive; it is often unexplainable and even it may seem miraculous. Survival stories also give us a renewed, uplifting look on life.

Out of all the survival stories I read, one in particular stood out. Maybe it is because I love animals, or maybe it just is unique. Every dog has its day. For Dosha, a 10-month old pit bull mix, April 15, 2003 was not it. Things got off to a bad start. In the morning when Dosha's owner let her out of the house, she ran across the road and was hit by a truck. She flew through the air, rolled to the ground, and gave every appearance of being dead. A police officer arrived and, to make sure, he shot Dosha in the head to end any possible suffering. Then a public works employee took her to the local animal control center, where she was placed in a freezer for dead animals awaiting disposal. Two hours later, Dosha's luck changed. A worker opened the freezer door by chance and found Dosha sitting up. She was alive. The veterinarian treated Dosha for hypothermia as well as for the gunshot wound. The bullet had traveled along Dosha's skull— barely missing her brain and settled in the skin under her jaw. Dosha was released from the veterinary clinic, returned to her astounded and joyful owners, and lived a normal healthy life. That dog had everything go wrong, but what started out to be a disastrous day for her, in the end turned out to be her lucky day.

In Laura Day's book, *Crisis*, it states that the moment your life falls apart is also the moment your new one begins. It is the moment when illusion and deception fall away and naked truth emerges. Crisis can be painful, but when dealt with head on, it can also be a source of power, hope and vision—and the start of the life you really want. Crisis can be the most authentic version of self-transformation. Points of crisis bring us face to face with our deepest doubts and fears, and our most essential aspirations—and this means that our response to change is every bit as important as the change itself. In her book, Laura Day offers practical tools for turning the lowest times into the greatest gifts. Getting through crisis is part acceptance and part reinvention—and Laura's book provides invaluable lessons for closing one chapter and beginning the next. She states that rock bottom can be the best place to start. Laura Day helps readers to embrace where they are, then pick up and renew from that point.

The article in People magazine on amazing stories of survival and Laura Day's book have helped me greatly through my crisis. There was a stage in my life when I desperately sought assurance from others, but Laura's advice was inspiring: "Go through a day in which you are your only source of comfort." Up to then I was addicted to getting approval from others. If I did not get a call from at least one friend on any single day I would feel abandoned. Laura advises everyone in crisis to remember all the times that you successfully navigated through past crises, and assure yourself you can do it again. I have mentioned earlier some of those "crisis" times in my life, and thank God I survived. As they say in the old country: "I am still above ground."

Like many travelers, last January 2006, while on my way with my friend Father Bob on Continental Airlines, I learned a significant lesson when the flight attendant demonstrated the usual safety exercises. I've heard the drill so many times I usually don't pay full attention. But the one that touched me most this particular flight was the oxygen routine. The stewardess said if the oxygen mask drops to make sure you *put on your own mask before helping others*. I learned a lesson from that; I must take care of myself first, take care of my health, take my vitamins and eat properly. I need to have the strength to go through the storm to regain my lost self. I need to have the strength to build a bridge between my old self and my new self. I needed the strength to rebuild my life determined not to ignore any physical signs of a medical problem.

Many years ago, in the eighties, I was part of a group (led by Jeff Biggiani) dedicated to helping the homeless in New York City. We collected sleeping bags and brought them to the NYC street people. I remember placing a sleeping bag inside a man's makeshift shelter. As I pressed down on the sleeping bag, to my horror, I was stabbed by a syringe needle. It was during the AIDS epidemic in the USA. I was terrified—what would I do? I went into denial mode and dismissed it from my mind; after all I was young and healthy, I would be fine. I could have made a major crisis out of it, but I was too busy helping the poor, so I didn't think about myself. That could have been a mistake but as it turned out, I went on with my life and I was fine.

Of all the fifty survival stories graciously told in the April 2006 issue of *People* magazine, I would have chosen the worst one of them over my personal story of the false accusation of me allegedly molesting two little sisters in 1980. For me, personally, there is no more horrific crime than the violation of a child. The very mention of the "M" word seers the core of my soul. It has become a festering sore that never seems to heal. After almost four years of unrelenting struggle to clear my name, the fight goes on, and the light at the end of the tunnel often turns out to be the headlights of an oncoming freight train to knock me down and plough over me time after time.

My nighttime ritual is to watch Larry King Live on CNN. Many of his guests are survivors. One such survivor was Warren McDonald. According to Warren, on the night of April 9, 1997, he took his last step as a complete human being. He set off to climb Mt. Bowen on Hinchinbrook Island off the east coast of Australia. But what began as a two-day adventure suddenly turned into a nightmare, when a huge rock slipped off the mountain crushing McDonald beneath it for two long days and nights, while his companion searched for him.

The accident changed McDonald's life forever. He described on the Larry King show an extraordinary story of survival in the face of overwhelming odds. What I found even more unbelievable, after having both legs amputated, a few years later Warren climbed to the top of Africa's tallest mountain.

His story helped me put my difficulties into perspective. However, I still feel like I am in some kind of suspended animation, time swirling around me like a fog. Ideally, I should live for the moment, because that is the only certainty I have. Time is precious and every second should be appreciated and enjoyed as if it's my last. But now in the midst of pain and darkness time can't pass quickly enough.

At this juncture the beautiful dissertation, the *Desiderata* comes to mind: "*You are a child of the universe no less than the trees and the stars... with all its sham and drudgery and broken dreams. It is still a beautiful world.*"

The Church, with all of its flaws, is still a beautiful church, the ever beautiful Bride of Christ. Jesus said, "I will be with you always until the end of the world."

At this time, in the year 2006 in fact, this very day as I write these pages, Friday, May 16, 2006, a major attack is being perpetrated against the Church in a worldwide release of a major motion movie entitled *The DiVinci Code*. The author of the book with the same name is Dan Brown, and the movie directed and produced by Ron Howard tries to undermine the very foundation of Christianity by portraying Jesus as having had an affair with Mary Magdalene and fathering a child with her, a daughter that she took to France and who eventually married a prince of France. The movie claims that the Holy Grail is not really the chalice used by Jesus at The Last Supper but the blood line of Jesus. The movie goes on to implicate the religious group Opus Dei as responsible for the cover up, and eventually is responsible for the murder of an individual who was about to reveal the so-called scandal. The book and the movie are pure fiction, not an ounce of truth to any of it. Unfortunately, there is always the danger of the people of God being confused and their faith shaken. But as Jesus said, "The gates of hell shall not prevail against it."

CHAPTER 44

RESISTING NEGATIVITY

Sometimes I went into stress remission, but usually not for long before I would suffer a relapse and be back where I started. I didn't think I could ever feel normal again. I felt that maybe I was permanently damaged, that I wouldn't survive all of this. Then I read Robin S. Sharma's book, *The Monk Who Sold His Ferrari*. It provided me with a formula for survival. It helped me to take control of my life. It gave me the turnoff switch I desperately needed to stop the constant replay of the awful attack on my character.

I believe that God inspired Robin S. Sharma to write her book to save people like me who were destined for self-destruction—often I thought of suicide as the only way to stop the mental pain. It became my bible, my comfort cushion as it were, when I relapsed and fell off my mental wagon. I had become addicted to negative thoughts and easily slid down the slippery slope of obsessive negative thinking. I took refuge by quickly opening Robin's book and reading what for me were her most helpful passages, which I had outlined with a yellow marker, such as: "Care for your thoughts as you would your most prized possessions," and "'I can' is more important than your IQ," and "If you hope to make remarkable improvements in your outer world you must first start within and change the caliber of your thoughts."

Thinking negative thoughts sometimes became a compulsive-obsessive behavior: basically a bad habit. I thought, "I've got to do something to break this bad habit and develop a healthy mind free to act as God created it. Free of being a slave to my dysfunctional mind and free to think positive uplifting thoughts and be capable again of seeing the world in all its beauty; to again see the roses and notice the sun shining." And as Robin Sharma says, "I must never allow the calendar or the clock to blind me to the fact that each moment in life is a miracle, a mystery, a gift." Not a "drag" pulling me down to a sad and a worrisome state of existence, which is not really living, but like a dead man walking.

Negative thoughts only pollute your mind like sewage water. As we have developed the technology to purify water, we must develop a psychological technology to purify our minds. I believe that Robin Sharma's work is a major step forward in that direction.

I pray that God will give me the strength to take back control of my mind. Give me back full ownership of the dwelling of my mind and kick out the tyrannical intruder that has stolen my peace of mind. I want to die to my old mind and receive a brand new healthy mind, returning to the mind of my childhood, pure and uncontaminated and to begin again to live a full and happy life.

To share with you a technique I used to clear my tortured mind: I would sometimes create an imaginary blackboard in my mind, write the word "accusation" on the board and then with a vengeance erase the word and write: "I am innocent; this whole 'thing' is a lie, a travesty of justice. Evil people did this to me. Evil, Evil, Evil; Bad, Bad, Bad." I would mentally focus on that writing for as long as I could, until reality set in and then I was back where I started.

Robin Sharma suggests applying opposition thinking to every negative thought that enters your mind. Allowing my mind to entertain negative thoughts—even one—is like an alcoholic taking one drink and thinking he can get away with it.

I often tried, as it were, to slam the door of my mind closed to keep out the negative thoughts; alas somehow they would sneak back in and again take over and enslave me to more torture. As Robin Sharma says, "I must wage war against thoughts that have crept into the palace of my mind. They will see that they are unwanted and leave like unwelcome visitors."

I must stop mulling over petty things that drag me down into the crisis and chaos. I must not stay a prisoner of my past but become an architect of my future. "Time slips through our hands like grains of sand, never to return again. Those who use time wisely from an early age are rewarded with rich and satisfying lives." (from *The Monk Who Sold His Ferrari*)

Jesus said, "Unless you lose yourself you will never find yourself." Preoccupation with "self" is a dysfunctional and unhappy existence. The wise men of the East call it "shedding the shackles of self." Robin S. Sharma says, "When we are born we are crying while the world rejoices." She suggests that we should live our lives in such a way that when we die, the world cries while we are rejoicing.

Some tell me, "Be patient—the truth will eventually come out and you will be exonerated." It is now going on four years, and I am getting discouraged.

I never enjoyed the virtue of patience and that only adds to my pain. My canonist has made progress and seems focused and smart. This should give me comfort; after all, I am in capable hands. However, because of my poor self-worth and chronic lack of patience, the situation gets progressively worse. Like a mouse I am on the treadmill of life—going around and around but not getting any place; or like a broken record repeating, repeating, repeating the same message. Like a car I am stuck in between gears, not going forward or backwards. Consequently, my impatient nature only gets worse. Someone said, "Patience is part of the equipment we need if we are going to cope with life." As a priest, the sin people confess to me the most is lack of patience, and I found that was particularly true of mothers. Of course, I am convinced my impatience is genetic; my mother had very little patience. At Lenten time, practicing patience was people's greatest determination while it made me feel a little better knowing that I'm not alone.

As children most of us were taught that "patience is a virtue." It is, but it is also a sign of strength. Patience is particularly difficult for a type-A personality like me. Some people claim emphatically that patience becomes easier as it becomes a habit. I wish I had learned to develop patience in my early days. Now that I am in a crisis it is too late—my impatience has developed into depression which is a double whammy. I have the gift of perseverance in spite of my impatience. For me, giving up is not a choice. Unfortunately, the hanging in there is not a pleasant experience; but failure is not part of my vocabulary. I am lucky that my closest friends have patience with my impatience and flaws.

Thomas Edison is supposed to have said, "Success in anything we do is one percent inspiration and ninety-nine percent perspiration." At this stage, I have to believe that nothing worthwhile has ever been achieved without patience—at least patient endurance. I have more endurance than patience. For me, patience is utter determination to achieve my goal and I am absolutely determined to prove my innocence, even while I suffer mentally and physically because of my impatience.

I've become more and more impatient with the lack of progress in my legal attempts to solve the problem. My lawyers, civil and canon, were important in their attempts to rescue me from the hands of people out to destroy me. I asked for quick results, my impatient nature becoming more and more frustrated because I couldn't go on living in this psychological pain. I went to the gym once or twice a week and sometimes had a massage. Every little thing helped even if it was in tiny increments. My head was always someplace else. My thoughts were all over the place. I kept thinking how horrible I felt. I was scared of everything out of the ordinary—even children screaming and yelling as they joyfully played, screeching brakes in cars traveling on the street below my apartment. Even going to movies was problematic, violent scenes would freak me out and I must have walked out of more movies than I can count; of course any friends that were with me walked out also—they understood what I was going through.

My negative mind controls me and I feel helpless. That is not me, and I miss being me. I've lost at least twenty pounds and have begun to age beyond my years. Life is for the living, I'm dead on the inside. I don't think I will ever be able to return to my vibrant active healthy days. However, my brain is wounded and it isn't going to heal overnight. Even when positive news comes, like a call from my canonist, April 4, 2006, that indicated I might be exonerated. I was excited, but cautious, asking myself, "Is this really true?" Could it bounce back and hit me in the face once again? No matter, this was a letter of hope in the midst of pain and confusion; a boost in my efforts to survive a despicable attack on my character. There is a stigma to it that makes you want to hide, ashamed of even being accused of such an act, even though I know I am completely innocent.

Behind the calm, outward appearance, the civil investigation of my alleged crime continued unabated. It began in February of 2003 and lasted a year, until March 2004 when it was determined there was no substantial evidence to proceed with a civil trial. During this period, I had to pretend nothing was wrong; going on with my hectic parish ministry, daily public mass, anointing the sick and dying, funeral masses, first communions, confirmation preparation and confirmation ceremonies, constant office meetings with needy people, running a large child care center and grammar school, proceeding with building of new buildings to keep up with the needs of a growing parish.

Still throughout this first year under the cloud of an investigation, my mind was bombarded with worry about the accusation, but I had no choice, the ministry had to go on. And then came the day I received a copy of a letter sent by my bishop to Rome to have me removed from the priesthood immediately—ex officio to Cardinal Joseph Ratzenger, now Pope Benedict XVI, that I was a danger to the people of God. That news sent me into the darkest place I had ever been in, the darkness was blinding if that is possible. However, I had to face the world with a brave public face. My outside demeanor was very different than my inward disposition of sadness and disappointment and negative emotions.

Close to four years later I can barely remember the details of events, one day has just slipped into the next.

CHAPTER 45

UNITED FLIGHT 93

I have just seen the movie *United Flight 93*, and I observed what courage really is. Radical fundamental Muslims, misguided young men, inflicted terror upon the passengers of this flight. These evil people had taken control of innocent people's lives, determined to kill all of them and destroy the capital White House of the USA as a punishment to western civilization. But with tremendous courage the passengers on the flight "stood up" to the terrorists and successfully prevented them from carrying out their evil mission, ultimately sacrificing their own lives. To all Americans they are truly heroes. In the face of all odds and knowing that they would likely lose their own lives, they would not and could not ignore the evil intentions of their attackers.

You will always have evil people in the world, even those who claim to have deep faith in God, maybe even because of it. The attack on my personal life was carried out by people who claim to be the leaders of the people of God, even though they knew in their hearts I was innocent. But like the passengers of Flight 93, I am fighting back. I will not allow them to highjack my life even though they have all the power and I am powerless. Ultimately truth will prevail. My mission is possible but will not be easy. I will not surrender. Like the passengers and terrorists all died, my attackers may bring me down because of their superior positions, but eventually they will collapse under the weight of the truth. Rome and the Russian empire were not destroyed from the outside. They collapsed on the inside. Someone once said to John Paul II: "You did an amazing thing in bringing down Communism, the evil empire." He replied, "That was easy, all I had to do was shake the apple tree and all those rotten apples fell off." There are at least five former executives of the diocese who tried to destroy me. What I would call five rotten apples.

I will not stop shaking the tree until all those rotten apples fall off and face up to the truth—that their attack on me was unconscionable, and ask for forgiveness before they have to meet their maker at their own natural deaths. I forgive them but I cannot forget what they did to me. It is indelible in my mind, irremovable. God forgive them, even though they knew exactly what they were doing..

CHAPTER 46

OPTIMISM & PESSIMISM

There is an amusing story I used to tell when I was in the active ministry. There were two little boys in a family, one was an eternal optimist; the other an eternal pessimist. For Christmas, as an experiment, the parents decided to give a piece of horse manure to the optimistic kid, and loads of toys to the pessimistic kid. After the two kids got up in the morning and picked up their gifts from under the Christmas tree, the parents asked the pessimistic kid what he got. "I got all these toys I have to put together," he complained. "They are a mess! What a pain!" The parents then asked the optimistic kid what he got for Christmas. "I think I got a horse," he yelled, "but I can't find him."

I personally qualify as the pessimistic kid. I always think of the worst—a definite worrier. I am just like my dad; he was tortured with worry. He would always think of "the worst."

So often in transition I believe I am waiting on God to show me what to do, but in fact He may be waiting on me. What is God waiting for? Perhaps to see how badly I want to be with Him. Will I keep seeking Him, even when I do not hear or feel Him, or will I give up the effort? God may also be giving me time to become whole in some area of my emotional life. I am not always ready to receive direction from God when I think I am. God is interested in my well-being. He wants me to succeed in my future endeavors. He wants me to be prepared for what lies ahead. He is for me, not against me.

I get great spiritual guidance from reading the book of Elijah. Elijah learned of threats being made against him by the King's wife, Jezebel, and he fled into the desert. There he collapsed under a juniper tree and asked the Lord to take his life. Elijah was exhausted without hope. Like me, he had been through an intensive ordeal. A chapter in his life had closed. Now he was in transition and he was telling God how he felt, he was giving up: he was ready to quit, he wanted relief. I have felt like this, as I've already mentioned.

But God did not answer Elijah right away. God waited until Elijah slept and then He sent an angel with only a simple word: "Get up and eat." (1 Kings 19:5) Elijah did as the angel instructed and lay down again, only to be touched by the angel a second time and given the same command. As he was told to do, Elijah ate and drank, and then he commenced a forty day journey to Mount Horeb, "The Mountain of God." Elijah was told to go and stand on the mountain and prepare for the Lord to come by. Elijah retreated into a cave as a great and powerful wind tore the mountain apart and shattered the rocks, but the Lord was not in the wind. After the wind there was an earthquake, but the Lord was not in the earthquake. After the earthquake came a fire, but the Lord was not in the fire; and after the fire came a gentle breeze. When Elijah heard it, he pulled his cloak away from his face and went out and stood in the mouth of the cave. He felt the presence of God. Now at last, God was going to address the prophet's concerns, and give him instructions. God came to Elijah in a gentle breeze.

God will bring me out of my transition gradually. The prophet was depressed, despairing, afraid, and ready to die when he fled to the dessert and collapsed under the juniper tree. God knew he needed a rest. Elijah needed simple nourishment the pronouncement of a grand plan for his future. Once the prophet was strong enough, he was able to take a journey to The Mountain of God. On the journey Elijah regained his confidence. He was no longer fleeing from Jezebel, but moving toward God. He was walking in wholeness, not running in fear.

God made his presence known to Elijah in a gentle whisper; God was not in the drama— the wind, the earthquake, or the fire. The prophet was able to perk up on God's whisper because he himself was quiet, he was back to center. God did not need to speak to his prophet with fireworks; he could reach him with the slightest sound—because Elijah was ready—because he was still.

I personally need to slow down. I need to learn a lesson from Elijah—I need to meditate on the beatitude: "He will bring me beside still waters, He will refresh my soul." God spoke to Elijah and gave him specific direction. Once the time is right, God will do the same for me. Paul wrote in 1 Cor 2:9: "The eye has not seen, the ear has not heard what God has prepared for those who love Him." In my transition I am lead to believe that God is preparing something beautiful and extraordinary for me. Something my finite mind cannot imagine. He will bring good out of my circumstances. That is my hope and my dream.

Billy Graham's daughter Ruth in her *Principles for Reflection* states, "Excessive busyness can be a trap. Make time for rest during transition. Learn to be still. Spend time with God. He will give you direction when He is ready and when He knows you are ready." Scripture promises that He will make all things to work together for good for those who love God and to those who are called according to His purpose. (Rom: 8)

God will bring life out of what looks dead. He will make our mess ultimately into something beautiful. He promises: "I will repay you for the years the locusts have eaten." (Joel 2:25)

CHAPTER 47

GOD IS FAITHFUL

As I have stated over and over, "I need a quick fix," but I have to realize by now that God works gradually. How often I have tried to rush with my own schedules and plans. I am overwhelmed with the darkness of it all, with God's leisure. I wanted to have things settled, and to know what I can count on. I want a plan. But someone has said it is out of mercy that God does not reveal the future all at once; rather He graciously unfolds it for us over time. I fully agree. There are so many things in my life I now am thankful for that I did not foresee. They would have overwhelmed me. I needed a gradual awakening.

My life has not turned out as I imagined it when I was ordained. I expected happy endings: but God did not fit into that box, and I am glad. If I had my way, life would have been easy and I would not have needed God very much. Consequently I would have missed opportunities to know Him better. I would have lived perhaps unable to recognize His faithfulness. If life were perfect, who would need a builder? God, as they say is in the construction business, and He is not finished with me yet. God has shown me that the only way to wait in darkness is to hang on to Him, to trust Him completely, to believe in His desire and ability to redeem what is lost or ruined.

As I drive my car I have observed a profound lesson. I always remember the "red" lights, but I never remember the "green" lights. I just cross through the green lights totally unaware of the ease by which I travel; but suddenly I am brought to a screeching halt at the sight of a red light. I get annoyed and feel like I always get the red lights—forgetting the innumerable green lights I just had gone through.

CHAPTER 48

THE FIRE OF SUFFERING

God allows problems to draw one closer to Him. In Psalm 34:18 it says: "The Lord is close to the brokenhearted; He rescues those who are crushed in spirit." My most profound and intimate experience of worship is in my darkest days, when my heart is broken, when I feel abandoned, when I am out of options, when the pain is great—and I turn to God alone. It was during that time I learned to pray the most authentic, heartfelt, and honest-to-God prayers. When we are in pain, we don't have the energy for superficial prayers. When life is easy, we may slip by with knowing about Jesus, by imitating Him and quoting Him, and speaking of Him. But only in suffering will we know and experience Jesus. We learn things about God in suffering that we can't learn any other way.

God could have kept Joseph out of jail, kept Daniel out of the lions' den, kept Jeremiah from being tossed into a slimy pit, kept Paul from being shipwrecked three times, and kept the three young men from being thrown into a blazing furnace—but he did not. He let those problems happen, and every one of these persons was drawn closer to God as a result. He could have prevented the plot against me, but he did not and I have drawn closer to Him.

Problems force us to look to God and depend on Him instead of on ourselves. Paul states this truth in 2 Cor. 1:9: "We felt we were doomed to die and saw how powerless we were to help ourselves. But that was good, for then we put everything in the hands of God, who alone could save us." You will never know that God is all you need until God is all you have got.

Regardless of the cause, none of your problems could happen without God's permission. Everything that happens to a child of God is father-filtered, and He intends to use it for good even when Satan and others mean it for bad.

(Rom. 28-29): "We know that God causes everything to work together for the good of those who love God and are called according to His purpose for them. For God knew His people in advance, and He chose them to become like His son."

Every problem is a character building opportunity, and the more difficult it is, the greater the potential for building spiritual muscle and moral fiber. St. Paul said in Rom. 5: 3-4: "We know that these troubles produce patience, and patience produces character." What happens outwardly in our lives is not as important as what happens inside you. Your circumstances are temporary, but your character will last forever.

Scripture compares trials and suffering to a metal refiner's fire that burnt away the impurities. Peter said in 1 Peter 1:7: "In this you greatly rejoice, though now for a little while you may have had to suffer grief in all kinds of trials. These have come so that your faith—of greater worth than gold, which perishes even though refined by fire—may be proved genuine and result in praise, glory, and honor when Jesus is revealed." A silversmith was asked, "How do you know when the silver is pure?" He replied: "When I see my reflection in it."

When you have been refined by trials, people can see Jesus' reflection in you. James said in James 1:3: "Because you know that the testing of your faith develops perseverance."

We can rejoice in knowing that God is going through the pain with us. We do not serve God at a distance—instead, He enters into our suffering. Rick Warren said in his book, *The Purpose Driven Life*: "If you are facing trouble right now, don't ask: 'Why me?' instead ask, 'What do you want me to learn?' Then trust God and keep on doing what's right. You need to stick it out, staying with God's plan so you will be there for the promised completion."

Heb. 10:36 says: "Don't give up, grow up."

CHAPTER 49

NOW IS THE HOUR

The hour came for me to leave my father, mother, brothers and sisters, my whole family and fly to America to begin my ministry as a priest. Every person has his or her hour. For the law student, it is the bar. For the airline pilot, the Federal examiner. For the pregnant woman, when she gives birth. For the bride, when she walks down the aisle. For the father, when he gets the bills. When our hour comes, we all tighten up.

So it is no surprise, given His true humanity, that Jesus was tense in the scene from Mat. 26:43. Jesus looked up to heaven and said: "Father the hour has come. Give glory to your son that your son may give glory to you."

St. Paul's final hour: "I have fought the good fight, I have run the course, a crown of precious jewels awaits me."

I recall a popular song when I was a teenager: "Now is the hour when we must say good-bye. Soon we will be sailing across the great divide."

Every time we say the *Hail Mary*: "Holy Mary mother of God pray for us sinners now and in the hour of our death, Amen."

I once asked my mother if she was afraid to die. She answered: "Why should I be? All my life I have prayed for a happy death when I said the Hail Mary."

Jesus, being God as well as human, knew what that hour meant: the most demanding suffering ever to be recorded. One man called to die for all mankind; once and for all and ever, taking with Him into His agony all the sins of all people of all time.

No wonder temptation hit Him: "What should I say, Father save me from this hour? But it was for this that I came to this hour." He did not flinch. He stayed the course. His hour is a strange one. At first sight He says: "The hour has come for the son of man to be glorified." Glorified? Yes, because He is doing the will of His father. Son though He was, He learned obedience from what He suffered; and when perfected, He became the source of eternal salvation for all who obey him.

"Christ Jesus has now taken his place at the right hand of God. Our faith rests on Jesus who endured the cross for the sake of the joy that lay before him."

Then He compares himself to the grain of wheat: "Unless the grain of wheat falls to the earth and dies, it remains just a grain of wheat; but if it dies, it brings forth much fruit." Indeed His dying will bring forth much fruit, namely your salvation, mine, and all mankind's. Yes, He will be glorified in the beauty and splendor of a redeemed mankind, a new humanity springing up from the dying "grain of wheat."

CHAPTER 50

PROMISED LAND

On September 17, 2006, I find myself reflecting on my journey...

Having ministered for forty years in the priesthood, I had reached the year I could retire. As required by the rules of the diocese I had to apply for permission to retire one year prior to my fortieth year. My bishop gracefully granted my request. It was with great anticipation that I looked forward to the day I would be free of responsibility of running a large parish. However, as I was about to step into the promised land of a relaxed and free environment, my dream ended and became a nightmare. Moses in the Old Testament led the Jewish people for forty years through the desert, but as he was about to enter the Promised Land he too entered a nightmare. His forty years of wandering, like his forty days on the mountaintop, ended in frustration rather than fulfillment. Somehow, Moses was able to reconcile himself with the God who had demanded so much of him and taken so much from him. How did he do it? How does a person get over that bitterness, that sense of being cheated by life?

Sometimes I think if only I could erase that painful memory from my brain that makes it hard for me to enjoy today and contemplate tomorrow with hope. For some people, their memories are global: thoughts of war, earthquakes, floods, or other disasters. We would be better off if the media didn't remind us of those global catastrophes. It seems like everything reminds me of the tragedy that happened to me. Instead of enjoying the promised land of my retirement I am suffering through hell on earth. Like Moses, I had dreamed of a perfect existence. However, I am beginning to believe this is an experience many people experience. The dream vacation that turned out to be a bore; the job that had been a lifelong dream that, when one attains it, is a disaster. The dream is a source of hope with the reality too often being a letdown.

In using the inspiring biblical story of Moses, Harold Kushner in his invaluable book entitled, *Overcoming Life's Disappointments*, reassures us that disappointments in life can be overcome and mysteriously can often be the very stepping stones that launch us toward the destiny God intends for us.

A psychiatrist, Dr. George Vaillant, states: "If you're aware of your disappointments, but at the same time thankful for the good, contentment comes more easily." In Valliant's words, "People who make lemonade out of lemons fare better (in old age) than people who turn molehills into mountains."

I am led to believe that few people get everything they yearn for, and most of us don't get everything we deserve. Unfortunately in my case, the false accusation against me hurt not only me personally, but hundreds if not thousands of former parishioners who loved me and felt their lives enriched by my ministry. That injects guilt into the fabric of my life. I have to ask myself if these good people have rejected my words to them, saying to themselves: "He was a fraud. Why should I have listened to him?" And then possibly find themselves back to their old selves; languishing in whatever was bothering them at the time. I think of Moses at the end of his life, this man who had climbed mountains to bring the word of God to mankind. Climbing one last mountain for a glimpse of the land he would never set foot on. On that last day, was he remembering triumphs, the Exodus, the sea divided, the establishing of the covenant? Or was he remembering the complaints of an ungrateful nation? I would like to think he remembered it all and decided that the good days outnumbered the bad days.

As I look back "post conspiracy," I, like Moses must remember the triumphs through my forty years of my priestly life and believe that the good days outnumbered the bad days. These thoughts help me to see my life as love gained and love lost: of acceptance and rejection of memories that continue to thrill, and of memories that continue to hurt, of people who were close to me who are now distant. I no doubt failed at things, but I have to be realistic and conclude that is an inevitable part of being human.

Harold Kushner ends his book with thoughts reminiscent of my own life. He states, "If I have been brave enough to love and sometimes I won and sometimes I lost. If I have cared enough to try, and sometimes it worked and sometimes it didn't. If I have been bold enough to dream and found myself with some dreams that came true and a lot of broken pieces of dreams that didn't, that fell on earth and shattered. Then I can look back from the mountaintop I now find myself standing on. Like Moses, I can realize how full my life has been and how richly I am blessed. As they say, 'Ask too much of life and you virtually guarantee heartbreak, disappointment and the risk of thinking of yourself as a failure.' So, I must choose to emphasize pride rather than regret, gratitude rather than bitterness, praise rather than envy."

As I write this journal on the very day, September 17, 2006, Pope Benedict XVI made a negative statement about the founder of the Muslims—Mohammed. There was an instant Muslim revolt around the world—he was burnt in effigy and called "a Hitler and a Mussolini." Pope Benedict quickly realized he had made a horrific mistake and tried to apologize for the remark, but it was too late. The harm was done. The Vatican announced to the world that the Pope felt terrible. My heart goes out to him; I feel his pain and he must be inconsolable. But he is a human and like Moses his soaring triumphs are offset by a simple oversight. I hope like Moses as the new leader of the people of God, he is resilient. Like all of us he must weather the disillusionment of the pain of criticism and condemnation, and respond to his broken heart with understanding rather than bitterness and despair. No human being is perfect. The best people will make mistakes, but we must not give in to despair and believe that tomorrow can be better than today.

Holocaust survivor Elli Wiesel said, "It is a fine thing to begin again after what you worked for has been taken from you." Harold Kushner says, "When part of your world has collapsed, make do with what you have left and don't stop celebrating."

Harold also says, "Some people buffeted by misfortune have found themselves capable of resilience because they did not have to face their problems alone. One of the things that doubles the emotional pain when things go badly is the fear that people will abandon us."

CHAPTER 51

THE STRUGGLE

From when I can remember as a child, I had massive obstacles to overcome. Many of these obstacles I have already laid out in former pages. But, I would not and could not give up—I had a goal to be a priest and nothing would prevent me from achieving that dream. I could enumerate hundreds of reasons why I should have quit, but for me personally, that was impossible.

In the early seventies, while driving to New York City, my car was robbed of everything in it. I felt violated and vulnerable. I asked myself how this could happen. I no longer felt secure and for the longest time I kept looking over my shoulder. Realizing I am vulnerable keeps me humble, and defines me.

Vulnerability prepares us to understand others, to be compassionate to the sick and downtrodden. Every year, while on vacation with my friend, Monsignor Bob Carroll, without fail we would pass a poor man on the sidewalk with no legs, holding a tin can; maybe once in awhile we would throw a dime in the can. But most of the time we felt uncomfortable, just seeing him; at least I did. Inside I would resent him being there—he just made me feel guilty. He probably made me aware of my own inability and that in fear my own incapacities will be exposed, and resist the possibility that others would see my weaknesses. I would never take the chance that people would love me for my weaknesses. I had a compulsion to always show my strengths. I spent a lot of my time trying to show that the pastor, director of certain diocesan agencies was in charge, clinging to the myth of authority and power to make myself feel important. So when I met up with the false accusation and it was public knowledge, I fell apart.

It is only vulnerability that prepares us to face real life, warts and all. It is acceptance of the limits of the self that makes us open, and it is confidence in the talents of others that makes us secure. Without loss we would be haughty and aloof. It is the conviction that I need others that saves me in times of trouble. It is the unacceptability that could destroy me at the end. It is not a question of just losing my priesthood that would destroy me, but the thought of living a useless life, being a nothing until death.

If I do not get my priesthood back, I will never feel fully alive again. I know from my psychological training that bodes badly for me. But I am determined to finish what I began. I remember as a child seeing a picture of an old priest kneeling in prayer and underneath was written, "I have fought the good fight. I have run the course and now there remains for me my rightful reward." I remember saying to myself, "That's me, that is the way I want my life to end." And so I intend to keep trying, even if it is unattainable. No matter how hard it may be, no matter how hopeless it may appear; even being open to the possibility that things will stay the way they are, perhaps indefinitely, bearing what I must no matter how unbearable.

Survival is how to live when there is little left to live for. I see life differently than I ever saw it before. It is not the nature of the struggle that counts. What counts is the effect of my particular struggle on me.

We all remember where we were when President Kennedy was shot. When the Towers fell, I remember where I was when I opened that registered letter. It marked me for life. It will never be undone. It will forever leave me timid and unsure of myself. It leaves me shamed. On the count of ten, I will get up and fight on. Joan Chittister, in her book, *Seared by Struggle - Transformed by Hope,* says, "When we know the meaning of what it is to struggle with something in life, we become totally human."

Before my name appeared in the newspaper, with no way to defend myself, I was able to look at another person's tarnished name and not think twice about it. Now at the sight of a newspaper I feel traumatized, terrified to look at it in case I would see my picture or read my name. I am now much more tolerable and less judgmental than I was prior to the attack on my character. I am told, no one comes out of struggle the same way they went in. Personally I've become more sensitive to the effects of the world around me on real people. I was transformed, I am more conscious of other people's pain.

On this first week of October 2006, three schools around the country experienced horror with the unimaginable massacre of dozens of little children in cold blood. What was especially painful to hear about was the massacre of several children in a one-room schoolhouse in the Amish countryside in Pennsylvania. Here was a community of people who wanted to live a simple, quiet life, untouched by the awful things happening in the modern world. Now, the violence came to them and they will never be the same.

The struggle that threatens to destroy us is whatever we cannot imagine living without. When I received that letter from my bishop, I felt like I was kicked in the stomach by a horse. How could I go on living without my priesthood? However, as I struggle through this ordeal once in a while I have to admit maybe what happened to me was in some strange way a blessing. A thirteenth century Persian poet, Rumi, put it this way:

> *I saw Grief drinking a cup of sorrow and called out, "It tastes sweet does it not?"*

> *"You've caught me," Grief answered, "and you've ruined my business. How can I sell sorrow when you know it's a blessing?"*

Hope is to remember where you have been before and know that God is waiting for you someplace else now, to go on and try something new. In the face of despair hope helps us discover how much life we can still make with whatever of it we have left. Hope is about allowing ourselves to let go of the present, to believe in the future we cannot see but can trust in God.

CHAPTER 52

JUSTICE

God has promised that if we will put our trust in Him, He will pay us back for all the unfair things that have happened to us: "I the Lord love what is right. I deplore robbery and injustice." In my case someone lied about me and their misinformation destroyed my reputation. A good friend, my bishop, betrayed me. These losses left indelible scars, causing me to want to hold on to my grief; having feelings to seek revenge. In fact, many people encouraged me to do so. The slogan, "Don't get mad, get even!" is a common accepted principle in America.

But I believe that is not God's plan for me. If I want to live my best life now, I must learn to trust God to bring about justice in my life. The Bible says, "God is a just God and He will settle and solve the cases of His people." (Hebrews 10:30)

We know the one who said, "Vengeance is mine, I will repay." That means you don't have to go around trying to pay everybody back for the wrong things they've done to you. I don't have to go around trying to get even with people. God is my vindicator. I need to start letting God fight my battles for me. Let God settle my case. God has promised if I turn matters over to Him and let Him handle them His way, He'll make my wrongs right. He'll bring justice into my life.

It takes faith to believe that God wants to vindicate me, but I am convinced He really does. He sent Father John into my life as my canon lawyer and he is working tirelessly for me. I can't make the mistake of sinking down to my offender's level, getting into arguments and fighting. That will just make matters worse for me. I must leave it up to God. Take the high road and respond in love and watch what God will do.

I will do it God's way. He'll not only fight my battles for me, but in the end I will come out better off than I was before. Sometimes God allows us to go through certain things to test us. God is interested in seeing how I am going to respond. I will not become negative, bitter or angry. I will not develop a vindictive attitude, always trying to pay people back.

I pray I pass that test so God can exonerate me. I hope to keep a good attitude and start trusting God to make it up to me. I am not working merely for the bishop. I am not employed merely by the Church. I am working for God and God sees every wrong that is being done to me. God is keeping good records. He is closely watching my situation and He said that He's going to pay me back—and when God pays back, he always pays back in abundance.

When God wants me exonerated, it doesn't matter whether my former bishop likes me or not; my future is not dependant on what my bishop does or doesn't do. God is in control.

The Bible says that exoneration doesn't come from the north, south, east, or west. In other words, exoneration doesn't come from my former bishop or his associates; exoneration comes from almighty God and when God says it is time for me to be set free, all the forces of darkness cannot hold me down. I will be exonerated.

Moreover, God will not allow somebody to continually mistreat me. If I will do my part, keep a good attitude and turn my circumstances over to Him, sooner or later God will bring justice into my life. Sometimes when I don't see anything happening month after month, year after year, it's tempting to become manipulative, to attempt to make things happen in my time. When I do that, I risk interfering with God's plan and purposes, creating another mess for Him to clean up and possibly even keeping God from doing what He really wants to do in my situation. It doesn't matter how people are treating me. I will keep doing the right thing; I will not get offended; I will not let them get me upset; I will not try to pay them back, returning evil for evil. I will continue extending forgiveness; keep responding in love. I know if I do that, then when it comes time for me to be exonerated, God will make sure it happens. He'll make sure I get everything I deserve and more.

The key is I must turn it over to God. Let Him do it His way. As the saying goes, "I can go my way, you can go your way, but someday we got to go His way." I must let Him do it His way. The scripture says, "Never avenge yourselves, but leave the way open for God's wrath." If I try to pay people back I am closing the door for God to do it. I can either do it God's way, or I can do it my way. If I'm going to let God handle it, I can't have the attitude of, "I'm going to show them what I'm made of!" That will prevent God from avenging me His way. If I want to keep that door open so God can bring true justice into my life, I have to totally turn it over to Him. Somebody may be saying nasty things about me behind my back. My attitude is, "No big deal. God's got me covered. He's going to make it up to me."

I find this a liberating way to live. If I truly understand that I don't have to fix everything that happens to me, I don't have to get all upset and worried and try to pay somebody back for what they did or didn't do. I don't have to get sad or try to manipulate the situation. I know that God is fighting my battle and He has promised to make my wrongs right, I can walk with a new confidence, with a spring in my step, a smile on my face, and a song in my heart. I am free.

My friend, Father Bob, keeps telling me: "The greater the struggle, the greater the reward." The scripture says, "Don't get tired of doing what's right for in due season you shall reap if you don't faint."

I must trust God to bring justice in His timing, not mine. Sometimes it doesn't happen overnight. My spiritual director tells me, "You're going to have to do the right thing when the wrong thing is happening to you and it may be a long time before you see any kind of change. It may require a strong will on your part and a determination to trust despite the odds."

When David was just a young man, he was anointed by the prophet Samuel to be the next King of Israel. Not long after that, he defeated the giant Goliath, and he became an instant hero throughout the Land. People loved him, and his popularity ratings soared off the charts. But King Saul, Israel's ruler at the time, became extremely jealous of David and started doing all sorts of unfair things to him. Sometimes Saul would get sick and David would play his harp for the King, soothing his mind and helping Saul to feel better. But one day as David was playing the harp for him; Saul suddenly picked up his spear and hurled it at David! The spear barely missed him. David ran out of the room, fearing for his life. When he realized that Saul was trying to kill him, he fled to the mountains to hide. He had to live on the run, going from cave to cave.

Think of it. David hadn't done anything wrong. He had treated Saul with respect and honor, yet Saul turned around and paid him back by attempting to kill him. Don't you know David could easily have been bitter? He could have easily said, "God, why is this man trying to hurt me? I didn't do anything to him. God, I thought you chose me to be King. What's going on here?" But David didn't do that. He kept a good attitude, refusing to hurt Saul, even when he had the opportunity. Although, Saul wasn't treating him right, David still respected Saul's position of authority.

My former bishop had authority over me and I was being treated unfairly. I know that what they did was wrong, and they probably knew it, too; I am tempted to treat the bishop with distain. It's easy to rationalize or justify a wrong attitude toward him. After all, my bishop is rude. He's ungodly. Thus, I don't have to treat him respectfully.

The truth is, whether he is behaving correctly or not, God expects us to honor his position of authority. I can't in good conscience make excuses and try to justify in my mind why I am free to speak or act disrespectfully toward that person.

It's easy to respect those in positions of authority as long as they are being kind to us, or when we agree with that person. But the true test comes when you get a "Saul" in your life: when somebody treats you unfairly for no apparent reason.

What happened to me wasn't fair, it wasn't right, and the accusation was totally false. I wasn't treated as I deserved; absolutely no justice, no recourse. I could have harbored anger and resentment in my heart toward some of those people, but I let those hard feelings go. I spoke to God: "I know you will eventually bring justice into my life."

YEAR FIVE (2007)

CHAPTER 53

THE TRIAL OF ST. JOAN OF ARC

The Inquisition was invented by the Church in the 14th Century to burn heretics at the stake.

Joan of Arc's trial was one of the most outstanding trials of the Inquisition. Joan was born in the village of Domremy on January 6, 1412, during the worst of times; the Hundred Years War was on the verge of blotting France out of existence; and the Black Death of Europe was creating famine and poverty.

Joan was the fourth of the five children of Jacques d'Arc and Isabelle Romee. Her parents were farmers. Both of Joan's parents were devout "good Catholics." Nothing extraordinary is reported about Joan's earlier childhood. She was baptized by the church of Domremy. Like most girls, she picked flowers and wove them into wreaths and garlands in the month of May. She would hang these wreaths on the "Ladies Tree" in order to honor Mary, the Mother of God. She was a very devout child. She would kneel and cross herself whenever she heard the church bells ring. She was charitable; she gave alms to the poor, nursed the sick. It was her mother who taught her the basic prayers, the "Our Father," the "Hail Mary," and the credo.

The extraordinary in her life started to take place when Joan was about thirteen. That was when she reported first having heard voices. She was in her father's garden, she told the inquisitor, the first time she heard the voice. "It was a day in summer at about noon." The voices taught her to be devout—to go to mass often, to pray, and they encouraged her to save France.

Joan lived a rather normal life for several years after she began to hear her voices. She must have continued to do her chores in those years—sewing, spinning, and farming. Joan remained silent about her voices. Years later, at her trial, she claimed that she did not inform her parents about the voices or what they said for fear that they would not let her embark on her mission. The voices called Joan to military action and to save France. She had to raise the siege of Orleans, crown the King, liberate the Duke of Orleans, and deliver France from the English.

Joan was sold to Archbishop Cauchon on March 21, 1430. He had Joan imprisoned in a small cell in the tower of the castle at Rowen. She was put in leg irons and chained by the waist to a large block of wood while she was in her cell. It is said by historians that Joan's Rowen trial was unfair, illegal, political, extremely biased, and that it was brutal.

The English tried with all of their might to dispel the very notion that God could have wanted France to win the war. This is why they staged an inquisition; an official Church trial to deal with Joan; for it was only the Church that could determine whether Joan's claim was authentic or not. The English did not go through with a fair inquisition. Had they wanted a fair hearing on Joan's case, they would have gone to Rome, where Pope Martin V may just have given Joan his blessing. They put the matter of Joan's inquisition in hands that would ensure an outcome that was favorable to them. This was the reason why they let one of their most devoted pawns, Bishop Pierre Cauchon, direct the ecclesiastical proceedings. The English needed Joan to be wrong. So Cauchon had to use every means at his disposal to have Joan discredited and eliminated. This was why he made Joan's condemnation as a heretic, her excommunication, and her death by fire his quest. This was what was at stake at Joan's trial. It was what makes the end of Joan's life such an incredible clash of wills.

Proceedings began on January 9, 1431, and they ended on May 30 of that same year. Many prospective members of the court refused to take part in the trial. The most vociferous was Nicholas de Houppeville, a priest from the diocese of Rowen, who pointed out that there were several reasons why the trial was gravely flawed. Cauchon's response was to have the priest reprimanded and imprisoned.

Cauchon had sent people to the towns where Joan was well known to try to uncover unsavory information about her. He needed some crime with which to accuse her in order to begin his trial. Inquisitional trials were supposed to be based on *diffamatio* charges which were well established before the trial began. But his runners came back empty handed, nothing even vaguely suspicious. The fact that Cauchon had no *diffamatio* meant that he would have to interrogate Joan in order to establish charges against her. That prospect was not a pleasing one. It meant that he would not have a solid case against Joan, unless she confessed to some grave crime. More importantly, it made the proceedings highly irregular from a legal point of view. It was virtually unheard of for a heresy trial to be based exclusively on the interrogation of the accused without anyone, including the accused herself, knowing what charge was being brought against her. Cauchon's first objective was, therefore, to find charges that would stick to Joan and which would make her claim to have been "sent by God to liberate France" sound heretical or false. Cauchon's mission was to find some way of insinuating that Joan's quest was not divinely inspired, that her mystical experiences, her conversations with her voices, were not authentic.

Despite the rocky beginning of his trial, Cauchon was confident. He had promised the English a beautiful trial and he intended to give them one, and he had every reason to be confident. He narrowed the possible causes of Joan's hearing voices down to three, a physical disorder, a mental disorder, and witchcraft.

Joan let the court know that she had no intention of succumbing to its pressure tactics. She refused to recite the *Our Father* until she was allowed to confess before a priest. She refused to swear that she would not attempt to escape.

After a month of interrogations, Cauchon had Jean d'Estivet draw up a list of articles of indictment. d'Estivet came up with seventy. Most of them were based upon twisted accounts of Joan's own testimony. Some called for the case to be sent to the Pope in Rome. On April 12, however, the University of Paris gave Cauchon its approval for the articles and that was enough for him. Joan got very sick and she asked for the sacraments. She was afraid that she would die. But she was not given the sacraments.

On May 9, Joan was threatened with torture, but still she did not submit to the court's judgments on the matter of her voices. Cauchon was at a loss. On May 24, Cauchon came up with his most brilliant play. He took Joan to the cemetery of St. Oven where he had several platforms and a large scaffold built. In front of a large crowd he told Joan that she would burn if she did not submit to the church militant. Joan once again asked to be brought to the Pope: "I appeal to God and to our Holy Father the Pope." She was ignored and told that the Pope was too far away to be called upon.

Two days later Joan was condemned to death and burned at the stake. That morning a monk, Martin Ladvenu, heard her confession and Joan asked for the Eucharist. Ladvenu was not sure whether he should give it to her—she was excommunicated. He consulted Cauchon who told the Dominican to "Give her the sacrament of the Eucharist and anything she asks."

Joan's death teaches us as much as her life does—Joan was betrayed and shame on the Church for one of its darkest moments in its history. Christ again was betrayed and Cauchon was the Judas.

CHAPTER 54

SHEPHERDS AND THEIR SHEEP

You would think the Church would learn a lesson from its history and that something even close to the Inquisition of the Middle Ages would never happen again. Unfortunately, and as usual, history repeats itself. Sure enough, here we are in the 21st Century, 600 years later and low and behold the Inquisition raises its ugly head again. Modern day bishops have become the great "Inquisitors" and a new witch hunt has begun—any priest can be accused of a crime against a minor, either through an anonymous letter, a phone call, or a conspiracy by disgruntled parishioners. The priest would be immediately censured and driven out of his parish; found guilty before he could prove himself innocent: a feat almost impossible to accomplish, once the accusation is made.

In my case, my former bishop writes an official letter to the Pope demanding my immediate laicization, ex officio; this time not even a trial or a personal discussion of any kind. No recourse of any sort was allowed me. No communication was possible—I was shunned by the diocese and my brother priests. My name erased from the official records. My life was essentially evaporated.

Finally, four years later, Rome responds and demands an ecclesiastical trial. But months have passed and I am still left hanging in the breeze, left out to dry. "Shrivel up and go away," seems to be the message to me. There are no accusers, and so the diocese is faced with a huge embarrassment and possibly a major lawsuit. The diocese has made one of the biggest mistakes of its life. And yet, I am still left in the dark, suffering indescribable, emotional pain; living alone in a one bedroom apartment 45 minutes drive from my former parish of 23 years, lost and isolated, and forbidden from having any contact with my former parishioners, in effect my church family.

Now Rome demands a trial and the diocese is trying to wiggle out of it hoping I would disappear or die, and they would be rid of the problem. The leadership is running scared and is trying to cover its own skin, after years of neglect, when bishops ignored the sickness of pedophilia and kept passing these priests around from one parish to another causing horrific damage to even more children. Now that they are confronted by their awful ignorance, they have reversed 180 degrees and gone to the opposite direction condemning *innocent*, as well as guilty priests. I am a victim of that Episcopal madness and caught up in its craziness. Bishops are no longer shepherds of the flock but more like wolves out to devour the flock.

Power corrupts; ultimate power ultimately corrupts suffering from Mad Bishop's Disease. Like Chaucon, my former bishop and his cronies are trying to set up a "beautiful trial" hoping eventually to make me look guilty of a nonexistent charge. Conscience, justice, the truth have no bearing on it. They stretch everything to try to cover all angles. Like Joan d' Arc, they already have searched the "attics" of my life to try and find "unsavory stuff" that would make me look bad. If they can't find anything they will invent some.

Where can I go from here to get my good name back? How can I even begin to repair the damage done to children and adults of my beloved family of St. Rose? Ever since I can remember, from when I reached the use of reason, I wanted to be a priest. As a child, I built an altar to Mary the Mother of Jesus, an altar made with shoeboxes and covered with blue linen given to me by my mother. I placed a vase of flowers on the altar every week. I remember, on my way home from the little one room school in Colemanswell Co., Charleville, as I walked by, my neighbor, Josie Driscall, would give me a bunch of her beautiful roses from her rose garden. I would put these in the vase of my shrine to Mary. As a young boy, I loved missions and I would ride my bicycle to most of the local churches either in Charleville, Newtown, Shandrum, or Colemanswell. The preacher who would preach with "hell, fire, and brimstone" was always my favorite. My mother recited the rosary with the whole family every night before we went to bed. I remember my poor gentle dad would fall asleep in the middle of the recitation. He had just come in from working a hard day on the farm, so it was understandable for any of us; the recitation of the rosary needs great effort to stay alert.

Not being able to celebrate a public mass is like a death to me, a terrible loss. I grieve for my beloved priesthood. I have suffered through four of the five psychological stages of grief, as outlined by psychologist, Kubler-Ross:

(1) shock
(2) denial
(3) anger

(4) depression

(5) acceptance

I will never reach the fifth stage of acceptance. I will fight to my last breath for the restoration of my priesthood. I will one day rise from the ashes to live my life to the fullest and again be able to preside at the altar of God, and feed God's people with the food of life. That is my calling that is my dream, no matter how hopeless it may appear; no matter how far, no matter how long. St. Joan of Arc is my hero—I ask her guidance and strength, finally declared a saint by the very Church that condemned her, and excommunicated her, and turned her over to the State to be burned alive, and her ashes thrown into the Seine in France. She was an extraordinary woman with extraordinary virtues and strength; at a time when women were treated as second class citizens with no rights.

*   *   *

Since the major scandal broke out in Boston in 2002, bishops around the country have behaved badly and made a bad thing worse. Their uncanny behavior is a scandal all by itself to the people of God. The sheep no longer follow them because they no longer recognize their voices; these bishops have become strangers to their people. The bishops should be ashamed of themselves and hang their heads in failure. I came so that they might have life and have it more abundantly. I am the good shepherd. A good shepherd lays down his life for the sheep. Many bishops today are cowards; scared of the media and the press. Jesus says, "I am the good shepherd and I know mine and mine knows me. My sheep hear my voice, I know them and they follow me. I give them eternal life and they shall never perish. No one can take them out of my hand."

I am confident I am in the hands of Jesus and no one can take me out of His hands, not even a bishop. I believe a pedophile priest is not a real priest. The day he was ordained there was a substantial impediment to his ordination, and now if it can be fully substantiated by a psychologist team; that priest gently and charitably must be removed and given proper psychological care and respect, he is mentally sick and needs all of the Church's medical care. In no way should the loving Church of Christ drive him out like a "mad dog" and run him down. He suffers from an obsessive, compulsive behavior, uncontrollable and incurable. Maybe someday with proper psychological counseling and supervision he may, like an alcoholic, become a recovering pedophiliac.

Unfortunately for the bishops this charitable process, they think, would be politically incorrect and make them a target of the media and press. Until bishops return to their vocation as shepherds, the sheep will continue to be wounded and scattered. How long O Lord will your Church be led by some spineless cowards; burying their heads in the sand and pretending they can hide behind their imperial mansions, unconscious and brain dead to the real world? Oh how I cry for poor Mother Church, a mother mistreated and abused by her favorite sons. I pray for the rising up of leaders like Cardinal Dulles, John Paul II, Bishop Serratelli, and other courageous bishops, who have handled this crisis with a calm and discerning mind, with tenderness and kindness.

CHAPTER 55

MY ECCLESIASTICAL TRIAL

January 23, 2007

As I reflect on the past four years, I remember weeks, even months, when I sheltered myself because I was bruised and afraid of more hurt. At times I didn't have the energy or motivation to reach out to others; I feared being an embarrassment to them. I lost interest in the people and activities I had once enjoyed. I gravitated toward a self-imposed isolation. I attributed all of my best qualities to the priesthood that was taken away from me; feeling that I was a worthless person without my priesthood. At times my own gifts and strengths were not apparent to me. I screened out many unhappy or uncomfortable experiences by ignoring them. I used denial as a largely unconscious mechanism to protect myself from anxiety and from hurtful reality. The philosopher Descartes said, "I think, therefore I am." Since I tried not to think, therefore I was nothing; void and empty. I had a dysfunctional belief that if I didn't think, nothing could happen to me. I often chose to numb my brain and just stare at a blank wall while avoiding human contact and feeling nothingness. The lights were out and I was not in. All my attempts to prove my innocence felt null and void; an exercise in futility...each one had failed.

But today is January 22, 2007: twenty-four hours before the trial of my life begins. It is a particularly dreary day of snow and ice indicative of what has been happening to my life. I have done everything in my power to clear my name. Now my life will be in the hands of three judges as I face an ecclesiastical trial.

*   *   *

My ecclesiastical trail began on January 23, 2007. I was not in attendance for this portion of the hearing. But the events of the day were related to me by my cannon lawyer:

The two sisters were first to go before the judges one by one. Then Detective Reedy testified—the one who began this whole shamble. The one who convinced the girls that "Father McCarthy molested you when you were children," even though they denied having any memories whatsoever of such a thing happening. He invoked the technique prevalent in the seventies called 'suppressed memory.' He had said to them, "You don't remember it because it was so painful and awful that you just buried it…but he did molest you." After several intense barrages at them, they allowed themselves to become convinced those awful things actually happened to them.

Now on January 23, 2007 before three judges of canon law, they gave supposedly a detailed account of the alleged molestation.

The two sisters, one at a time, sat at the head table. On their left sat their canon lawyer, Father Vincent G. On their right sat my canon lawyer, Father John Farley In front, at a separate table, sat the three judges who were doctors of canon law. On the extreme left, sat the head canonist. On the extreme right sat the stenographer.

To follow are the questions that were presented to the two daughters of Mrs. Snedo, the alleged victims:

1. Where did this alleged molestation occur and how did it happen?

2. Was your mother present when you were supposedly molested?

3. During the past 23 years, did you or your family discuss this alleged happening, and if so, with whom?

4. What is the detective's name who came to your house, and what exactly did he say to you?

5. Did he tell you: "You don't remember it, because it was so painful and awful; you just buried it?"

6. Did you "go along" with what he said?

7. Did you object to his assertions?

8. Did two older women speak to you or your mother about the alleged molestation and if so, when, who were they, and what did they say?

9. When did you first hear of the lawyer named John Cestone, and did he at any time represent you or your mother?

10. Who retained and paid him as your lawyer?

11. Was your lawyer retained by others to keep the family from talking about the accusation?

12. Were you angry at Father McCarthy for calling DYFS to your house?

13. After your father died, did the DYFS issue get worse?

14. Did you think this was a plot to destroy Father McCarthy?

15. Why were the police frequently at your home?

16. Did it ever occur to you to go to the police and report the plot?

17. Did your dad drink—was he an alcoholic?

18. Do you remember Father McCarthy ever being at your house—if so, how often?

19. What else do you know about this whole thing that we have not specifically asked about?

20. Molestation was never mentioned for 23 years; why?

21. Did your father, Mr. Snedo, ever touch you improperly or molest you?

These 21 questions were presented beforehand to the judges by my canon lawyer, Father John Farley, of which they were free to use at their discretion. Unlike a civil trial, the accused is not allowed in the courtroom when the accusers or their witnesses give testimony. Also, unlike a civil trial, there is no cross examination in an ecclesiastical trial. (Both situations leave the accused at a disadvantage, at a more likely risk of being convicted—and this needs to be changed!) Therefore, since I was not in the room, I do not know which questions were asked or how the questions were answered. But Fr. Farley later assured me that the sisters had contradicted one another and were not consistent or credible.

After the two sisters' testimony, Detective Reedy was called to testify. But before he would testify, he asked for immunity stating he was concerned that a major lawsuit against him could result from him testifying. The chief canonist of the court assured him it was a canonical trial and he shouldn't worry. However, after the detective testified, the chief canonist himself testified to the court regarding the unusual request of the detective. Obviously, if the detective was telling the truth, why would he be concerned about a lawsuit? His credibility was immediately suspect.

This confirmed my belief, from the beginning, that he was a rogue detective working under the radar of the prosecutor's office; and who was hired by one or both of the conspirators to bring me down. I recall that after four months the prosecutor's office had declared the case ended, because the evidence was too weak and it fell outside the statute of limitations. Yet, Detective Reedy restarted the case, and eventually mailed a completely bogus report to my bishop, adding the nonsense that I had visited the Snedo home *seven* times and brought puppets with me each time to dupe the sisters with.

$$* \quad * \quad *$$

Finally, my portion of the hearing was scheduled for January 30, 2007 at 10:00 a.m. The trial was held under top secrecy to avoid the media and the press. I left my apartment in Sayreville, NJ about 8:00 a.m. and drove on the New Jersey Garden State Parkway for an hour. Then I got off the parkway and went on Rte. 3 West. I was over an hour early so I drove a short distance to the Holy Face Monastery in Clifton. There I prayed for about forty-five minutes and lit some candles asking the Sacred Heart of Jesus and Pope John Paul II for spiritual guidance, especially the guidance of the Holy Spirit. Then I proceeded to the parking lot of the court building. I got out of my car and walked to the main entrance, through the double door, down the corridor to the desk where a young man sat. I announced my name and asked for directions to the trial room.

After a short time, a priest arrived and took me to the top floor. I felt numb and the whole thing was like an out of body experience. Was this really happening to me? Or was I dreaming it? Finally we arrived at the trial room, where all the official participants shook my hand; everyone looked very serious—no smiles whatsoever. I sat down at the head of the table within the same setting as I previously described. For a moment there was complete silence. Then the head judge asked me to read my opening statement. Father John had already prepared me for that, telling me to just give a broad outline of what already had occurred. I opened my sheet of paper and read the following:

"My brothers and sisters, good morning. I would like to give you just a short synopsis of what has happened to me over the past terrible four years. My name is William Malachy McCarthy and I have been a priest for forty-three years. It is my understanding that I am charged with having allegedly molested two little sisters between the ages of six and seven years old and that I used one of my puppets to do this in their family home about twenty-five years ago while I was pastor of Saint Rose of Lima, East Hanover, NJ.

"I wish to state most emphatically that I have never sexually molested anyone, child or adult. More specifically that I have never sexually molested either one of those two little sisters. I never sat them on my lap. I visited their family only once; that was to explain to their mother why the children could not be admitted to our parish school. That was a very brief visit during which I did not encounter these children.

"In my preaching at Saint Rose of Lima, I sometimes used puppets to help make a point during the homily at the children's liturgy. I never brought those puppets to anyone's home. In fact, I never used those puppets anywhere off church property except for one occasion when I was persuaded to take them to a charitable public event in Newark.

"I am devastated by these charges. For almost four years I have been excluded from all public ministries. I trust that these deliberations will result in my being totally exonerated and that I will be permitted to resume public ministry as a priest in good standing.

"Now, I would be pleased to respond to any questions which you may have."

*   *   *

The first judge asked me the first question:

Question:	Monsignor McCarthy, I would like to know why you went to the Snedo house in the first place?
My answer:	I went there because Mrs. Snedo was very upset that her children were not accepted into Saint Rose of Lima School. She felt they were being discriminated against because they were poor. I went to the house and knocked on the door. Mrs. Snedo came out and seemed excited to see me, thinking, I suppose, that I was there to explain that the school principal had changed her mind and the children could come to the school after all. She insisted that I look at all the pictures on the walls all over the house. However, eventually I explained to her she indeed had a lovely family but unfortunately the principle of the school felt, after a preliminary test, that they needed more attention than Saint Rose of Lima was able to provide. That made Mrs. Snedo agitated and I quickly left the house and went home. Mrs. Snedo continued to call Sister Mary, the principal, and myself frequently. One night she was on the phone

pleading her case when suddenly she yelled: "Here comes the father and he will 'f**k up' the kids for the rest of the night." I was horrified and the next morning, I called DYFS and asked them to investigate the family for possible sexual abuse. A few days later, the father, Mr. Snedo, came to my office and was very upset that I had called DYFS. I felt sorry for him and told him his wife had misled me into thinking that something could be wrong. I immediately called DYFS back and convinced them that maybe I had made a mistake and taken Mrs. Snedo literally; but having spoken to the father, I feel everything is okay and the children are safe. After that encounter, for over twenty years, I never heard nor saw the Snedo family again. In fact, I felt they had maybe moved to another town.

Question: (from the second judge) Why now do you think they are making the accusation that you went to the house seven times with a puppet, and were drunk, and molested them seven times?

My answer: I believe Detective Reedy had convinced them that I, in fact, molested them—claiming, "They didn't remember it because it was so painful and hurtful that you buried it." He was obviously using the "suppressed memory" technique with them. The mother told Doctor Frank Ferese and me that at first the girls did not want to go along with him, but eventually he obviously convinced them that these things happened to them.

Question: (from the third judge) Why was Detective Reedy so persistent in his questioning of the girls?

My answer: When I went to the prosecutor's office he said to me that the family didn't accuse me of this—it was two women who came in the office and made the accusations.

Question: Why would those two women make such an accusation? What was their motivation?

My answer: At first I couldn't imagine who these two women were. But eventually, I realized who they possibly were. Several years prior, an elderly woman left me $25,000 in her will. Her daughter objected and was furious. She and another woman had me brought before my bishop, claiming I had conned the poor woman into leaving me all that money. The Vicar General interviewed all of us and eventually dismissed the case as frivolous. Obviously these women were not happy, and some years later, when the pedophile scandal broke in the media and there was a constant story practically every night on the six o'clock news when more and more priests were being accused. It is my conviction that it was then these women saw their chance to go to the prosecutor's office and accuse me of molesting two little sisters in their neighborhood. Those women were well aware of the conflict that took place twenty-three years prior when they were not accepted into the school and that the whole family was hurt by the situation. I guess in their minds, I as the pastor, by not accepting them in the school had somehow abused them. Now was an opportune time for them to invent the story about sexual abuse.

Question: What motivated the anonymous letter?

My answer: Detective Reedy tried to find the author of the letter, but since he was unable, the letter lost its significance. The theme of the letter was that I molested little girls using puppets. That, I believe, was why he injected the use of the puppets when I allegedly went to the Snedo house.

Question: Did you ever go to a parishioner's house with a puppet?

My answer: No, never once did I operate the puppets in any home. With the one exception of a charity event, the puppets were never used outside the church property.

*   *   *

222

After my testimony, my other witnesses were interrogated. The second witness, Sil G. was interrogated at 11:30 on January 30, 2007. Sil had known Mrs. Snedo, and they were friends at the time of the alleged incident. *For the record, I did not have to swear on the Bible, but all the others did*:

Question:	Sil G., do you swear to tell the truth, the whole truth and nothing but the truth?
S.G. answer:	I do.
Question:	May we have your account?
S.G. answer:	On returning from a working assignment in Spain, I heard about the accusation of Monsignor McCarthy, and I heard through the grapevine that it was the Snedo family. I went to the house and spoke to the mother. The mother said emphatically, "He never molested my children, and if he did I would have choked him."

* * *

The third witness was Dr. Ferese, a friend of mine.

Question:	Dr. Ferese, how are you connected to Monsignor McCarthy?
Dr. F. answer:	He was my pastor for twenty-three years.
Question:	How are you involved in this case?
Dr. F. answer:	Father McCarthy and I, after the civil trial was dismissed, went to visit the Snedo family to reconcile with them. Mrs. Snedo walked to the car and spoke to Father McCarthy and myself saying: "Father McCarthy, we didn't accuse you of anything; it was a detective that came around here and tried to convince my daughters that you molested them. They protested and refused to go along with him. However, he eventually prevailed."
Question:	Why do you think they eventually went along with him?
Dr. F. answer:	Detective Reedy obviously convinced them with

223

a sordid, elaborate story that was totally false. Supposedly using detective jargon, "You don't remember it because it was so awful and bad that you buried it, but this is what happened." This method of "recall," which was popular in the seventies, is now looked upon with disdain among most psychologists. Many people's lives were ruined. In Montclair, NJ, a childcare director was accused of molesting several children and was convicted and jailed, only to be totally exonerated a few years later. Her life was completely destroyed. Now this innocent priest has become a victim of a similar situation. Surely by now, we should all have learned from the past and not repeat history. This is an awful attack on an innocent priest. As a practicing clinical psychologist for thirty-seven years I can say with every fiber of my being, without hesitation, Father McCarthy is an innocent man. He does not possess the characteristics of an individual who would commit the horrible and horrendous act of child abuse. I beg you to fight the wrong that has been done to this innocent man and remove the cloud that has cast darkness and suspicion on a good and wholesome life of service for over forty years as a priest in the image of Christ and his ministry. He is the stuff all priests should be made of. All of my words cannot express the joy he brought to the people of Saint Rose of Lima for the past twenty-three years. His life for forty years was like the light of Christ, dispelling the darkness that surrounded people's lives in sickness and death. Now, I ask you to keep his priesthood alive, so he can continue to help others.

*   *   *

Another three witnesses were interviewed on January 30, 2007.

The first witness was attorney George D.; the former prosecutor. He originally became involved prior to the dismissal of my civil trial, back in 2003, when all civil charges against me were dropped.

Question:	What do you have to say in defense of Father McCarthy?
G.D. answer:	I interviewed Father McCarthy in my office. After less than ten minutes I knew he was innocent.
Question:	How come?
G.D. answer:	Once he stated that he called DYFS [Division of Youth and Family Services] to investigate the family, I knew he was innocent. Who in their right mind would call DYFS to initiate an investigation, if he, himself, was responsible for the abuse?
Question:	Any other observations?
G.D. answer:	After forty years as a lawyer, I need only look into the eyes of an accused individual and I can tell if he or she is telling the truth or lying. Looking into the eyes of Father McCarthy, I strongly felt he was telling the truth.

*   *   *

The second witness was Rocco Fuschetto from Argus Investigative Services in Scotch Plains, NJ. After my lawyer, Gerry Rooney, suspected that the polygraph Detective Reedy had orchestrated was rigged in order to intimidate me into a confession, he sent me to Mr. Fuschetto, who he felt would be unbiased, for a second test.

Question:	What can you testify about Father McCarthy?
R.F. answer:	I gave him a polygraph test and he passed it comprehensively.
Question:	Why do you think he failed the first test?
R.F. answer:	The polygraph, known as the lie detector, could also serve as the truth detector when properly administered. It is an investigative tool and doesn't make the examiner judge and jury. It has reliability and validity when all the criteria for ethical examination are met. The test becomes totally invalid following an interrogation due to lack of food, anger, confusion, and poor formulation of the questions presented. Father

McCarthy's first test met all of the above negative criteria resulting in an invalid test. Also, it was rather obvious that the instrument was used as a tool for interrogation and intimidation to try to get a confession. Many times it works, especially for individuals who do not understand what is happening and why.

*   *   *

The third witness was Dr. Jenson.

Question:	What evidence do you have for Father McCarthy?
Dr. J. answer:	I have known Father McCarthy since he came to Saint Rose of Lima. He baptized both my children. I assisted him as a teacher in the confirmation program at summer bible school, and during Christmas and Easter Masses. Father McCarthy is a charismatic individual. His distinctive preaching, especially at the children's masses, was often enhanced by his talents as a ventriloquist. The children eagerly anticipated the arrival of Rolly, his puppet sidekick. Father McCarthy would sometimes use the puppet to explain truths to the youngsters in an enjoyable manner.
Question:	Do you have any knowledge of ventriloquism?
Dr. J. answer:	Personally, I am knowledgeable on the subject of using ventriloquism to teach in the public schools in an entertaining way. For many years, Father McCarthy has invited me to join him on the altar during a portion of the special family masses on the feasts of Christmas and Easter.
Question:	What exactly would you do?
Dr. J. answer:	At Christmas, I utilized my little boy puppet, Georgie, who was so excited about the arrival of Santa Claus. Father McCarthy and his Santa Claus puppet patiently explained to Georgie as well as to all the children in attendance that

Christmas is about the arrival of Jesus. It was quite a powerful message for the standing room only congregation of families to hear Father McCarthy have Santa explain that Christmas is all about Jesus, and not Santa and not just about presents, but about love. On Easter, I utilized my little girl puppet, Georgette, who was often dressed up in a bonnet for the Easter Masses. She learned from Father McCarthy, that Jesus was the light of the world and that Easter eggs and the Easter bunny symbolized how life for us was a rebirth, our own resurrection—just like that of our Lord Jesus Christ. Father McCarthy explained the meaning of these biblical truths to the children, assisted by his puppet Rolly, who was all dressed in yellow, courtesy of Sister Ann Brennen.

Question: What qualifications do you have to know the value of using puppets in church?

Dr. J. answer: Having earned my doctoral degree, I consider myself an educated person. Therefore I know the importance of using creativity to teach students when trying to convey a message. As I used puppets in school and in church to instruct the children, so did Father McCarthy.

Question: How do you feel about the accusation that Father McCarthy sometimes used the puppets to molest children?

Dr. J. answer: I am sickened and offended by these accusations against him. They have turned a beautiful and talented ministry into something twisted and ugly. I was always pleased and proud to be a part of this ministry. Yet, now it has become tarnished. I am shocked and saddened to think that someone would accuse Father McCarthy of using this beautiful ministry in a negative way. He always had the best of intentions and was open and forthright in his words and actions. I cannot imagine that he would ever even consider using his God-given talents to molest or hurt a child.

Question:	How would you describe Father McCarthy?
Dr. J. answer:	I feel that Father McCarthy exemplifies what it means to be a good and faithful servant of God; and I hope you will find it in your heart to restore him to the dignity of his former self.

*   *   *

SUMMARY:

A private detective was commissioned by my cannon lawyer. The following is the summary that was entered and subsequently allowed as evidence in my canonical trial:

"I interviewed Mrs. Snedo, the girl's mother, at her home. The interview was unannounced. The home appeared neat and clean. Mrs. Snedo appeared composed and lucid. The interview was conducted voluntarily.

Upon reviewing my interview with Mrs. Snedo, it is evident inconsistencies exist between her statements and statements made previously by the daughters, Nora and Mary and the father, Mike Snedo. The daughter's statements have been documented by the County Prosecutor's office.

Mrs. Snedo states that Father McCarthy visited the Snedo home on two occasions.

Father McCarthy's puppet was not present during his visits to the Snedo home.

Mrs. Snedo states that both of Father McCarthy's visits occurred within a time period of approximately one week.

Mrs. Snedo states that she was not aware of, or suspicious of, any inappropriate behavior between Father McCarthy and Nora and Mary.

Mrs. Snedo is not aware of any threats made by Father McCarthy to her, or her children in regards to DYFS.

Mrs. Snedo does not believe Nora and Mary were aware of DYFS, or the function of DYFS at the time in question.

*   *   *

The trial formally ended on January 30, 2007. Now my canon lawyer, Father John Farley and the promoter of Justice, Father Vincent G., are in the process of preparing a brief to present to the judges.

In a canonical court, the three judges are complete strangers to the accused, who does not know their names or where they came from.

The judges each returned to their respective localities, three different dioceses.

It would not be until nine months later that they would be able to reconvene and reach a final unanimous decision. The following chapters detail my life during these arduous, agonizing nine months, as I awaited the canonical decision of whether they would find me innocent or guilty.

CHAPTER 56

THE GUERNICA

Picasso expressed his consternation in the famous painting; of which I have had a print on the walls of my various homes for as long as I can remember. I too was very angry as to what was done to me but I turned my anger inward, which expressed itself in terrible depression, tearing me apart psychologically.

Picasso painted the oil on canvas entitled *Guernica*, one of the most impressive war-themed paintings of our times. *Guernica*, which received its name from the small Basque City, was completely bombarded in 1937 during the Spanish Civil War.

At this time, Picasso was working on the sketches for the walls of the Spanish Pavilion for the universal expository in Paris. The news of the bombing of Guernica made Picasso renounce the design he had planned. Instead he created an economical personal scenario, where he expressed his personal consternation and anger in an accusation against cruelty and war. There is a poem by Picasso entitled *The Dream and Lie of Franco* as a poetic commentary on *Guernica*.

"Children's screams, women's screams, screams of flowers, screams of rocks and wood, screams of bricks, of beds, of chairs, of curtains, of casseroles, of cats and papers, screams of scratching scents, smoke screams itching in the boulder of the screams cooking in the kettle and the shower of birds which flood the sea; a mass of a torn shredded world—everything screaming out with anger and rage against injustice."

This enormous painting was created in almost 50 studios, in a minimum amount of time and was finished in the summer of 1937. Picasso arranged for the painting to be taken to Madrid only after the fall of Fascism. After a long period of time in the Museum of Modem Art in New York, the painting can be currently found in the Centre de Arte de Reina Sofia in Madrid as a national symbol and an exhortation to collective conscientiousness.

Picasso has always been my favorite painter; he spent a lifetime as he famously said, "Learning how to paint like a child." I had the pleasure of visiting his museum in Malaga, Spain in December of 2004 while visiting my sister just outside Malaga in Fungiorolla. The collection of his paintings, drawings, and sculptures are displayed in the Picasso Museum, a group of 204 works generously donated and loaned by Christine and Bernard Picasso, the artist's daughter-in-law and grandson.

However, the painting entitled *Guernica* is my favorite; especially now in my hour of pain and suffering. Like Picasso, I feel torn apart and in shreds; screaming silently on the inside. I identify with the chaos depicted in the painting, I can meditate on it for hours on end and each time I see something new. It is a source of inspiration and comfort for me.

I have looked at that painting for years and years and always saw something entirely different, something interesting and unusual; but now this painting has meaning for me personally, meaning for my life, my sadness, my fear, the chaos in my mind-confusion of the nth degree. There is a well-known phrase: "No pain no gain." I have suffered much, but I have gained a closer relationship with the suffering Christ which is worth more than money can buy. In the end it turns out to be an enormous blessing. To whom much is given much will be expected. The gift of the priesthood was given to me, consequently much is expected of me, even in the face of a terrible conspiracy.

A year or so after I was falsely accused, I removed the *Guernica* print from its frame and added to the "shredding" with a shredded miter, shredded church, shredded cross, shredded roman collar, shredded stole, shredded priest's head, shredded staff (Crozier); all an expression of my personal consternation and anger at what was done to me by the very institution I faithfully served for 40 years. The impetuous actions of the diocese left my life in shreds.

When I first read that infamous letter from my former bishop seeking to censure me, I could not stop screaming; it was a horror of huge magnitude, a type of psychological Tsunami as occurred in South Asia in 2004, crushing me to near death. I was hyperventilating, unable to breathe, finally collapsing on the couch of my living room semi-unconscious, mentally paralyzed. In the presence of children, I felt terribly threatened and frightened. I who had worked all my life to protect children, to educate them, to take care of them; now I was terrified at even the sight of children. The world as I had known it had come to an end. With patient endurance, I survive in a kind of limbo, waiting for my exoneration.

As John Milton says in *Paradise Lost* "They also serve whom only stand and wait." As I wait I push forward, all uphill slowly but surely, like the little train "that could," climbing up the hill saying, "I think I can, I think I can, I think I can;" finally saying "I know I can, I know I can—I can. I could." When adversity stares one in the face then you know what you're made of. In December of 2004, a Tsunami tidal wave hit South East Asia. 155,000 people died, however, millions survived in spite of tremendous odds, saving others on their way.

With God's help I will survive and go on to inspire others in similar circumstances. I am sure I'm not the only priest who has been or will be falsely accused. I hope my suffering will not be in vain; that others will be encouraged to keep on fighting for their freedom. In John 14:23-25, Jesus says to his disciples: "Peace I leave with you, my peace I give to you ... do not let your hearts be troubled or afraid."

There are many fascinating stories and legends about the great magician and illusionist Harry Houdini. Houdini had a standing challenge that he could get out of any locked jail within 60 minutes, providing they would let him enter the cell in his regular street clothes and not watch him work. There is a story about a little town in the British Isles that decided to take Houdini up on his challenge. The town had just completed the building of a state-of-the-art, escape-proof jail, and they invited Houdini to come and try to break out of it. Houdini accepted the challenge. Wearing his regular street clothes, Houdini was taken to the cell. A locksmith turned the lock and closed the massive steel door. Then the townspeople who had gathered left Houdini to work his "magic."

Houdini had hidden a long flexible steel rod in his belt, which he used to try and trip the lock. But the lock would not trip. He continued to work, but the lock would not give. Thirty minutes went by. He kept his ear close to the lock to hear it trip, but nothing. Forty-five minutes, an hour had passed. After two hours, Houdini was ready to admit defeat. Perspiring and exhausted, the defeated illusionist leaned against the door and, to his amazement, it opened.

The townspeople had never locked the door. It was their trick on the great escape artist. The door was only locked in Houdini's mind.

We sometimes live our lives behind locked doors—doors locked spiritually and mentally. Fear, disappointment, and distrust imprison us from living life to its most joyful and most fulfilling end. The night before he died, Jesus left his followers the gift of his peace.

Christ's peace, however, is much more than a "spiritual tranquilizer" (as Thomas Merton called it) or a mental and emotional garrison we construct to protect us from unpleasant conflict. The peace of Christ is the hope in the things of God, the assurance that the love of God is ours, the awareness of God's presence in every moment of our lives. To embrace Christ's gift of peace

232

is to understand and celebrate our connectedness to one another, as children of the same God in whose love and justice we center our attitudes and values. The peace that Jesus leaves us is not a passive acquiescence to the absence of hostility and conflict; the peace of Jesus is a mindset, a constant seeking out of God's presence in all things and places, an awareness of love, justice and mercy, an understanding of our "connectedness" to God and to one another as children of the same God. Peace, as given by Christ, is a perspective that shapes all of our actions, behavior and values.

It is the only "master key" of faith and trust that will open our lives to living a full life. Fear is the enemy. In the well-known hymn, *Be Not Afraid*, it states:

> *Be not afraid.*
> *I go before you always.*
> *Come follow me,*
> *and I will give you rest.*
> *You shall cross the barren dessert,*
> *but you shall not die of thirst.*
> *You shall wander far in safety,*
> *though you do not know the way.*
> *You shall speak your words in foreign lands,*
> *and all will understand.*
> *You shall see the face of God and live.*

Sometimes I ask myself if I could only let go of my negative thoughts, thoughts of gloom and doom, would I be free? Unfortunately, I don't seem to be able to let go. I am reminded of the man who went into the forest crying, "Please take away my sadness." Suddenly he saw the wise sage of the woods with his hands around a tree. The man yelled, "O wise sage, please help me to let go of my sadness."

The wise sage said, "I will as soon as this tree lets go of me."

"But," says the man, "the tree is not holding on to you; you are holding on to the tree."

Immediately the sage let go of the tree and ran into the forest.

The man realized the lesson: the sadness was not holding on to him, he was holding on to the sadness.

This story has a great impact on me and helps me a little bit at a time to let go of my negative thoughts. They are not holding on to me, I am holding on to them.

I know I can get through this. I'm strong and I am surrounded by people who care and constantly pray for me. I am greatly encouraged by the following poem, that I return to often:

THE OAK TREE

by Johnny Ray Ryder, Jr.

A mighty wind blew night and day.
It stole the oak tree's leaves away.
They snapped its boughs and pulled its bark,
Until the oak was tired and stark.
But still the oak tree held its ground,
While other trees fell all around.
The weary wind gave up and spoke:
"How can you still be standing Oak?"
The oak tree said, "I know that you,
Can break each branch of mine in two,
Carry every leaf away,
Shake my limbs, and make me sway.
But I have roots stretched in the earth,
Growing stronger since my birth,
You'll never touch them, for you see,
They are the deepest part of me.
Until today, I wasn't sure,
Of just how much I could endure.
But now I've found, with thanks to you,
I'm stronger than I ever knew."

CHAPTER 57

THE PERFECT STORM

The conspiracy against me was similar to a perfect storm.

Many elements and factors go to make a "perfect storm," including the temperature of the ocean, the closeness of land, the track of the storm, its destination, the width of the eye, where it will hit land, the density of the population, the vulnerability of the homes, etc. It develops a life of its own and nothing can stop it. It leaves great devastation in its wake—homes destroyed and many lives lost.

Many elements and situations converged to cause me unbelievable pain and suffering. The attack kept coming in from all sides, becoming more and more frightening—my life was in mortal danger. All the events that followed took on a life of its own—it seemed unstoppable going faster and faster rising to a crescendo, a climax like a boiling kettle getting closer and closer to becoming steam. The more I tried to save myself the more ominous things became. I was like a drowning man desperately grabbing for something to hold on to. The more I tried the worse things became.

Now I am reduced to waiting for a verdict. If I could only float until the storm died down, the situation might be better for me, but my nature is to stay alert and pray with every ounce of energy I can muster.

As I look back I see that sometimes I was winning the battle but losing the war. What was I to do? I was totally innocent, but it didn't seem to matter. I was doomed to forces "closing in" around me, very powerful people; even Rome itself was determined to destroy me.

Every time I thought a door was opening for me, it only shut in my face. Sometimes I would see a light at the end of the tunnel only to see it grow dimmer and dimmer, and finally disappear. It was torture—even my faith in God began to wane. At times I was unable to pray. Darkness engulfed me—I began to lose hope but God always seems to come to my rescue and inspires me to continue to fight the good fight toward exoneration.

The waiting is exasperating. I feel like David verses Goliath. I am confronted by a giant institution. David was equipped only with a sling and a stone. He brought down Goliath with a single stone and faith in God. I believe I too can succeed with the stone of my faith and determination.

In a short shattering cataclysm, the carefully prepared and implemented ministry of 40 years was reduced to rubble. If I win, I will have to rebuild my priesthood and reputation and conquer the giant of blatant injustice. As Raymond Donovan said after he was accused of wrongdoing in the state department and then exonerated: "Where do I go from here to get my reputation back?"

CHAPTER 58

ROOMS OF MY HEART

Jesus said, "In my Father's house there are many mansions." In my heart there are many rooms. Rooms for those I love. Some rooms are larger than others, some more special than others; but each is different, because I love each memory and each individual differently. I used to believe that everyone has a set amount of love to spread around. But experiencing the near death of my priesthood changed that. My priesthood had the holiest room of my heart. Now that room has been violated by a false accusation. What do I do with this room or space in my heart that I can so clearly identify as empty ... as aching ... as hurting, so much that it must be broken? Do I put something else in that space? Do I shut that door and pretend nothing ever happened there? Or even worse, do I frequently go in there and pretend that the past is the present and that I never suffered the loss? Or do I open the door and peek into the darkness, forgetting that there are other places and feelings in my life.

It is a room in which I can stay just to ponder and reflect on the memory of what once was. It is good to go to that room in my heart and remember all I learned there. The day I first went there, the day I was ordained, June 8, 1963; the day I gave my first blessing to my mother as she knelt before me and then to each member of my family one by one. To remember each parish family that I was assigned to; to recall the way I grew, the way I was loved by the people of those parishes. The day I was reassigned to another parish and the huge amount of people who turned out to say good-bye to me. To remember the person I am today as a result of having been there, in that time living out my priesthood. Would I ever put something else in the room of my priesthood, no—never! My priesthood has its own room forever; that room belongs to my priesthood and to nothing else.

When I want to remember happier days, I slip silently away to a special place in my heart and open the door and whisper with all the love my memory allows, "I'm so glad you are still here—be at peace—ad multos annos."

My little one bedroom apartment in Sayreville, NJ became another room of my heart, a kind of museum that holds special items that symbolize life that once existed. Significant artifacts remind me of my world as it then was—standing in corners or places or hanging on my walls.

In front of the main window of my living room is a large wooden boat that I purchased in Acapulco in 1975. I bought it on the streets from a vendor for $25. It was constructed by inmates at some jail in Mexico. Bringing it back on the plane was a problem because of its size. The stewardess refused to have it in the cabin of the plane. Suddenly, the pilot showed up and suggested it be put in the cockpit of the plane; so this boat was brought to Newark Airport in the cockpit of a Continental airliner. It has special significance for me because scripture describes the Church as the "bark" of Peter. This boat has a special room in my heart; it is a symbol of the Church I served for 40 years.

On the right hand wall of my living room hangs panoramic pictures of my family home in Shandrum, Ireland called Shandrum House. Immediately underneath are other panoramic pictures of my parish church buildings. Unfortunately, the new regime demolished the "frontage" pulling down a beautiful shrine and water fountain and removing all the decorative stone. Thank God I still have the pictures of the frontage as it was before I retired. I often sit on my couch and meditate for hours upon these special significant pictures. It centers me and brings me back to where I lived out 23 years of my life. Underneath the picture is a very special "wood design" donated to me by the Eucharistic ministers, arranged and designed by my friend, Doris O'Dea. It honors my term as pastor of my beloved St. Rose for 23 years. Next to that wall is my special shrine with many of my favorite statues—that is my prayer corner, a holy place in the heart of my home. On the wall down the stairs are displayed many of the accolades I received while at St. Rose.

Looking at these gifts always boosts my spirit. On the opposite wall are pictures of vacation times with my friend Monsignor Paul Knauer and myself riding horses along the lakes of Killarney. Above that is a picture of Monsignor Bob Carrol and myself at a famous restaurant in Acapulco, Mexico. Next to it is a picture of my special friend Ron DeSena handing me the winning ticket from the raffle drum at our annual parish ball.

MY HOME
SHANDRUM HOUSE, CHARLEVILLE
COUNTY CORK, IRELAND

Ron DeSena and myself. Ron was my right hand man in running the parish of my beloved St. Rose of Lima. Ron was the president of the parish council and an active member for 23 years of my pastorate. Every year he ran a golf tournament, a "high class" event, ending with an elaborate formal dinner.

Myself on the left and Father Paul Knauer riding horses around the lakes of Killarney, Ireland in the summer of 1972.

Next to those pictures is a painting by one of my favorite local painters (artist) from my home in Morris County, New Jersey—John Bradley. It is a beautiful artistic description of Connemarra County, Mayo, Ireland. As I look at this painting, it connects me to my childhood roots. When Cromwell the English General ethnically cleansed all of Ireland in the 17th Century, he drove the entire population of ten million people into Connaught, a barren tiny section of northwest Ireland. To survive in this barren ground, each family retained a plot about the size of an acre. They dug up stones from the ground and made a dividing fence around a little thatched cottage made of stone and mud consisting of one room in which often large families had to survive. They cultivated their piece of land and grew vegetables, mostly potatoes, as food for the family, at least until the famine in 1845 when two-thirds of the population either died of starvation or immigrated to America.

It was at this time that President John F. Kennedy's family and President Regan's family immigrated to America. It was a time of absolute poverty and devastation, but in the midst of this tragedy is an amusing fable: "People tried to cross the Atlantic in old makeshift boats in which many lost their lives in the rough seas. The story goes that this poor old woman embarked on one of these "tubs" carrying all her belongings: a goat, and a few pieces of furniture. Halfway across the Atlantic a huge whale attacked the little boat. As was the superstition at the time, something had to be cast overboard to distract the whale. So the captain threw out the goat, and of course the whale completely swallowed the goat. But the whale continued to attack the boat, so they threw out the woman's chair. Again the whale swallowed the chair, but still was not satisfied. Finally, they cast lots and the poor old woman was chosen and dumped overboard, only to be devoured by the whale. Somehow, as the story goes, the whale continued to follow the boat and the crew managed to lure the whale into New York harbor where it became "beached." They cut open the whale and lo and behold there was the old woman sitting on the chair milking the goat... end of story.

The population of Ireland dropped from ten million to three million people. Gradually the people fought their way back to their original farms. To this day these little plots of land surrounded by stone fences still exist in Co. Mayo Ireland.

For me to observe John Bradley's painting in my living room brings me back to this tragic time in the history of my native land, and the indescribable suffering of millions of people who desperately tried to survive in the most difficult of circumstances.

My suffering pales in retrospect and humbles me and helps put my loss in perspective.

In my kitchen is a newspaper article containing many pictures of my

25th anniversary celebration. Next to that is a picture of my parish staff standing next to me on the occasion of my elevation to Monsignor. In the little sanctuary of my small apartment is my book of the 25th anniversary of the founding of St. Rose of Lima parish, containing the entire history of my parish family.

I could describe many more defining moments of my pastorate. But I share this with you to emphasize my little "hideaway" refuge in my heart in the midst of a shattered world. "Pain that falls drop by drop upon the mansion of my heart so that in my times of despair comes wisdom through the awesome grace of God."

The mind is in its own place, it can make a hell out of heaven or a heaven out of hell. But the rooms of my heart remain sacred and intact, and with God's grace will one day be restored to its former glory, pumping new life throughout my entire being and letting me live again a full and happy life.

"Wherever a man walks faithfully in the ways that God has marked out for him, Providence, as the Christian says, will be on that man's side." (Henry Ward Beecher)

"Surely goodness and mercy shall follow me all the days of my life. Hence we may be sure that the days of adversity, as well as days of prosperity are full of blessings." (Hudson Taylor)

"For He shall give His angels charge over you, to keep you in all your ways. In their hands they shall bear you up, lest you dash your foot against a stone." (Psalm 91:9-12)

Finally, there is my childhood room in the old family homestead called Shandrum House. My brother Dannie and his wife Nora (mentioned earlier in this book) preserve this room as a kind of shrine in my memory. Anytime I go home I sleep in that exact same room and am filled with childhood memories. I remember the desk I studied at for hours during my school years. I remember the front window I looked out from, sometimes for hours when I was sick or in a sad or pensive mood.

All of the above rooms are rooms of the mansion of my heart, filled with varied memories; of course the room of my tainted priesthood tortures me with unbelievable mental anguish; consequently living my life as if it were on the dark side of the moon.

I did receive an abundance of mail offering me psychological support. A card or letter was like a summer rain that could make ever the desert bloom, but ironically going to pick my mail up was traumatic for me. I was terrified I would receive a letter from the diocese further attacking me or accusing me of some kind of violation of the rules or the ban against me. I was forbidden to go into my parish family church to even say a prayer, or to spend time in the Eucharistic Room for a visit to the Blessed Sacrament, a program I had established the last few years before I retired. It was called the Perpetual Adoration Room which I participated in first thing in the morning and last thing at night. This Perpetual Adoration Room was a sacred room of my heart, a room in which I felt the presence of God in a way beyond nature itself; it was a supernatural presence more present than other people in the room. It was always a mountaintop experience for me. As it says in Matt. 17:2: "Jesus took Peter, James, and John up to the mountain to pray; as he was praying, he was transfigured before them. His face shone like the sun, and his clothes became as white as the light ... Peter said to Jesus, 'Lord it is good for us to be here...' while he was still speaking, a bright cloud enveloped them, and a voice from the cloud said, 'This is my Son whom I love, with Him I am well pleased. Listen to Him.' When the disciples heard this, they fell facedown to the ground, terrified. But Jesus came and touched them. 'Get up,' He said, 'don't be afraid.' When they looked up, they saw no one except Jesus."

While I meditated in the Perpetual Adoration Room, I silently listened to Jesus speak to my heart and I too like Peter, James, and John did not want to leave. I often felt caught up in the presence of God and lost touch with this world and the things around me.

Jesus has shown me how much I must suffer for his name. In the Perpetual Adoration Room, I would consider on my knees the mystery of God's love for us that He didn't want to leave us orphans. For Christ knew our hunger for himself. He knew that I would be lost without him. My hope is literally embodied with his glorified humanity in the Eucharist, which is the living memorial of his death and resurrection. My faith assures me that it is the selfsame risen Savior who now sacramentally offers himself to me in communion as the bread of life, and who offers his perpetual presence for my adoration.

In the old Baltimore Cathachism, the first question was, "Why did God make you?" The answer was, "To know Him, to love Him, to serve Him here on earth, so we can live happily with Him forever in heaven." The Eucharist gives us a taste of heaven. It is pleasant to spend time with him, to feel the infinite love present in his heart. To spend an hour resting in Jesus is truly a Holy Hour. A guarantee that we will live happily with him for all eternity. The holy room in my heart of my priesthood is the same holy room in my heart of the Holy Eucharist. Without the priesthood, there is no Eucharist, without the Eucharist there is no priesthood. You can't have one without the other, they are synonymous. That is how Jesus shows me how much I must suffer for His name.

CHAPTER 59

DISILLUSIONED

I no longer believe that our Church functions in reality the way it does on paper. I no longer take for granted that I am safe just because I am innocent. I've seen that closing our eyes and praying our bishops will keep us safe isn't what creates real safety. I know that everyone is human, capable of making mistakes, acting carelessly, being selfish—including myself. I also know that every one of us also has the capacity to do the opposite; to ask questions, to listen closely and carefully for the truth; to learn to act out of compassion and wisdom, instead of fear. To see how it is possible to help save lives justly, asking and acting ethically. Personally, I have seen how much one person can live through. I have seen how determination can make it possible for any one of us to take the ugliest circumstances imaginable and come out the other side with something beautiful. I have also seen that exoneration isn't something that just happens. We have to work for it.

Jesus said, "Woe to you scribes ... you tie up heavy burdens hard to bear, and lay them on the shoulders of others; but you are unwilling to lift a finger to move them ... blind guides! You strain out a gnat but swallow a camel ... you have neglected the weightier matters of the law: justice and mercy."

Sister Helen Prejean in her book, *Dead Man Walking*, says, "Long in advance the condemned man knows that he is going to be killed and that the only thing that can save him is a reprieve. In any case, he cannot intervene, make a plea outside himself, or convince anyone. Everything goes on outside him. He is no longer a man but a thing, waiting to be handled by the executioners ... This explains the odd submissiveness that is customary in the condemned at the moment of their execution."

I too feel like a condemned man; no recourse; just left lingering in darkness and hopelessness, groping about trying to find answers to my dilemma. On

Holy Thursday, March 24, 2005, I got a phone call from my new bishop, Bishop Arthur Serratelli. I was surprised and excited, hoping for good news of exoneration. However, I received nothing of substance and consequently the "call" hurt me more than helped me; setting me back into even deeper sadness like a dead man walking around, putting on my "best face" possible to the outside world. From the beginning, my former bishop and his associates declared me guilty and a death sentence was sought from Rome without once calling for a thorough review of my basic rights, and callously allowing the injustice to remain in place.

I used to think that the Church provided sanctuary for the innocent, even for the guilty. But now I know differently. It defends the unborn and condemns the death penalty, and yet executes the souls of innocent priests without the slightest qualms of conscience. In fact, it prides itself in condemning accused priests, irrespective of whether they are innocent or guilty. Anything that would make them look good in the eyes of the press or the media—political correctness. Like Pilate, they wash their hands and go into hiding behind the walls of their chancery offices. What happened to the way of Jesus, who sided with the poor, dispossessed and the despised, and the isolated?

"Blessed are those who are persecuted because of righteousness, for theirs is the Kingdom of Heaven." (Matt. 5-10:ll) There are no words strong enough to describe the torture I endured. But as Pope John Paul II said at the canonization of Padre Pio, "A chosen person must experience misunderstanding." He also said, "Suffering is a gift from God." As I have mentioned earlier, the conspiracy was a blessing. I, in an unusual way, no longer wonder if I am loved or, as in the past, felt loved only for who I was as a priest; now having lost everything I feel more loved than ever and have gotten emotionally closer to loved ones more than ever before.

On the weekend of the 9th and 10th of April, my friends Doris and Dennis Odea invited me to their beautiful Long Beach Island home. It was a weekend of great emotional healing. When I came home to my apartment in Sayreville, NJ, I went immediately to my mailbox. Lo and behold there was a letter from my new bishop. I immediately opened it and I couldn't believe what I was reading, an invitation to his home; obviously to discuss my case. Just the Thursday before Holy Thursday I felt the bishop, by his calling me, was not helping me, but for the first time since 2003, I saw some hope. Does Bishop Serratelli finally see the truth? I wait anxiously for final resolution and exoneration.

This letter was the first "sign" in almost three years of a possible reprieve from the death sentence of my priesthood and a significant relief from my state of hopelessness. On April 2, 2005, when the Pope died, the whole Catholic world fell prostrate with grief, and yet when I died psychologically on March of 2003, it felt like I was totally alone and abandoned, as Jesus felt on the cross.

What does it feel like to see three thousand men, women, and children incinerated and crushed to ashes in the span of a few seconds? Anyone who was watching television on September 11, 2001 now knows. But most of us know nothing of the sort. To have watched as did I and millions the World Trade Center, absorbing two jet planes, along with the lives of thousands and to have felt, above all things, disbelief, suggests some form of neurological impairment.

In March of 2005, we were all transfixed to our TV sets as Terry Schiavo's fate was being debated. Elected officials voted to give her, as it were, a stay of execution (not removing her feeding tubes) while the federal judges ignored the pleas of her parents and millions of other people, and let her die of starvation, claiming she was in a persistent vegetative state.

During that feverish debate over life or death, I listened to a lady on Larry King Live on CNN. Her name was Kate Adamson; she was declared in a PUT state by her doctors and given up for dead. However, her husband wouldn't give up on her and insisted she had at least minimal consciousness. He got her to blink her eyes at "yes" or "no" questions. He put a sign over her bed: "This is a human being aware of what is happening; be careful what you say." With aggressive physical therapy, she eventually revived and went on to lead a practically normal life. She even wrote a book of her experience entitled *Kate's Journey*, revealing her nightmare of paralysis and inability to communicate with the outside world. Like Terri Schiavo, she was given up for dead, but unlike with Terri, her husband never gave up. Reading her book you experience along with Kate what it's like to be a "vegetable," while awake and aware of everything that is going on—and then the inspiring, triumphant, powerful and joyful person she is today. Why did the world not listen to Kate's story during Terri's struggle to communicate with the outside world?

I prefer the "never give up" message contained within the pages of *Kate's Journey*, the story of bouncing back against all odds. Her experience with the numerous challenges she faced in her own life has inspired me to overcome my own suffering now more than ever. *Kate's Journey* took me on an emotional ride, but left me convinced that with hard work, strength of will, and the power of prayer, anything is possible. I will now always remember her strength and courage whenever I feel defeated, mainly because she has been there, and helped me appreciate the power of the human spirit. Her life of courage and tenacity, despite the odds, is an inspirational lesson for me personally and indeed for all people in hopeless situations.

Finally, I feel that my arms are not too small to wrap around my unspeakable grief and pain. I continue to pray, "Dear Jesus, anoint Bishop

Serratelli and Father John with wisdom and courage and strength to liberate me from the grasp of evil people—deadly enemies out to destroy me."

Erma Bombeck wrote, *If Life is a Bowl of Cherries, What am I Doing in the Pits?* I can relate! Life feels like the bottom has fallen out of the barrel and everything has caved in. As it says in Psalms 116:8: "I have delivered your life from death, your eyes from tears, and your feet from stumbling and falling. When you need relief, come to me in spirit and truth, and you will find it." This Psalm gave me much comfort. I have never prayed so much in my life as I did during this time.

I'm reminded of the story about the teacup. The refiner's fire was so intense that the teacup screamed, "What are you doing to me?" But it was the fire that made the teacup into a beautiful work of art. God was molding the teacup into something exquisite. Just like the teacup, I was forced into a pottery oven of circumstances, trembling and afraid. I discovered there was nothing I could do but stand there and burn until God delivered me from death to life. I believe God has been molding my life; as the Bible says, "Trials come to test our faith; to produce in us the quality of endurance." It is comforting to know that God is only a prayer away. Because this conspiracy is an indelible scar in my mind and heart, I take refuge in the constant soothing balm that prayer provides.

*   *   *

At the Nuremberg trials it was stated: "The crime which we seek to condemn and punish has been so calculated, so malignant, and so devastating, that civilization cannot tolerate their being ignored because it cannot survive their being repeated."

I wish my life could be simple again. On the other hand, I have absolute confidence in my mission. Just winning my case is no longer enough for me. Things have to change. Notably to find a way to make sure that no innocent priest ever has to go through what I did, but I also intend to push for major reform of the ecclesiastical court system in order to "clean up the mess." Nothing less would be good enough. I absolutely have to win my case; it is my only objective. Without being exonerated, my priestly ministry is over.

The diocese is an unchecked bureaucracy that has allowed lives of innocent priests to be ruined. It's despicable; there is no other way to describe it. In my case, there was nothing I could do to help myself. I could only wait for things to happen as I watched them snowball into a huge disaster. The accusation caught me off guard—the problem was that if the diocese had been fair and kept the accusation confidential until I was proven guilty or innocent, I would have had time to understand what was happening and prepare. I was, as it were, thrown under a bus. The Church had no regard or even an interest in the truth. When my former bishop acted out of order in sending a letter to Rome to have me laicized, did he realize, or even care about, the stress he caused me? Why did he not have some semblance of decency and wait until the trial was conducted?

I was steamrolled by the unfair system and I had to fight back. The gray area and the waiting used to drive me crazy. Part of the reason was that all of my mental energy was going into fighting the accusation, which was so surreal, as I had no idea what was going to happen next. The accusation had absolutely no solid foundation, thus the zeal with which I was persecuted by my former bishop totally confused me. The idea that I could possibly molest a child was so farfetched that finally after months of having my life turned upside down with the character assassination and bullying by the diocese, I was unspeakably exhausted.

Despite all the progress we had made in mounting my defense with my canonist, Father John Farley, nothing was happening in the diocese to move my case forward. Four years after the accusation, the delay lingers on. It appears there is no end of my case in sight. The frustration of the people who loved me is great, for they are convinced of my innocence.

The canonical trial has come and gone for months and nothing has happened. The superficial accusation of priests is unfair and in need of major reform. The Church has failed to protect us priests from injustice. The Church became the "enemy" and all it takes is a *suspicion* to halt a priest's ministry and put his reputation on doubt. What is to stop *anybody* from writing an anonymous letter accusing a priest of molesting a minor and immediately put his hard-earned reputation in doubt and wrecking his life? It is way too easy to presume guilt. There needs to be accountability for cases where there is harmful presumption without solid proof. Priests need to have more of a say in their fates, rather than having them determined behind closed doors.

Unquestionably there needs to be positive meaningful change to the ecclesiastical tribunal system. They have never been truly challenged. It is time for priests around the world to speak out for major reform. It needs to change so that innocent priests like me can get a fair shake—and I'm going to keep fighting until it is done. If I don't keep up the struggle, my life's work will be in vain.

CHAPTER 60

A CALCULATED ACT

What happened to me was not a random act; it was a conscious deliberate attempt to destroy me. It was a conspiracy of two women who had a vendetta against me, because of a "Last Will and Testament" situation, which I have already elaborated on earlier. These women left nothing to chance and carried out their crime with cunning detail; getting a written guarantee of protection and anonymity from the prosecutor's office before they accused me of this totally false crime; and then as it were "hid in the bushes" and watched as the awful attack took place against me.

Leaders of even simple ordinary positions such as pastors of local churches are not without their adversaries who will go to any extent to hurt them. During the "pedophile" eruption in the USA, the media was inundated with countless accusations of priests. People were bombarded with this phenomena, it was in the "air" as it were. Consequently, anyone with a grudge against a priest was motivated to seize the opportunity to make a hit. So these two conspirators saw their chance to destroy me, hatched their plot, and the rest is history. My former bishop lost his head while all about him were losing theirs. The bishops, hounded by the media, made rash decisions and were reckless and impetuous in censuring their priests under their care. They behaved badly and history will judge them severely. Instead of being good shepherds they were marauders and false shepherds who scattered the sheep and caused immense psychological damage. When their flocks were attacked they saw the wolf of the media coming and ran away. They were cowards. Instead of calmly investigating accusations, they rushed to judgment and caused extraordinary damage to innocent priests.

It seems the only member of the hierarchy to keep his cool was Cardinal Joseph Ratzinger. Cardinal Joseph Ratzinger was elected Supreme Pontiff on

Tuesday, April 19, 2005. It gave me great joy, because he was the one who saved my life by refusing to accept my bishop's mandate that I be removed from the priesthood ex officio. Cardinal Ratzinger refused and wrote to the diocese demanding a trial. Cardinal Ratzinger took seriously the sex abuse of minors in the United States. He set up a special office within the congregation of the protection of the faith and morals to deal with the crisis in the United States. He made a statement that the United States media and press were blowing the issue out of proportion; that only one percent of American priests were pedophiles. Of course, even one pedophilic act against a child would be one too many. As I mentioned earlier, I consider a sexual act against a child the worst possible crime.

Above all, Pope Benedict XVI is my hero, an honest, humble servant of the church. I hope and pray that he will reform the seminaries of the world and root out individuals with a propensity toward obsessive, compulsive unnatural sexual behavior. To me, priests and especially pastors are some of the most underappreciated people. Hundreds of thousands of them unselfishly minister to their people 24 hours a day. And all you hear about are the handful of bad priests. Priests get bad press because of the evil acts of a tiny minority. As some priests said on TV on the occasion of John Paul II's funeral, being a priest today is as exciting as being a member of the British Royal family. Even before the conspiracy against me, I often refrained from wearing the Roman collar in public; I felt a target of suspicious people, asking themselves, "Is he or isn't he?" When they attack one of us they attack all of us. I think it is both galvanizing the Church and getting the Church back on its feet. As good priests, we have got to restore pride in ourselves, we've got to have pride in our Church; and priests have to show the world that the vast majority of us are pure, holy, and good. We must bond as a Church and bond as a community. As good priests we must find meaning in our suffering and say to the world, "I will not surrender my priesthood. You will not take my spirit, because you know what? I am still here."

Because of all I've been through, I know one thing—it's not going to help me to ask "Why me? What have I done to deserve this? Why has God allowed this to happen to me?" Those are not my questions. Although it's natural for victims and survivors of tragedies to ask them, it also implies that something so horrible should happen to someone else; that I should somehow be immune to do the most difficult challenges in life, but that it is understandable if someone else is not. I prefer asking, "Why not me?" Let it be me over any of my brother priests, especially let it be me over my close priest friends. Did someone else deserve it more? Of course not. It's like when people say the person who did this to me will "get his," or "What goes around comes around." People tend to say if that's true, what did I do to deserve this round? No one, and I mean no one, deserves to have misfortune befall them.

But be sure as there is life, we will all be tested at some point. It may not be to the degree that I was—it may be less, it may be more—but the crossroads are everywhere and in facing this, it is my roughest test yet. I know I'd like myself better in the end if I won, not by being a victim, but by being a fighter. That's the kind of survivor I want to be.

One calculated act of hate changed my life forever. So I ask all who may read this book, do a calculated act of *kindness* every day of your life.

CHAPTER 61

IN SPITE OF INNOCENCE

Right or wrong, any professionals who come into daily contact with children have a high probability of becoming entangled in negative publicity—especially priests more than any other profession. Priests have become targets of the probing nature of the press. The members of the press view the alleged crimes as a violation of trust and present the cases to the public from that perspective. Now, after all this time, especially since the outbreak in Boston with Cardinal Law, the media coverage feeds the public's mistrust of priests, which causes Catholics to want to limit legal or Church protection of priests.

Reporters are currently able to use dark quotes from unnamed sources, report the name of the accused and protect the privacy of the alleged accuser or victim by withholding their names. In my case, two little sisters, ages 6 and 7 years old, were allegedly involved; and so the press used different ages of the girls to divert the public away from possible identification. The reporter is shielded from any errors by the First Amendment, as long as the story was written in "good faith."

Based on my experience, it is my conviction that if a priest is accused of a crime, there needs to be a level of privacy until a determination of the validity of the allegation can be made. A priest can never regain his reputation under current reporting procedures, because once accused their reputation is permanently tarnished. I agree that in order to make sure that victims of abuse are not re-traumatized, the media and the courts disguise their identity. This protection is meant as a shield. But when a false allegation is made, the protection becomes a double edged sword. The accused is defenseless to keep his name and reputation from being soiled because the Church and the media are allowed to report *his* name. This policy needs to be reexamined. Because of the rise in false allegations, the accused should be afforded anonymity until a determination or admission can be obtained. Without anonymity the accused cannot return to normal life after his ordeal because of the societal stigma attached to him, even if he is found completely innocent of all wrongdoing.

Anonymity for accused priests will not place minors in jeopardy, because the vast majority of abuse cases are false allegations. Of the few pedophile priests giving the Catholic Church a bad name, the priests who commit crimes against minors taint every priest. Now it appears that priests are seen by many people, Catholic or non-Catholics, as pedophiles until they can prove they are not. There is a growing perception by modern society that the priest has done something wrong if an accusation is made, no matter how frivolous. In the media's naming of accused alleged abusers, the public needs to be conscious of the shortcomings of media reports. Relying only on media coverage to form an opinion of events is dangerous. Several protections need to be added. People need to be educated that the problem of abuse is no more prevalent with priests than with other trusted professionals.

Several protective measures need to be taken to ensure that personal animosities are not leading to a false allegation, as what happened in my case. Among the protections are the guidelines I suggest:

1. Initial screening of the report by a neutral party to ascertain whether the accusations are valid and verifiable.

2. Thorough investigation of the allegations prior to criminal reporting to the media, or priest removal.

3. Findings of the investigation should be made available to the accused priest and his attorney.

Right now adult accusers can fabricate and get away with it. No one should be immune from the law. Accusers must know the consequences for their actions and need to be subject to a lawsuit if the allegation is conclusively proven false. All dioceses should be more attuned to the investigative process.

Children must be listened to. Allegations must be investigated, but children must not *automatically* be believed. Another resolution to the increase in false allegations made against a priest is for parents to be made accountable for their children's accusations—especially in situations where it is eventually proven the parents put their children up to it, in some cases for revenge, and in others for monetary gain (e.g., a trumped up lawsuit). Every diocese must take meticulous measures to ensure that priests are as protected from false allegations as those who are making them.

This great country was founded upon the principle of the presumption of innocence until proven guilty. The Church, the very institution that puts itself forward as the epitome of justice, must guarantee the rights of priests who are falsely accused. My advice to all my brother priests:

1. Protect yourself at all costs from the appearance of too close contact with minors.

2. Priests, I believe, can no longer hug children; stay away—at least a handshake away.

3. Never allow yourself to be in a one-on-one setting with a minor, especially behind closed doors.

4. Priests must be always alert to how vulnerable they are to being victims of false allegations, and act accordingly.

Old Mother Church after centuries of experience, put rules in place to protect its priests:

1. A screen must be in place between the penitent and the priest in the confessional.

2. At the end of mass, priests must return to the sacristy.

After Vatican II, confessional rooms replaced the old partitioned booth confessionals. The priest, after mass, went to the door of the church to greet people, often grabbing children in their arms and hugging them. I strongly believe that that day is gone. Even touching adults, especially women, can easily be misinterpreted if someone wants to twist it to their malicious purposes.

If a priest is accused, that priest needs to remain silent and immediately retain a lawyer. If I had chosen silence from the moment that detective first accused me, and referred him to my lawyer, I would not be in the position I am in today. As my lawyer, Gerry Rooney, told me, "Priests are too trusting." At first I felt that Detective Reedy was being my friend, and had my best interests at heart; when in fact he was my deadly enemy. He was only interested in ultimately getting me to sign a confession. I knew I was innocent, thus believed I had nothing to fear, and only wanted to clear my name. I naively felt I could just sit down with Det. Reedy and convince him that I was totally innocent. I now realize he had a whole hidden agenda. In his mind, Det. Reedy already had me tried and found guilty before he even met me.

Often priests don't get an attorney because they believe they have done nothing wrong. They have blind faith that the system will deal with their situation fairly. A priest accused needs to realize that he is likely to be presumed guilty until proven innocent.

Falsely accused priests want to believe their bishop will protect them. After all, he is a shepherd, he is required to protect his attacked sheep; but too often Church officials have their own agenda. They are busy protecting themselves against possible civil suits. It is not in the dioceses' best interests to believe a priest is innocent because the allegation carries so much weight in society. Thus, they generally believe the best course of action in all instances is to presume guilt first and sort out the facts later.

Even if they have done nothing wrong, priests should get an attorney, and remain quiet—which also means not talking to reporters. It's too easy for words to get twisted.

Because of this atmosphere of epidemic accusations, the Church has lost its moorings and consequently now is flawed. But the Church is still the Bride of Christ, pure, holy and undefiled. The Church has to be scrupulously careful in screening its candidates for ordination. When the Church ordains sexually healthy, good priests, the church needs to protect them.

During the Salem Witch Trials an individual would be ostracized by the people because of an allegation. To determine guilt these accused often were cast into a river or pond. If the accused *did not* drown, they were assumed to be a witch. Conversely, drowning proved their innocence—but a lot of good it did them at that point...damned if you were, dead if you weren't.

The phenomenon of abuse in the Church resembles that part of American history. To improve the ecclesiastical system, "protections" to avoid "drowning" priests because of false accusations, must be put in place. Courageous bishops must step forward and *protect* their priests by thoroughly examining the accusations before impulsively driving a priest out of his parish as if chasing a mad dog.

Why, I ask, doing 40 years of active duty in my diocese, and having attended numerous clergy conferences, was the subject of pedophile behavior never discussed? Obviously bishops must have known that at least a small percentage of their priests were habitually involved in the despicable crime of pedophile behavior. Why did they not educate and inform their priests of this evil virus that lurked among us? It was a hidden secret within chancery walls; not until the Boston dioceses in the late 1990's did the bishops finally react. Then they added insult to injury by turning 180 degrees and enacting laws that hurt innocent as well as guilty priests.

Priests have become the most vulnerable people imaginable. Priests by virtue of their basic calling are expected to be another Christ. The Christ who said, "Let the little children come to me, for theirs is the Kingdom of heaven." In my experience as a parish priest, children gravitated toward me and clung to me like a magnet. Playing with children on the playground gave me immense pleasure and joy. I was doing what Jesus would do. That day is gone; the Church has lost its innocence. Now priests must protect themselves by staying at a distance and looking on parishioners, adults and children, as potential accusers. "Greet—don't touch" must be the motto. And never visit the homes of parishioners alone. When Jesus sent out the disciples two by two, He had a healthy method in mind. A priest should at all times visit parishioners with a companion minister. Protection is guaranteed with dual ministry.

It seems the Church is standing on its head and all decency and common sense has disappeared. The Church of America has lost its first love, its first enthusiasm. It must find its way back by following the directives of St. John to the Church of Ephesus first: "Remember your first love and enthusiasm as a Church in a new country. Secondly, remember the height from which you have fallen. Thirdly, repent and do the things you did at first. He who has an ear, let him hear what the spirit says to the Churches. To him who overcomes, I will give the right to eat from the tree of life which is in the paradise of God."

It is my conviction, the darker the night, the brighter the stars. The Church of America may be in a time of darkness, but many bright stars like Bishop Sarratelli of the Paterson Diocese of New Jersey and many more wonderful bishops and servants of the Church will eventually dispel the darkness and restore the Church to its former glory, including Monsignor Robert Carroll, Father Jack Catoir, Cardinal Dulles, Monsignor John Demkovich; and of happy memory Pope John Paul II, and Mother Teresa. Still shining stars in a dark world.

And I would be remiss if I did not mention a rising star in the Church, Mother Antonea known as the "Prison Angel," who in the middle of her life found her life's calling, At the age of fifty, this remarkable woman left her comfortable world in suburban Los Angeles to dedicate her life to caring for the poorest of the poor, the inmates in one of Mexico's most notorious jails. Carrying little more than a Spanish dictionary and a toothbrush, she moved into a cell to live among prisoners, who ranged from petty thieves to some of the most powerful drug lords in Mexican history. Twenty-eight years later she still lives in that Tijuana cell, and the unstoppable force for her good works has become legendary. Mother Teresa met with her, and Pope John Paul II blessed her. Presidents in the USA and Mexico have lauded her work, and she has now founded a religious community named the Servants of the Eleventh Hour, designed to give older women—many of them widowed or divorced—a way to bring new meaning to their lives. From a new home in a small, cold cell she has profoundly affected the lives of thousands of people, not only prisoners and guards, but many well-to-do Californians whose lives she has enriched by drawing them into her ever widening work.

CHAPTER 62

THE HORROR OF FALSE
CONFESSIONS

I was appalled by the behavior of the detective assigned to my case. It is no doubt the dirtiest secret in the darkest corner of law enforcement leading constantly to the scandal of wrong man convictions. It is a national disgrace. From what happened to me I can easily understand how a blameless person could be falsely accused and wrongfully convicted. I was completely naive that such an evil process existed, a kind of conspiracy of silence. It was always my belief that miscarriages of justice hardly ever occurred.

It is awful that the approved police methods can create guilt by compelling confused and browbeaten people to admit to crimes they did not commit, and then be handed over to prosecutors more interested in winning than in making sure that justice is done.

Interrogation detectives pretend to believe that everyone who confesses is guilty—never mind the power of suggestion and intimidation. It is immoral behavior. I became a citizen of the United States in 1968. It was one of the happiest days of my life. I felt safe in a country of just and fair laws. I don't think so anymore. I have discovered the country's dirty secrets of profound injustice inside the legal system that would make our founding fathers turn in their graves.

Father Joe, an honest and decent human being, was also falsely accused of touching a young girl when he gave her a hug at her grandmother's funeral. This particular girl was for years under a psychiatrist's care. At one stage on being asked if anybody ever touched her, she said yes, Father Joe. The psychiatrist reported this to the police—who then came to the rectory and took Father Joe to the police station and questioned him for five hours, and finally got him to sign a confession. He was eventually arrested and tried in a civil court. However, the girl, a few months later, finally accused her own father of molesting her, and not the priest. The case was dismissed and Father Joe was free to go. When Father Joe went to the Vicar General of the diocese and asked to be reinstated to the priesthood, he was refused with, "We know, Father Joe, you are innocent, but we are afraid of the media and the press." What injustice? How this Vicar General can live with his conscience is beyond me. Father Joe was condemned to a lifetime in limbo.

Many critical reforms are needed in the Church's justice system and of course in the entire American justice system; such as the need to record interrogations and have a greater professional disdain for cases built on the forced extraction of so-called admissions. How could this great country and indeed the Church itself be part of ruinous mistreatment of an individual?

In hindsight, I now believe that Detective Reedy had a hidden agenda in his treatment of me; and his ultimate goal was getting a signed confession. My guilt or innocence was completely irrelevant to him. The polygraph test was rigged for me to purposely fail; then he immediately walked me through a series of dark corridors with keys clanging to a dark, dingy room, where he sat me down and said: "Well now, we have a stack of evidence against you, and we know you are guilty, so just sign a guilty confession and we can all go home."

I cannot believe Detective Reedy was suggesting, was insisting, that I had committed something revolting to my very nature. What a violation of one of my most treasured beliefs, in the innocence and purity of a child. I adamantly refused, saying, "I will never sign my name to a lie—never!"

He began to berate me and used abusive language. He insisted that I had failed the polygraph test and that he totally believed in the infallibility of the polygraph; so how dare I question its veracity. This harassment went on for hours.

Finally, I told him I had to leave as I had a Pre Cana to conduct that night. In a fit of rage, raising his voice and becoming red in the face, he told me I could go.

Obviously, he couldn't accept that he had failed. He thought he had a sitting duck and all he had to do was shoot me down. He went to this extreme knowing that the case was going nowhere, because supposedly it fell under the statute of limitations. What were his reasons for such ferocity and madness? I am convinced he felt compelled to satisfy the requests of my conspirators who wanted my "head on a platter." Either that or he just wanted a quickly closed case. And nothing would be more convenient than an autographed confession. That was his "payoff" and he had failed. I can think of no other logical reason for his uncontrollable aggression.

My refusal to sign must have infuriated him, for he wrote up a report that was completely false. Now the story had drastically changed. According to his final report, I had gone to the Snedo house not once, but *seven* times with a puppet and molested the two little sisters at the kitchen table— and in this version, he aged sisters a few years now making them nine and ten years old. (Perhaps Det. Reedy thought this would keep the alleged crime within the statute of limitations?) The obvious question is: "Where were the parents?" Two other obvious questions: "Why would I have gone to that house after refusing to accept the children in the school? — And after I had called DYFS to investigate the family for abuse?" A lunatic wouldn't believe such an outrageous story.

It is common knowledge that the prosecuting technique in the USA is to regard a conviction as a personal victory calculated to enhance the prestige of the investigating detective. A feather is his cap or as it were; another notch in his gun handle.

Are there detectives psychologically programmed so that their consciences are anaesthetized to any feeling of guilt? Otherwise, how can they live with themselves, extracting false confessions with false pretenses; exposing a person's mind to relentless nonstop interrogation? Extracting at any cost an admission of guilt and using browbeating methods of coercion upon an already exhausted individual? To make matters worse, in criminal cases where justice has been miscarried, authorities will fight furiously to avoid any admission of their own mistakes. This gives an illusion of the law's universal rectitude. Fear of loss of face is often the overriding factor, and the obsessive need to protect themselves from the obvious appearance of being not prosecutors but persecutors by rejecting any suggestion of error, much less delinquency.

During my third year in exile, I remember reading that on the third week of May in 2005, five black kids were released from prison. They had been wrongfully convicted of molesting and brutally beating a Central Park jogger. They were convicted and found guilty after confessing to committing the crime. Obviously, at least one of them was browbeaten and forced to make a false confession, because several years later, an unknown individual confessed to the crime and his confession was corroborated. Seven years is a long time to spend behind bars for a crime you did not commit.

I am told that in the process of getting a suspect to sign a confession of guilt, he is regularly given a fake lie detector test, all "legal," and the suspect is then told that he lied in denying he had committed the crime. Then all kinds of mental manipulation is applied on the suspect for hours upon hours until the suspect is exhausted and confused and eventually there occurs what is known as a "coerced-internalized confession." This is a statement from a book entitled *Conviction of the Innocent* by Donald Connery. He went on to say that even Galileo confessed that the sun and all the stars revolved around the motionless earth rather than face the wrath of the Church.

The influence tactics routinely used in interrogations are sufficiently powerful to cause some innocent persons to at least temporarily come to believe that they have committed a serious crime. Claims that the suspect "blacked out" recollections of the crime often figure prominently in accounts of seriously disputed confessions.

An innocent suspect who naively assumes that police officers would not lie, is likely to experience confusion, anxiety, distress, and might ultimately come to doubt his or her memory.

The interrogator is trained to ignore normal rules of decent human conduct by lying freely. Also, police deception is likely to be more effective against an innocent person or first time offender than against a hardened criminal.

It should be a nationwide requirement that all detective interrogations are audio and video taped. If my interrogator, Detective Reedy, had been taped, he could not have radically changed his report to the prosecutor, and ultimately to my former bishop. This is nothing less than an abuse of power, and arrogance of power—happening not years ago in the dark ages, but today right here and now. If I was familiar with the evil process of police interrogation, I would have protected myself with a simple tape recorder in my pocket and the world would have learned word for word what transpired, and that detective would be nailed for making a false report.

It is now clear to me as a citizen of this great country that two things must be done to reduce this brutal mental process. In addition to videotaping all investigations from its inception to its conclusion, police need to produce corroboration for the confession. Then the person can say without hesitating, "If you can't convince me, you can't convince the prosecutor, you can't convince the judge, you can't convince the jury, and here is the clear evidence (audio-video recording) that proves it. If a detective or policeman knows it is only his word against the accused, then they willfully fabricate the entire story—and that is exactly what happened to me.

When I finally read his report, which was not given to my canon lawyer until a year later, I did not recognize a word of the actual dialogue that took place behind closed doors. Detective Reedy had "made up" a horrific story designed to shock and outrage anyone who read it, especially the prosecutor and my bishop. This detective knew he had nothing of substance to charge me with; but if he had a confession, the so-called statute of limitations would go out the window and he could have me arrested and incarcerated. But I am convinced he was motivated by a "payoff" from my conspirators and had learned from them the new rules in the Church with all of its loopholes. He knew that all that was necessary to get me destroyed by the Church was a convincing report from the detective; that the investigation alone would prove that I was guilty, and that if it was not for the statute of limitations I would be thrown in jail (the actual statement of the detective). Now, that statement through a fake interrogation became my judge and jury, and my fate was signed and sealed by not only the Church, but by public opinion with the diocese intentionally revealing the detective's report to the press and media.

Ordinary people and indeed I myself (before what happened to me personally) wouldn't believe that a person would confess to something he or she didn't do. But now I know differently. I know that with a limited ability to understand your situation, or a limited self-regard, you just might, and there are other circumstances when a confession might seem quite sensible no matter how innocent you might be.

It is now well established that a confession can, and in fact, be forced out of a completely innocent person, thus calling into question the so-called public noble claim that America is a society of justice. But inside closed doors of the American justice system is, in fact, a sometimes obnoxious injustice.

I would like to further protect my fellow Americans, especially my brother priests from falling into the trap of feeling as I wrongfully felt: "I haven't done anything wrong, and after all only a criminal really needs an attorney, and the truth will eventually come out in the wash."

The general belief, an innocent person would never confess to a crime he did not commit, should be forever erased from the "collective consciousness" of Americans. Anybody, regardless of their social or intelligence status, after going through the brutal process allowed in this free society, is a sitting duck for making a false confession.

What I would want to teach any American, especially my brother priests if they are questioned by law enforcement personnel is to say immediately: "I would like to have an attorney present during my interrogation." A confession is in my humble belief the product of police viciousness, the product of the political necessity to close a case. It is nothing less than that. I suspect that detectives are trained to do this, and it is all terribly routine. It is my hope and prayer that this brutal system is regulated by a more humane society, especially in a great country like America that prides itself in being the land of the free. Because of my naivety of the law enforcement system, all I stood for was stolen from me overnight.

Donald Connery also states in his book, *Convicting the Innocent*, "In the occasions I have seen on false confessions, there is only one conclusion; they would rather kill an innocent man than admit to having made a mistake, because the politics of it simply mediate for that."

Perhaps the most important matter a person with an accusation can know is that most of the people who loved and accepted you before the attack will love and protect you after the attack. For too long I felt like an outcast, but today I am much more confident with my lot in life. I didn't do anything wrong, no matter what some people or the media says. Today people are far more tolerant than they were years ago. America loves a comeback kid and that is my goal. To climb back up from the deepest hole I have ever been in.

I have discovered that one of life's great milestones is when a person can look back and be almost as thankful for the setbacks as for the victories. Gradually it dawned on me that success and failure are not opposite poles, they are part of the same picture; the picture of a full life where you have ups and downs.

In my lowest moments, I would try to disguise myself in public wearing a cap with a peak in the back, an old brown jacket I hadn't worn for years, and a large pair of dark glasses. However, no matter how much I tried to disguise myself, every now and then someone would recognize me; their reaction was always a surprise to me. Usually they would get carried away and greet me with great exuberance, unreservedly hugging me and expressing gratitude for some favor I had done for them as their priest, or later as their pastor, often mentioning favors I had done for them which I had totally forgotten. After the encounter, I had mixed feelings of gratitude and sadness, which took me some time to recover my composure. Sometimes I would hear someone call my name out, but I would keep walking, pretending I didn't hear them or giving them the impression that it wasn't really me. I guess I was fooling nobody but myself. I felt so psychologically fragile that the slightest invasion of my life was traumatic for me.

Since the conspiracy I feel like I am continuously pushing a big rock up a steep hill, often falling back down, but always starting all over again and pushing a little higher each time. A tough hill to climb, but never climbing alone, I find peace in a stanza from Oscar Hammerstein's 1945 Broadway musical play *Carousel*:

> *When you walk through a storm,*
> *hold your head up high, and don't be afraid of the dark.*
> *Walk on, walk on with hope in your heart,*
> *and you'll never walk alone.*

The message of that song reminds me that even though my life had been tossed and blown, if I continue to climb, if I keep up the struggle to exonerate myself, I can do anything. I am continually amazed at the incredible power of the human spirit to survive the worst possible attack. There is no way to get around pain but through it; and there is always a better world at the other side.

264

CHAPTER 63

STILL STANDING

They say you never know what Mother Nature will throw at you. Now it can be said, you never know what Mother Church will throw at you—especially if you are a priest. During the worst hurricane season of history in the year 2005, Hurricane Katrina and Hurricane Rita devastated the Gulf Coast. America was unprepared to cope with nature's vicious attack. What went wrong? The President, the Louisiana governor and the mayor, were all "asleep at the wheel" as it were.

The "Church hurricane" of the pedophile revelation of 2001 took the Church by storm and the bishops were "asleep at the wheel." Frightened and confused, the bishops scrambled to protect themselves. Quickly, a control charter was put in place; a "zero tolerance" law was devised, no matter how long ago or superficial an accusation was made against a priest, the rules applied and the priest was removed.

Hundreds of priests across the country were caught up in this insanity with no recourse. I was one of those victims, but I was determined to be a victor and find strength through adversity. My attitude was I may have been knocked down, but I am not going to stay down.

I heard a story about a little boy who was in church with his mother; he could not sit still. He kept standing up in the pew. His mother kept telling him to sit down in the pew. He'd sit down for a while, and then he'd get back up. Finally, his mother put her hand on his shoulder and pushed him down on the pew. The boy looked up at his mother and said, "I may be sitting down on the outside, but I am standing up on the inside."

My situation may have forced me to sit down, but I see myself standing up on the inside. I feel as though life has caved in on top of me, knocking me off my feet and pushing me down. But I made a decision not to stay down;

rather to develop a victor's attitude and mentality of faith. I try not to allow myself to lapse into negative thinking, complaining, or blaming God. I told God I do not understand this, but I know You are still in control and You said all things would work together for my good. You said You would take this evil and turn it around and use it to my advantage. "So Heavenly Father, I thank You that You are going to bring me through this."

In Ephesians 6:13 it says, "When you've done everything you know how to do, just keep on standing firm." I have done my best, I've prayed. I've believed; I have placed my faith on the truth of God's word, but it just doesn't look like anything is happening, I am tempted to say: "What's the use? It's never going to change." But because of my faith, I can't give up. I keep standing, keep believing, and keep hoping. I know God will eventually reward me if I keep standing up on the inside. I will keep on getting up in my heart, mind, and soul. I have to have a victor's mentality. This thing is not going to defeat me. This thing is not going to forever steal my joy. I know I'm the victor and not the victim. I know when one door closes; God will open up a bigger and better door. Even if the enemy hits me with his best shot, his best will never be good enough. He may knock me down, but he cannot knock me out. When all is said and done, when the smoke clears and the dust settles, I'm still going to be standing strong. I must act on my will not simply on my emotions. I must do my part—as my dad used to say, "God can only help those who help themselves."

Sometimes we need a push. I was looking forward to my retirement, enjoying the twilight years of my life united with my family, brothers, sisters, nieces and nephews, my loved ones that I left forty years before I went to the USA to minister to the people of God. Now finally I could return and be with them again. But God pushed me out of my comfort zone; what I had proposed God had disposed. If this adversity had not happened, who knows where I would be? I probably would be living a life of comfort, putting God on the back burner, being a lazy Christian. God obviously wants me to be constantly growing, so he used adversity to get me moving forward. He allowed the pressure to push me and to stretch me. He knows just how much I can take, and in my distress God is mysteriously enlarging me.

I am amazed at what I can accomplish when God puts a little pressure on and gets me out of that safe zone and gets me into the FAITH zone. To continue to get to know him, to love him, to serve him, and with his continuing help to finally live forever with him in heaven.

* * *

On one of the walls of the concentration camp of Auschwitz, Poland was scribbled the words: "I believe in the sun even when it is not shining. I believe in love even when I'm not feeling it. I believe in God even when He is silent."

Revelations 21: *"And God shall wipe away all tears from their eyes and there shall be no more death, neither sorrow nor crying, neither shall there be any more pain for the former things had passed away."*

I felt lost in an unfamiliar world, when the former things passed away. I was me, but I was watching myself from somewhere outside of it all. How do I rebuild when I have lost so much of who I am? It seems like yesterday that I died when I received that letter that my former bishop sent to Rome to send me to the gallows for my priestly execution. The sound of my breaking heart was numbing and because of it there is psychological pain in my head that no one can comprehend. I am trying to make sense of my world torn apart. Tragedy is a bizarre irony in that it can be fascinating and mesmerizing and at the same time heart wrenching. This is hard to write. My stomach aches now as it did then.

And time seems to stand still as I continue waiting for the final verdict from the three canonical judges.

What will be the result of the ecclesiastical trial? The uncertainty of it all is extremely disturbing. I must fight my fate with my faith. I feel my life—my priestly life—has been taken hostage, not by a foreign power or terrorists, but by my very own people. I was not physically blindfolded, bound or gagged, but psychologically and spiritually. Don't cry for me, but cry for the Church. The Church has lost its soul. This is not constitutional. This is not America. Surely this is not the Church, the Bride of Christ.

As my lawyer, Gerry Rooney, said: "This is an injustice in our civil and criminal courts, and it should have been deemed an injustice by the Church."

Gerry then said to me, "Father McCarthy, the Church really screwed you."

I said to him, "Look what they did to Christ, and he was God."

Gerry nodded, "Well said."

CHAPTER 64

PERSEVERENCE

Morning, noon, and night I pray on my knees: "Dear John Paul II, please intercede for me to my beloved Sacred Heart, my Lord and Savior, to send His Holy Spirit on the members of the tribunal to convince them of my innocence; I am falsely accused. O Dear Jesus, you were falsely accused at the end of your life. You went into the Garden of Gethsemane and fell on your knees, pleading with the father to remove the chalice of suffering from your life. From the cross you felt abandoned and cried out, 'My God, my God, why have You forsaken me?'"

Many times I've felt like giving up ... "What's the use? God is not listening!" I find myself asking if He really exists at all ... "Is it all for nothing?" At times I could not feel his presence. Then I would feel guilty for such thoughts and feel even worse than ever for my doubts, and all alone with no hope.

Even in the midst of my disbelief I still kept pleading although I felt like I was uttering empty words. I would think, "Why would God listen to poor little me? Who am I when God has the whole world to listen to and all of its problems?" Then for a while, my prayer life would "dry up" like waling on a barren desert. I felt ashamed of myself until one day in September 2007. While I walked about Barnes & Noble bookstore, the cover of *Time* magazine caught my eye—there I saw a picture of Mother Teresa. I looked closer at the cover and read the bold block letters: "THE SECRET LIFE OF MOTHER TERESA" — in smaller print was the startling words: "Newly published letters reveal a beloved icon's fifty year crisis of faith!" What could that mean? I bought the magazine and went to my place of refuge on Long Branch in New Jersey and sat down to read her secret letters—now published for all to see. I was astounded and shocked at the revelation.

Mother Teresa's agony…a decade after her death coming to light in secret letters showed that she spent almost 50 years without sensing the presence of God in her life. What does her experience tell me about the value of doubt? Although those who witnessed her in prayer spoke of Teresa's serenity, her letters to superiors and confessors, chronicled a belief that her prayers were spurned or empty. "Jesus has a very special love for you, but as for me, the silence and the emptiness is so great that I look and do not see—listen and do not hear." (Mother Teresa to the Reverend Michael Van Der Peet, September 1979)

Mother Teresa directed Father Picachy: "Please destroy any letters or anything I have written." Consistent with her ongoing fight against pride, Teresa's rationale for suppressing her personal correspondence was, "I want the work to remain only His." If the letters become public, she explained to Father Picachy, people will think more of me and less of Jesus. Teresa considered the perceived absence of God in her life as her most shameful secret.

In my ministry, as a priest, I have known many people who have felt abandoned by God, and had doubts about God's existence; and yet have complete trust in God at the same time. Who would have thought that the person considered to be the most faithful woman in the world struggled so much with her faith? Who would have thought that the one to be the most ardent of believers could be a saint to the skeptics? However, doubt is a natural part of everyone's life, be it an average believer, or a world famous saint.

In 1968 Mother Teresa told a priest, "Inside it is all dark and I feel totally cut off from God." And yet she continued her work with the poor. In 1959, she wrote: "What do I labor for? If there is no God, there can be no soul—if there is no soul then Jesus, You also are not true." She frequently bemoaned an inability to pray: "I utter words of community prayers and try my utmost to get out of every word the sweetness it has to give, but my prayer of union is not there any longer. I no longer pray, referring almost casually to 'my darkness' and to Jesus as 'the absent one.'" There was one respite. In October 1958, Pope Pius XII died. Mother Teresa prayed to the deceased Pope for a proof that God is pleased with the society. Then and there she "rejoiced." Disappeared were the long darkness and the strange suffering that lasted for ten years.

A letter from 1995 discussed her spiritual dryness, and then she died in 1997. "Tell me Father, why is there so much pain and darkness in my soul?" In 1951 she wrote that the passion was the only aspect of Jesus' life that she was interested in sharing. "I want to drink only from his chalice of pain." So she did, although by all indications not in a way she had expected. After receiving an important prize in the Philippines during the 1960's, Mother Teresa stated: "This means nothing to me, because I don't have Him."

Mother Teresa's ambitions for her ministry were tremendous. She states:

"I want to love Jesus as He has never been loved before." Yet her letters are full of inner conflict about her accomplishments. Rather than simply giving all credit to God, she refused to take any credit for her accomplishments. For Mother Teresa, an occasion for a modicum of joy initiated a significant quantity of misery and her subsequent successes led her to perpetuate it.

It seems that starting her ministry may have marked a turning point in her relationship with Jesus, and she was finally in a place to fulfill. It seems she was the author of her own misery and even defined it as true misery. She considered herself the ultimate spouse to Jesus. Father Martin makes the analogy: "Let's say you fall in love, you get married and you believe with all your heart that marriage is a sacrament. Your wife gets a stroke; she's comatose and you will never experience her love again. It's like loving and caring for a person for fifty years and once in a while you complain to your spiritual director; but you know on the deepest level that she loves you even though she's silent. What you're doing makes sense."

Mother Teresa knew what she was doing made sense: "I can't express in words the gratitude I owe you for your kindness to me; for the first time in years, I have come to love the darkness. For I believe now that it is a part of a very, very small part of Jesus' darkness and pain on earth. You have taught me to accept it as a spiritual side of your work. Today I felt a deep joy that Jesus can't go anymore through the agony, but that He wants to go through it in 'Me.'"

The Reverend Joseph Newner, whom she met in the late 1950's and confided in somewhat later about her darkness, seems to have told her the three things she needed to hear: That there was no human remedy for it… that her very craving for God was a sure sign…and that the absence was in fact part of the spiritual side of her work for Jesus. This counsel clearly granted Teresa a great sense of release. For all that she had expected and even craved to share in Christ's passion, she had not anticipated that she might recapitulate the particular moment on the cross when He asks, "My God, my God why have You forsaken me?" It was the redeeming experience of her life when she realized that the might of her heart was the special share she had in Jesus' passion.

Despite her perception of God's "absence," Mother Teresa never let up on her work in His name. However, years later she said, "I just have the joy of having nothing—not even the reality of the presence of God in the Eucharist." She described her soul as an "ice block." She worried that she might turn a Judas to Jesus in this painful darkness. She stated, "If I ever become a saint, I will surely be one of darkness. I will continue to be absent from heaven to the light of those in darkness on earth." She also wrote, "I am willing to suffer for all eternity if this is possible." She writes to Jesus: "If this brings you glory, if souls are brought to You—with joy I accept all to the end of my life."

After reading the Mother Teresa story in *Time* magazine, my own story of sometimes not feeling the presence of God, and feeling my prayers fall on deaf ears, did not seem so unusual. And as far as my prayer life was concerned, I was in good company.

No matter what, I persevered in praying constantly for my exoneration.

CHAPTER 65

SCARRED

It's emotional trauma that leaves the deepest scars. When there is uncertainty, the imagination can wreck havoc on one's psyche. During the pedophile crisis, priests lived in an atmosphere of fear and terror, a period of uncertainty that indeed caused havoc in the psyche of many priests. The 6 o'clock news constantly announced that yet another priest was accused and removed from his ministry. Americans were bombarded with bad news about their priests. The subject was discussed everywhere from the supermarkets to the hairdressers and nail salons, to the corporations to the schools and colleges, and of course around the "water coolers" of every place imaginable.

As I listened to the gossip, it never occurred to me that I personally would be accused. After all, that was unthinkable. I was squeaky clean as far as that stuff was concerned, that only happened to other priests. I even entered into the fray of judging as guilty some of those I personally knew. "Yeah, he was always kind of different," etc. Priests were rounded up by their bishops, and because of the slightest accusations were declared guilty.

Did I write this journal to remain sane, or to try to understand the terrifying insanity that has erupted in the Church? I write this journal to preserve a record of the ordeal I endured in the retirement years of my life.

Having survived, I have to give some meaning to my survival. By writing and publishing this journal, maybe I can inspire others not to get discouraged. Justice will eventually prevail; also I feel a moral obligation to tell the world that not all priests who are accused are automatically guilty; and to try to prevent bishops and their accomplices from thinking they are above the law—especially the moral law—and that all accused priests should be considered innocent until proven guilty.

I also write this journal because I believe this period of history will be judged one day, just as the Inquisition and Senator Joseph McCarthy's communist witch hunt period was.

Unfortunately, while I am well aware that I have many things to say, I don't always have the words to say them. The last thing in the world I even thought of was writing a book. But I feel compelled to give witness to what was done to me by evil people, even though they knew I was innocent. All the dictionary had to offer seemed impotent to adequately describe the psychological pain I endured in my innermost being. How could I find a way to describe the darkness that engulfed me? To be utterly beaten down by a man dressed up like a shepherd with a miter on his head that was supposed to represent the tongues of the fire of love that fell on the heads of the apostles at Pentecost; and carrying a staff used by the shepherds to protect their sheep from attack by wolves, or to retrieve a sheep fallen into a crevice on the rough terrain of the hills of the Middle East. How was I to write of such a contradiction without my heart being broken and trembling with fear?

Deep down, my former bishop knew then as he does now that he was betraying the very essence of what he was supposed to stand for. After all, it deals with man's inhumanity to man. Only a priest who experienced what I experienced would know what it was like; others will never know. Having lived through this experience I cannot keep silent, no matter how difficult, if not impossible, to write about such an atrocity. A shepherd consciously and willfully tried to wound his "sheep" but thank God I persevered. For despite all my attempts to articulate the unspeakable accusation, my simple words will cry out for justice, and will not remain silent, and somehow will hopefully change the cruel, insensitive stance of those who should know better.

On the cover of *Time* magazine, when John Paul II was shot, were the bold words: "THEY SHOT GOD." With every false accusation of an innocent priest, the words could be repeated: "They shot God." Every priest is an *alter Christi*: a man endowed by God with a power not even given to the angels: the power to change bread and wine into the body and blood of Christ, the power to forgive sins. From the time I could reason, I thought only of God, longing for the day I would be ordained a priest, dedicated to Him, the soul of a child of God, called by Him to serve his people.

NEVER shall I forget the day that Detective Reedy walked into my office and accused me of a despicable crime that I can only describe with the "M" word. Never shall I forget that arrogance that assaulted my intelligence and common sense: "You don't remember it because it was so painful and awful you just buried it."

NEVER shall I forget that accusation that consumed my life forever.

NEVER shall I forget that attack that for a time deprived me of my desire to live.

NEVER shall I forget that time that murdered my God and my soul and turned my dreams to ashes.

NEVER shall I forget those things, even if I live to be a million years old. NEVER.

This was a time unlike all others when the one who offered the sacrifice on the altar was himself being sacrificed; not as a sacrifice of expiation but as a sacrifice of convenience, to cover up the sins of others. It is the only way I can make sense out of all of this. It is what keeps me from going insane.

I try to hold onto my memories of how things were, but things are different and will never be the same again. So many things went wrong, you'd think my name was Murphy, instead of McCarthy, from "Murphy's Law." Life is full of ironies. Someone once said, "If you want to make God laugh, tell him your future plans."

Not all of our dreams turn out the way we expect them to. Sometimes we wake up and find that life is different from what we had planned.

After the injustice and suffering I endured from a terrible false accusation, I swore never to ignore the pain and suffering of others. Yesterday, I visited the Poor Sisters of the nursing home in Totowa, NJ to visit my former pastor Monsignor Dennis Hayes on the occasion of his 95th birthday. I was his associate for six years in St. Cecelia Church in Rockaway, NJ. He was my favorite pastor and I was his favorite curate. It was the happiest six years of my priesthood. When I went into his room at the nursing home, even though he was awake and the staff told me he was as alert and as sharp as ever, when I told him who I was he wouldn't believe me. He said, "You are not the Father Bill McCarthy I know. There must be two Father McCarthy's. I don't see any resemblance whatsoever of the Bill McCarthy I knew. You don't have the vitality and alertness and lightheartedness I knew. I am searching my brain for something that would remind me of you, but I can't find anything whatsoever. I remember Father Bill McCarthy very well, but that is not the person I see before me." He felt my face with his hand and shook his head. "No, that's not you."

His remarks frightened me. I asked myself, has the terrible attack on me changed everything about me? I know I am not the same person I was before the conspiracy, but did a 95-year-old man sense and feel an enormous change in me, and feel the pain I had been through? He had no cognitive knowledge of what happened to me, but somehow at his sensitive old age he just said what he felt without realizing how he was making me feel. Nobody else would have the courage to tell me I showed the torture and pain in my face and demeanor. I know I had lost fifteen pounds and probably looked like I came out of a WWII concentration camp. Still, I didn't think I had changed all that much physically. I don't feel old in spite of what I am going through. I guess that is how most people feel as they age. The physical body ages, but the soul and spirit are spiritual and immaterial and consequently never age.

I remember the old saying, "Yesterday is history, tomorrow is a mystery, today is a gift. That's why they call it the present." In the days of my preaching homilies, I constantly reminded people to live for the "now"—that the journey is its own reward. As I spent time with Monsignor Hayes on his 95th birthday, I kept thinking that time was passing by too quickly, and that I was just getting older and living the senior years of my life. I began to realize that the older I get the faster the years seem to go by, and I know I will never have those years back again.

"To be or not to be, that is the question. Whether tis nobler in the mind to suffer the slings and arrows of outrageous fortune, or take arms against a sea of troubles, and by opposing end them? ... For who would bear the whips and scorns of time, the oppressor's wrong, the law's delay, the insolence of office." — *Hamlet*; William Shakespeare

CHAPTER 66

THE EXPLOSION

On September 8, 2007, the birthday of the Virgin Mary, at nine in the morning my phone rang. I picked up the receiver and said, "Good morning."

The voice on the other end was that of my canon lawyer. "This is Father John."

I asked Father John how he was doing.

He said, untypically buoyant, "I feel terrific."

"Okay," I took the bait, "why do you feel terrific?"

"The Chief Canonist called," he said excitedly. "He said you are unanimously declared exonerated!"

After four years of pent-up stress and anxiety, like a pressure cooker, I exploded into a fit of yelling, screaming, and then crying. I shouted into the receiver at the top of my voice, "Yes! Yes! Yes! Thank you! Thank you! Thank you!" over and over again. This outburst must have lasted five minutes. Finally I calmed down and returned to a somewhat normal state. At this stage, I thought Father John had hung up on me, thinking I had gone mad, and he was probably in the process of calling 911. However, I discovered he was still on the other end patiently waiting for me to recover and reconnect to him.

Surprisingly, he appeared real calm and collected, and just proceeded to give me directions about what to do now.

"You're not to tell anyone," he said, "until the paperwork returns from Rome, accepted and approved with the Vatican seal."

He then told me not to worry and this was routine; however it may take three to four months for everything to transpire. He advised me to be patient, go on with my life and do all the normal things I was already doing.

Sure, this is easy for him to say, I said in my own mind. *My life will never be back to "normal" again.* And sure enough, I still have flashbacks and once in a while panic attacks.

I feel like my body is deflated like a balloon when you let all the air out. The "pent up" feeling is gone, but it is replaced with a collapsed mental exhaustion feeling. Sometimes a numb feeling overtakes my whole body and I feel it is vibrating with emotions of various types.

The conspiracy caused extraordinary damage to my health. Now, however, I was able to turn the "off" button in my brain and stop the insistent worrying; and at last I wasn't running from myself anymore. I was at peace being alone in my apartment, rather than constantly having to drive to the beach to find solace in the sound of the ebbing ocean. The dull, heavy feeling in my stomach had also dissipated.

Stress takes a terrible toll on the body and the mind; and it is said to shorten one's lifespan. Now I felt like a load had been lifted off my head and shoulders. A feeling of being free from the long psychological jail I was subjected to for going on five years. I could almost fly. Also, the dark cloud that engulfed me was slowly rising and I could see more clearly the sun shining again.

CHAPTER 67

MY CHRISTMAS WISH OF 2007

On September 8, 2007 I knew I was exonerated by the Paterson Diocese Ecclesiastical court. It was a unanimous decision of all three judges that I was totally innocent of all accusations made against me. However I was forbidden to announce it to the public until Rome responded with the Vatican seal of approval. Father Farley informed me that it could take three to four months before Rome would send to the diocese the "Innocent Document" sealed and signed by the Vatican officials. In the meantime, I sent Christmas cards to many of my former parishioners with a hidden message, indicating that I was exonerated. I wrote, "Don't give up five minutes before the miracle happens." This was a message I believed God revealed to me on a bumper sticker as I was driving my car on the Garden State Parkway. At the lowest moment of my life, when I felt like giving up, there in front of me appeared the above saying, "Don't give up five minutes before the miracle happens." From that moment on I felt encouraged, that God was with me, and He would see to it that my prayers and the prayers of many would be answered—except it would not literally be five minutes but five long years of darkness. Many of my former parishioners were encouraged and interpreted my Christmas wish as being positive.

The majority of my former parishioners never doubted for a moment that I was innocent; this is why it was with great joy I found the quotation from Proverbs 10:17: "Good people will be remembered as a blessing," and proudly wrote it on the front of my Christmas card. The people of St. Rose have always been a blessing to me. It would break my heart if I ever disappointed them, and it would also break their hearts. When I left St. Rose, I left my heart in that parish. With God's help, I will return to finally celebrate my fortieth anniversary and retirement. Then there will be an honorable closure to my ministry as pastor and all will be well. I left as a victim but returned as a victor. I left accused but returned vindicated.

But the waiting *still* was not over. Even though I had been unanimously exonerated by the three judges who participated in my canonical trial, it would be approximately five more months before the Vatican sanctioned the verdict and I could once again go in public as a totally "free man."

CHAPTER 68

COMING OUT THE OTHER SIDE

We were childhood lovers, an absolute close intimate relationship between us.

Every morning after awakening I went to my knees and carried on a close conversation with my creator; and every night before I went to bed I again went on my knees and worshiped Christ, my Lord, and savior. Finally after much preparation we decided to tie the knot. I totally committed my entire life to serving my Bride, the Church. I remember it as if it were yesterday. But it was June 8, 1963. I went to the altar and vowed my life to Christ, for better or worse, for richer or poorer; in fact for all eternity; a priest forever according to the order of Melchesideck.

Jesus had asked me to give up my father and mother, my brothers and sisters, and follow Him. That I did without hesitation. It was a perfect marriage and I couldn't be happier. I was blessed with many children through spiritual birth. Today after forty years of bliss, Jesus and I decided to spend more intimate time together, somewhat removed from the daily grind of life, sometimes serving my Bride mechanically, doing a lot of holy things—working morning until night—but never becoming holy. Too busy with the kids, God's people, and in a way putting Christ on the back burner of my life. So the time came for more intimate quality time with my Bride, the Church, Christ himself.

Then a tragedy happened against my will and we were forced to separate. The powers on earth became my judge, jury, and executioner; and decided I was not worthy to be the servant of the Church. In fact, I was declared a danger to the people of God, and my Bride, the Church. I was forced to leave my family and go into exile. It was the darkest time of my life. A restraining order was issued against me as it were; never to go near my family, the parish, in any way.

I became a *persona non grata*. I pined night and day for my beautiful Bride, as Saint Paul described her as beautiful and undefiled—she was forever young. I was falsely accused of violating the most innocent of my parish family and I felt totally helpless to prove my innocence. It was totally against my nature. Jesus had told us, "Let the little children come to Me for theirs is the kingdom of heaven." To me they were the most innocent of God's creatures and, I was especially called to protect them and educate them in the things of God.

Now at the end of my days, I was accused of doing the opposite. My life was in a fog of confusion—how could this happen? I was plunged into severe depression; isolated and alone. My reputation ruined; my heart and my life scarred for life.

In Corinthians 15:51-52, I get comfort: "I shall be changed in a moment—in the twinkling of an eye." I will have arrived at the other side of the storm, asking myself: "How did I make it through to the other side? How has this ordeal transformed me? What will I know then that I did not know before?" I have gone through the fire of purification and come out cleansed of pride and arrogance, and have achieved a new level of humility. The unexpected I hope will have come into my life in the form of virtues, empathy, and compassion. I felt it's wounding and scourging at the pillar of life, by the hands of so-called leaders of God's people. But with patient endurance and "stick-to-itiveness" a wonderful beauty was born, especially empathy for other's sufferings. I am sure if, God forbid, in the future, I have to face dark times again, my previous experience will help make what I have to endure a lot less frightening.

Often it's the confrontation with what appears to be unsolvable that changes and renews us. When I was falsely accused I was plunged into sorrow and despair; but in a strange way I eventually awakened to a new me in spite of the fact that in my time of indescribable sorrow, I could not even imagine ever being happy again. I was irrevocably changed. Indeed in the past it comes to mind, times I felt so physically sick, I could never imagine ever feeling healthy and well again, and yet I did and then I could never imagine being so sick.

There comes to mind, times I suffered from debilitating migraine headaches that were almost beyond my physical endurance. There was a time when no medication was available to ease my migraine headaches. The best advice doctors had to offer was to go into a quiet dark place in total silence for several days. Fortunately, medical science came up with a smart drug named Imetrex. This nose spray went right to the source of the migraine and eliminated the pain. It changed my life. I no longer went about terrified of doing anything that would initiate the migraines; for instance, eating the wrong foods such as chocolate; or in my particular case, not protecting my head from cold weather. Consequently, during the entire winter I wore a warm cap and it protected me most of the time from the onset of the monster headache. Doctors finally discovered the cause of migraine. Supposedly the blood vessel in the back of one's neck constricts and in certain circumstances puts pressure on the brain causing immense pain. Now, thank God, many drugs are available that release the restriction of blood vessels and restore everything to normal, and stop the headache almost immediately. Now, thank God, I can't even remember the last time I got a migraine.

To return to the point I was making, when I felt that unbearable pain, I could not imagine feeling normal again; but as I mentioned before, I did, and then couldn't remember being so sick. My heart still hurts from the accusation. There is a grief that has not left me. I know, of course, this book would not be written if I had not been forced to dig so deeply into my innermost being.

With God's help someday, when I have gone through my own challenges and difficulties and come out at the other side, it is my full intention to reach out to other priests falsely accused, and I will have something priceless to share—my strength and my insight with those unfortunate priests. There is a certain maturity gained from having experienced so many struggles from the depths of my being as I have traveled the path of my own personal transformation. This is one of the most important discoveries about navigating those challenging times. Like a sailor coming home from a rough crossing, I look back at the treacherous seas I have crossed. At first emerging from the darkness, my eyes are still unaccustomed to bright light. I obviously have been on a journey that tested my inner strength. Suddenly I realize, the fog has lifted and the future looks clear. I feel more alive than ever.

As I look at the beauty of the earth, I must not forget that the beauty didn't just suddenly appear. Our mother earth has been tested, crushed, cracked, and shattered. Yet the effects of these difficulties have created some of the most breathtaking images imaginable. I would like to share with you a true story. In the early days of my priesthood, I traveled from America to perform the marriage of my nephew Carl and his beautiful fiancé. The marriage took place in the local church in Westport Co., Mayo. I expected the reception to take place in a restaurant close by.

However, my sister Vera, the mother of the groom, informed me that the reception was twenty miles away in Clifton, Connamara. At first, I was annoyed. Why travel so far when there are so many nice reception places close to the church? To make a long story short, we started out on our journey over the narrow twisting roads over rough mountain ranges to Clifton. Suddenly I realized we were entering a magical wonderland area of what must be Mother Nature's greatest creation—the sights of the rugged mountain sides reflecting several shades of green, brown, and yellow. The various shapes and sizes of the terrain made the twenty-mile journey to Clifton absolutely unmatchable to any place in the world. I was traveling with a friend, Jim Tunny, from America, and we were both mesmerized and couldn't believe such beauty could exist. We felt like we had landed on a different planet. We couldn't help but think about the fierce disruptive force of nature that created this sight that filled our hearts with wonder and awe. When we finally arrived at the reception, we couldn't help but exuberantly praise my sister for practically forcing us to go twenty miles that turned out to be one of life's exquisite gifts of nature's beauty for the both of us—an experience Jim and I still talk about thirty years later.

Strange, as I go through my own turbulent, shattered, crushed experience of my life, remembering what earthly violence must have produced that magical place in Connamara, I am reminded of the emotional earthquakes forming my existence and how I must have changed; creating hopefully an interesting, unusual personality that inspires others with what I have to offer. A lesson the earth of Connamara taught me, as Elizabeth Kubler-Ross aptly put it: "Should you shield the canyons from the windstorms, you would not see the beauty of their carvings."

My heart has its own canyons carved by grief and my heart is broken by the terrible accusation leveled against me. Consequently, I am wounded to the core and scarred in every aspect of my emotional life. I hope I can turn my scars into stars and be a shining light to dispel the darkness of the suffering of others. I no longer hide my scars, so others can see how you can survive near death experiences and learn from them; life does not end but merely changes. When other people notice scars in my personality, when they notice that something traumatic must have happened to me, I tell them the remarkable battle I fought and won—not without being severely psychologically wounded. I fought the war waged against me by the Goliath of the diocese. I won the war and won the fight. So I embrace my scars when others notice them; proudly saying these tell the remarkable story of how I was made brave and wise. By staying the course and not throwing in the towel; always trusting that there is life, hope, and renewal—even when it appears there is none.

We live in turbulent times masked by the almost universal war of radical Muslims and suicide bombers. People are in constant fear of a terrorist attack, especially in the big cities of America. Add to that the turbulence in the Church. It is easy to despair. Hatred penetrates mankind, causing unimaginable pain and suffering. We are at the heart of a brokenhearted world in which all of us have suffered trauma and experienced the most intense forms of grief, fear, and despair. A healed life is always a work in progress;

not a life devoid of all traces of suffering, but a life lived deeply, authentically, and compassionately at the same time.

I was accused of abusing two little sisters—all concocted in a conspiracy to destroy me: two women, unrelated to the sisters, angry at me because one's mother had chosen to endow me with $25,000 in her will; which I gave to charity. They saw their chance to destroy me, by throwing me into the pit of the pedophile scandal rocking the church. So they sold me out to the legal and ecclesiastical authorities accusing me of a false crime and enslaving me against my will. I was isolated and driven out of my parish family—forced to live a long depressing life, instead of what should have been my glorious retirement years.

I live now in a purgatorial world waiting for my freedom; a chance to start over, getting a new life, a fresh start. I must put my life back together again. Sometimes I feel like Humpty Dumpty—so fragmented that nothing can put me back together. C.S. Lewis once said, "God whispers to us in our pleasure, but he shouts to us in our pain."

* * *

I sometimes question why God is taking so long to rescue me from my dilemma. Winter is approaching and my canon lawyer, Father Farley tells me there still is no final verdict from Rome. That means living through this darkness in my little apartment during the months of November and December unable to escape to the beach where I was usually able to find solace and a little peace. I realized how difficult waiting can be. I have to say though, that the situation I find myself caught in, has offered me some benefit. For one thing, it's showing me so clearly I am not the master of time. Time is its own master and has its own space. It's a reality I have to accept. When God makes a way for me—that way takes time which requires patience on my part—and as I mentioned earlier, patience is my weakest virtue.

Father Farley, my ecclesiastical attorney is like a turtle, and I am like a butterfly. Father Farley is traveling at the rate of twenty-five miles an hour and I am traveling at the rate of one hundred miles an hour. I am addicted to shortcuts and quick fixes; however gradually I am seeing the wisdom of the slow pace of Father Farley. As time goes on, gradually but surely things and facts are revealed that favor my position, as I am forced to slow down and more and more see the wisdom of God. As philosophers say, "Those things that have immediate payoffs and results tend not to be as important in the long run, and things that move slowly, prove to be more significant."

Obviously, God is often making a way for me when I cannot even see his hand at work As this case drags out and it seems nothing is happening on my behalf, I am beginning to gradually realize that it is a gift of faith to be able to trust that God is at work in my frantic efforts to prove my innocence. I guess I am beginning to learn that I must wait without trying to rush God's time table. I am told that tolerating God's pace of time is the biggest part of an ultimate solution for the better. As time goes on, hidden facts have come out that clearly show my innocence; whereas if I had rushed the case, I may have missed the chance to clearly demonstrate my *total* innocence.

I am sure that people hearing my story for the first time must be very confused. My case is a multiple series of twists and turns and requires great patience and intelligence to sort out the story in its pure state. I remember one civil attorney recommended to me was an elderly man who fell asleep during my sincere attempt to give all the facts. I left his office totally deflated and discouraged. Here my priestly life was at stake and this guy appeared he could not care less. I obviously left that office, never to return.

One lawyer, George D., a former prosecutor said as I left his office, "Father McCarthy, after only speaking to you for fifteen minutes I am convinced of your innocence." I asked him how he could be so sure in such a short while. He said, "It was simple once I discovered that you called DYFS (Division of Youth and Family Services) to have the family investigated for possible abuse. I don't have to be a brain surgeon to know that someone who was accused of molesting two little sisters would either have to be incredibly dumb, or crazy, to call DYFS to have the very family he was being accused of molesting investigated. Obviously, if you had committed this horrific crime, your name would surface as the prime target of the investigation." Attorney George D. was the first person to give me hope. Now he is also anxiously "waiting in the wings" to hear the result of the ecclesiastical trial.

* * *

Some concepts in this section were inspired by three books:

How Did I Get Here (Barbara DeAngelis)
God's Answers To Life's Difficult Questions (Rick Warren)
God Will Make a Way (Dr. Henry Cloud and Dr. John Townsend)

These three books helped me greatly with my predicament. These books I highly recommend to anybody struggling with life's problems.

In the past, during my active ministry in the priesthood, often people would mention: "Father, your words today were specifically directed at me and have helped me immensely to deal with the problems I am going through. I felt you were talking directly to me. God answered my prayers and pleadings through you. Than you so much, Father. Now I will go home with a lighter burden and with greater insight as to how God is helping me. I no longer feel He has abandoned me."

Afterwards, I would thank God for using me to help people in stress. I felt privileged to have been chosen to be an instrument of God's healing. Now that I am suffering myself, I am more sensitive to the unseen hand of God in bringing me through the valley of darkness, and I see that I am not alone.

Little did those authors know they were writing for me? Some having a greater impact than others—some so absolutely profound that I have no doubt that God lead me to their books, and very often in the most unusual circumstances. In a maze of books in a books store, there was this one staring out at me; especially at times of my lowest moments. There was God walking by my side, leading me to the answer. Not hitting me over my head with a "two-by-four" but gently soothing my pain almost unconsciously through the surprising words of a particular author—sometimes leading me toward a greater awareness of God's interest in little me, a speck on the planet. I feel like asking, "How did I stumble on these books?" The answer comes to me loud and clear. I found these books and others, through the invisible hand of God.

Let me close with a poem that sums up what I've been trying to say:

UNEARTHED STRENGTH

I ask for health, that I might do better things;
I was given infirmity, that I might achieve greater things.
I asked for riches, that I might be happy;
I was given poverty, that I might be wise.
I asked for power, that I might have the praise of people;
I was given weakness, that I might feel the need of God.
I asked for all things, that I might enjoy life;
I was given life, that I might enjoy all things.
I got nothing I asked for, but everything I hoped for.
Almost despite myself, my unspoken prayers were answered.
I am among all people most richly blessed.

— Unknown Confederate Soldier

CHAPTER 69

TEARS OF SADNESS (THE BLUES)

Again feeling down, lonely, sad and blue, all alone in my little apartment; it is nine p.m., October 20, 2007. Immediately I turn the television to CNN. As usual, Larry King has a powerful story of survival that helps me beat the blues. His interview is with the rock legend, Eric Clapton.

Eric Clapton is one of my favorite guitarist-singers. I had no idea that his talent grew out of the pain in his life, just like the thorn bird who sings her best after being impaled by a thorn. Born illegitimate and raised by his grandparents, Eric never knew his mother until the age of nine. As a child, he found comfort playing the guitar; and eventually he became a worldwide superstar. His most enduring song was *Layla*. However, a failed love affair led him to the depths of despair, self-imposed seclusion, and a drug addiction to heroin. In time he beat his addictions, got married, and became a father. But as his life was rebounding, he was again tortured—by a horrible accident. His little four-year-old son, Connor, fell out of a penthouse window of a hotel in New York City and died instantly. Instead of once again killing his pain with drugs, this time Eric took refuge in his music, producing his most mournful and most beautiful song: *Tears in Heaven*. Clapton went on to achieve the pinnacle of success despite extraordinary sadness.

His compelling story helped me tremendously to beat the blues in my own life. It was another little morsel of encouragement to stay the course and live another day, one day at a time. Listening to the dark side of a famous person's life is both a reality check and a quick cure for the blues. It works like a charm every time. When thrown off course, it seems there are two kinds of people: there are the "hand wringers," while the others roll their sleeves up and plow full speed ahead. I must constantly try to be a "plow person" and plug my way through the muck of life. It's the only way to get out of this mess, to chase the negative thoughts out of my head and gain a little satisfaction through the process of making order out of chaos.

Another relief is observing the trees changing colors this autumn. Encouraging myself with these little challenges of self-improvement is lots of "good medicine" for my doldrums and low moments. It is a way to get out of being in the dumps. I have a tendency to wallow in the blues; it's my addiction. In a funny way, I think I take some odd pleasure in it. Maybe I need to go to some kind of rehab since it seems to work for the Hollywood crowd.

*   *   *

My friend, Father Bob, decided to get a dog from the local pound and bring it home. For a while everything was fine; but soon the dog got very possessive and began to attack people going to the rectory. So Father Bob knew he had to get rid of the dog. What was he to do? He would be forced to put it to sleep. As was typical of him, Father Bob started to pray for a solution. One day while walking the dog in the parking lot, a car on the street slams on the brakes, pulls in to the lot, and a little girl runs out yelling, "Brownie! Brownie!" Turns out it was her former pet that had been lost and she wanted him back. Father Bob's prayers were answered. A coincidence? Very unlikely.

The idea of my having a dog is out of the question. Pets are not allowed in my apartment complex—so much for having a companion dog. Consequently, I will have to live with having a bout of the blues once in a while.

*   *   *

I am back to feeling the blues; asking myself all kinds of scary questions: "What's going on? Haven't I waited long enough? Have they changed their minds?" Nine months since the trial, now two more months have passed and I am again experiencing the blues, and once again back to waiting and worrying.

This brings me back to where I began with Eric Clapton. He fought off the blues in his life with every ounce of energy he had. He kept climbing that mountain of drugs and alcohol, also going up two steps and falling back ten. Similar to my journey as earlier described, he too kept climbing. Now, finally at the top of the mountain, he is honored as one of the world's greatest survivors. With God's help, I will reach the top of my mountain. Totally exonerated and free; I too will be a survivor. Finally, I'll be able to stop crying after almost drowning in an ocean of tears.

CHAPTER 70

THE TELEPHONE CALL

On October 30, 2007, a high official of the diocese called me on the telephone, to confirm what Fr. John had told me over a month earlier. He said, "Mark this moment on your calendar. All three judges have signed the document of exoneration and they are in my possession."

He went on to say his secretary would need to Federal Express everything to the Vatican for their stamp of approval. I was elated that I was finally on the threshold of freedom. There was only one minor obstacle in my way to be restored to my full priesthood: Now I would just have to wait for the actual document sealed by the Vatican.

The diocesan official assured me this should take no more than roughly two months. God is great, praise Him from whom all blessings flow. In roughly 60 days I will get to feel *completely* vindicated.

Psalm 25-27: "May those who delight in my vindication shout for joy and gladness. May they always say, 'The Lord should be exalted who delight in the well being of his servant.' My tongue will speak of your righteousness and of your praises all day long."

Psalm 33:11: "The Lord is close to the brokenhearted and saves those who are crushed in spirit."

You would think that after waiting five years, two more months would be like a walk in the park? But you know me…the epitome of impatience…and besides, as I know from experience, a lot can happen in sixty days…

CHAPTER 71

JOYFUL

In the midst of all the trouble and strife in the world, how could God possibly expect us to "Be joyful always"? (1 Thess. 5:16) After all, when you have hit bottom in life, is it really possible to be joyful?

According to the apostle Paul, the answer is "Yes." In Paul's letter to the church at Philippe, he uses the words "joy" or "rejoice" over and over again even though he was languishing in jail at the time, and chained to a Roman guard while awaiting trial.

How could Paul speak of joy in the midst of that trial? During my ecclesiastical trial I was practically numb and almost in denial that this could be happening to me. Paul, however, remained joyful because he firmly believed that joy doesn't depend on our circumstances, but on God and our relationship to Him. In the book of Philippians, Paul outlines seven good reasons why even in the midst of trouble we should live our lives with great joy:

1. God, who began a good work in you, will carry it on to completion.

2. God works in you to will and to act according to His good pleasure.

3. God will give you grace to be always forgetting what is behind and straining toward what is ahead.

4. You don't have to be anxious about anything; but in everything, by prayer and petition, with thanksgiving, present your requests to God.

5. The peace of God, which transcends all understanding, will guard your heart and mind.

6. You can do everything through Him who gives you strength.

7. God will meet all your needs according to His glorious riches in Christ Jesus.

Consequently, in the midst of my ordeal, I too am confident that God will see to it that justice will prevail. I will eventually be exonerated. "The truth will set me free."

CHAPTER 72

THE SACRED HEART

I pray that 2008 is my very best year yet. May I be greatly blessed in the days and months to come as I grow closer to the Lord and allow Him to fulfill His purpose in my life. When I received a Christmas card in 2007 from a priest friend, and he wrote me these ten words: "I know that 2008 will be the best year of your life," I knew God inspired him to say this. After five years of darkness light was finally about to break through. I felt the power of the Sacred Heart of Jesus getting stronger and stronger. The shrine in my little apartment became my constant refuge. I constantly knelt on my knees before a picture of the Sacred Heart of Jesus—with a round white light—a globe burning steadily for five years. I must have changed every bulb in my apartment, but that bulb never died. It is as bright today as it was then. It is only a tiny bulb inside a white globe, but it still endures. That shrine is a holy place that puts me in touch with the presence of my loving Jesus. I feel safe there. I know I am in the safe hands of God. I look into His eyes and He looks into mine. Prayer has always been part of my life but now it *is* my life. Prayer has chosen me as my new way of life. I no longer feel alone, I feel the presence of Jesus. I feel the comfort of a mother, secure and confident.

In the past I was like a car in neutral. I would put my foot on the gas pedal but I was going no place. Now I know where I am going, I am on my way to freedom. I am riding into the light of grace and I can almost taste the amazing feeling of contentment. I am a survivor. The picture of the Sacred Heart has been part of my life since I was a child. It hung on the kitchen wall of my childhood home forever. It too had a little red light that no one remembers ever changing. I remember in the seminary carpentry workroom making a little wooden shrine for that light. That was back in the 1960s and it is still there. I had somewhat of a connection to it, but never like now. Now it has come alive and when I pray on my knees in front of that picture, I feel a real and powerful connection to the loving heart of Jesus.

Ultimately I know that my explanation of surviving the extreme attack on my very existence requires a connection to my personal Lord and Savior—my beloved Sacred Heart.

For a while I just lived on the edge of survival. It was my trust in the Sacred Heart of Jesus that helped me over the threshold to the end of my struggle; to survive the awful attack on who I was as a human being, and especially as a priest. I constantly went on my knees before the picture of the Sacred Heart of Jesus pleading, "Dear Jesus, my dear Sacred Heart, send your spirit of wisdom and strength to help me survive the final journey out of the darkness into the light of freedom and normalcy. I surrender my future to you. Please dear Sacred Heart; strengthen me in my efforts to bring my future dreams to fruition; that I will return in triumph to my beloved St. Rose of Lima to celebrate my long awaited retirement.

I left as a victim and I return as a victor. I am sprinting as hard as I can toward the finish line. I see it in sight and it pushes me forward. Dear Sacred Heart, be the wind beneath my wings, for I am exhausted, barely surviving and anxious I won't make it. Please dear Sacred Heart; don't give up now that I have come so far. The final sprint is the hardest because I am at my most tired. Five years of indescribable determination; the human spirit can only survive so long. But with the inspiration of the Holy Spirit, my human nature is encouraged by my supernatural nature. If I make it to the finish line, it will be a supernatural achievement—far beyond human endurance."

My constant mantra: "Dear Sacred Heart, bring me over the finish line in triumph."

My heart is aching with anticipation. What will it be like to be at peace again?

YEAR SIX (2008)

CHAPTER 73

FULL CIRCLE AND BEYOND

After being falsely accused of a despicable act; after my former bishop and his associates rushed to judgment and made an attempt to permanently remove me from the priesthood by asking Pope John Paul II to laicize me; I was exonerated by an ecclesiastical trial and unanimously declared totally innocent.

Following this judicial declaration, my *present* bishop, Bishop Serratelli wrote a letter to my successor, the current pastor of my beloved St. Rose of Lima Parish, conferring on me, now and forever, a title that translates as "a pastor retired with honor." I am deeply grateful to Bishop Serratelli for his kindness to me—in my regard, he is a bishop second to none. And now, thanks to him, this title will *permanently* appear in the parish bulletin underneath the name of the present pastor: *Monsignor William McCarthy, Pastor Emeritus.*

"Emeritus" is defined by Webster's dictionary as "a title for a person retired, but retaining one's title as an honor." The word "emeritus" is derived from the Latin *merere*, meaning "to earn or deserve." I am proud to have that title conferred upon me by Bishop Serratelli. I consider it to be delayed justice or full retribution for the evil done to me by my former bishop and three of his associates in the Chancery Office, who ignored my presumption of innocence, and the violation of canon law in the process as well.

To add to my joy of full-circle restoration to my priesthood, I received another special honor. Since I now reside within the diocese in Mechuchen, the presiding bishop, Paul G. Bootkowski, has received me into his diocese as an "Extem Priest," a canonical title meaning "Welcomed from another diocese." In fact, I am the only priest accepted into that diocese while belonging in good standing to another diocese. In effect, I am approved and welcomed canonically by two dioceses—a unique privilege, which explains the title of this chapter, Full Circle and *Beyond.*

CHAPTER 74

MONSIGNOR McCARTHY: FALSELY ACCUSED!

NEWSPAPER ARTICLE [EXCERPTED]:

After a five year ordeal of living under a cloud of suspicion, Monsignor William McCarthy, former pastor of St. Rose of Lima Church, East Hanover, New Jersey has been formally and finally exonerated of any wrongdoing in a case by a canon law court, by unanimous decision. Monsignor William McCarthy was unjustly accused of abuse of two sisters around five or six years of age in 1980, in the presence of their mother. Monsignor McCarthy has never been accused of any other improper conduct throughout his unblemished forty year career of service as a priest.

...Monsignor McCarthy's ordeal began shortly after he retired... as pastor of St. Rose of Lima Church. An anonymous letter alleging misconduct by him was [sent] to the county prosecutor. Although anonymous allegations proved baseless, an over-zealous detective pursued the case without regard for the reputation of Monsignor McCarthy... [even though]the mother [of the children]had denied that any inappropriate touching ever took place...

...The canonical trial was finally conducted in 2007. This deliberative process of calling witnesses before three judges concluded with their unanimous finding that Monsignor McCarthy was innocent and thus exonerated. Bishop Serratelli agreed with the findings and on November 21, 2007, forwarded them to Vatican for final approval. On April 28, 2008, the Vatican accepted the findings.

...Now Monsignor McCarthy looks forward to returning to St. Rose of Lima Church to celebrate his fortieth anniversary and retirement; plans that were put on hold five years ago when this nightmare began. Throughout this time, he never lost his faith in God's ultimate plan...

CHAPTER 75

THE MEDIA

I was exonerated and suddenly out of nowhere, the media began calling me on the phone. They were excited and anxious to interview me. They treated me like some kind of hero; I was totally surprised and pleased.

I was always of the opinion that when you are accused, you get smeared all over the front page of the newspapers, but when you are innocent, you end up in the corner of the back pages of the papers. However, I found the opposite was the case. My story was front page news!

I got a call from NBC-TV, Channel 4, asking me for an interview. They said they were on their way to my apartment and that they would arrive in an hour. Sure enough, they showed up at my front door with all of their equipment and came upstairs to my living room. Anchor woman, Pat Battle, sat down next to me and began asking me all the pertinent questions while the cameraman was zooming his camera around my apartment. He was talented, and while listening to the anchor woman's questions, he would focus his camera on areas that gave significance to what she was asking me. For example, while I was explaining that I celebrated a private mass on my dining room table, he took a shot of my chalice on the table along with the sacramentary and bible, and a shot of my vestments hanging on the dining room door. As I explained to Pat Battle how I prayed night and morning at a shrine to The Sacred Heart of Jesus, and how I knelt on a kneeler in front of the shrine, he zoomed in on that too.

When I finally saw the interview on the six o' clock news, I found it uplifting and inspiring; and it was far beyond my expectations. She intertwined the story of Cardinal Ratzinger and Pope Benedict XVI with his arms outstretched. It was most tastefully done and I was absolutely grateful to Pat Battle and her cameraman for their great performance.

After the feature aired, I was inundated with compliments from many people. The local newspapers likewise were excited and pleased for me. All of them gave me top front page placement.

The Star Ledger (Sat. May 3, 2008): "VATICAN CLEARS EAST HANOVER PRIEST OF ABUSE CHARGES"

The Morristown Record is known as an anti-Catholic paper, yet in my case their article was balanced and fair.

The Beacon, my very own diocesan paper, left a lot to be desired. When the accusation was first reported, it was smeared all over the front page of the paper, implying guilt with no reserve whatsoever. However, when I was proven innocent, the *Beacon* responded in the form of a very small restricted article on the fifteenth page. Many people protested. But the only response *The Beacon* offered was: "To have elaborated on the history of the case would only have served to once again cast a negative slant on the priesthood."

But, thank God, I did get some excellent coverage. *The Hanover Eagle* was the most explicit of them all. Across the front page in big block letters was the heading: "INNOCENT" — I have excerpted it as follows:

Hanover Eagle and Regional Weekly News [EXCERPTED]

Headline:

INNOCENT

Church reinstates former St. Rose pastor after rejecting sexual abuse charges.

EAST HANOVER TWP. - The Vatican has closed the case on Monsignor William McCarthy, the long-time priest of St. Rose of Lima Church...by completely exonerating him...[and] rejecting allegations he had sexually abused two little sisters in the 1980s.

...In a statement, [Bishop]Seratelli said, "Six years ago, allegations were made against Monsignor William McCarthy. A Church Tribunal, composed of canon lawyers from outside the diocese, concluded that it was not proven that he was guilty of the charge alleged against him. The Holy See has determined that the case is closed. Monsignor McCarthy is a priest in good standing and is free to exercise his priestly ministry as a retired priest..."

...The allegations against McCarthy surfaced in 2003 shortly after...[he] had retired as pastor of St. Rose when two women claimed he had molested them as children in the 1980s.

In a statement, Monsignor McCarthy said he was "unjustly accused of the abuse of two sisters around 6 or 7 years of age in 1980...

"I have never been accused of any other improper conduct throughout my unblemished 40-year career of service as a priest...

"My ordeal began shortly after an anonymous letter alleging misconduct by me was [sent to] the county prosecutor...

"Although the allegations proved baseless, an overzealous detective pursued the case without regard for my reputation...

"Moreover, the mother has denied that any inappropriate touching ever took place either at that meeting or thereafter..."

On April 28, the Vatican accepted the Paterson Diocese finding that McCarthy was innocent...

* * *

To follow are random samples of letters I received at or around my celebration on June 8, 2008. [EXCERPTED] I received hundreds of letters, so it was not possible to include all of them.

May 1, 2008

Dear Monsignor McCarthy,

Guy and I are absolutely over the moon with happiness. Finally the case is closed and you can reclaim your life. It never, never should have happened.

...Outside church this morning, everyone was smiling and talking about this fantastic news; we were all so happy for you, some with tears in our eyes. I can't tell you the wonderful feeling to know that you are able to return to your priestly duties.

...May the Good Lord fill your future with an abundance of blessings,

Anne Marie and Guy

*   *   *

Dear Father Bill,

...Isn't it true: "Delight yourself in the Lord and He will grant you the desires of your heart." Psalm 37:4

Your victory over this act of evil is our great joy! I know God must be saying, "Well done, good and faithful servant."

...You have demonstrated the deepest faith, greatest patience, and perseverance of Job. Therefore may you be blessed ten thousand fold for the months and years of anguish, sorrow and great suffering. Welcome now sunshine and happiness like a beautiful rainbow after a brutal storm.

All our love,
Theresa, Tom, and Anna

*   *   *

Our dearest Monsignor McCarthy,

...God Bless you as you celebrate your 40th anniversary. May He walk beside you and keep you in His heart always, and may He reward you abundantly for your untiring and unconditional dedication, devotion, and love to all those lives you touched.

With love and our best wishes,
Narie and Gerry

*   *   *

Dear Father McCarthy,

Congratulations on your 40th anniversary as a priest. We are grateful for all you loving support and encouragement to our family for so many years. There was never a moment we had a doubt of your total dedication and devotion to your office of priesthood.

...Always remember that there are many more good people in the world than bad. And like you taught us, in the end good always triumphs.

We love you always,
Deborah, Phil, Chris, Andrew, Kathryn, Sarah, Breana

* * *

Hi Father,
Wow! What a wonderful day. We are so very happy for you. I know Our Lord was holding you in the "Palm of His hand." Everyone was so excited, just as if we were waiting to see the Pope...

God Bless You!
Rosemary and Frank

* * *

Dear Monsignor McCarthy,
...Celebrating your achievement! Every day is a wonderful chance to be what you've dreamed... to do what you've imagined. Congratulations on making your dream come true.

With our love,
Bill and Pat

CHAPTER 76

THE WEEK THAT WAS

My canonical trial began the week of January 23, 2007. I testified before the panel of three judges on January 30, 2007. On the week of Saturday, September 8, 2007 a call came from my canon lawyer, Father Farley, that I was exonerated unanimously. Six months went by—between the start of the canonical trail on January 23, 2007 to September 8, 2007. Six months of psychological torture. From September 8, 2007, to October 30, 2007, the chief canonist collected all the signatures of those participating in the trial and sent the package of documents to the Vatican congregation for the defense of faith on October 31, 2007.

I waited for results from Rome from the first week of November 2007 until the week of April 28, 2008; approximately five months. The diocese sent emails to all the priests of the diocese making a public announcement that Monsignor McCarthy was exonerated and fully restored to the priesthood—a retired priest in good standing.

Finally back home to the priesthood, my first priestly ministry was at my priest friend's church in Sparta, New Jersey, Our Lady of the Lake. I participated with Bishop Serratelli and many priests at the confirmation ceremony and I publicly distributed Communion to the congregation.

On the week of May 4, 2008 at all the weekend masses at all the churches I served in for forty years, a public announcement was made by the pastors; reading the statement that follows:

"Six years ago, allegations were made against Monsignor William McCarthy. A Church Tribunal, composed of canon lawyers from outside the diocese, concluded that it was not proven that he was guilty of the charge alleged against him. The Holy See has determined that the case is closed. Monsignor McCarthy is a priest in good standing and is free to exercise his priestly ministry as a retired priest. During this very difficult time in his life, Monsignor McCarthy has been totally cooperative, faithful to his priesthood, and shown a great love for the Church."

*   *   *

The weekend of May 4, 2008 was a weekend of everlasting remembrance; a weekend of profound impact—a weekend in which I became a celebrity of sorts…all over the newspapers and featured as a special on Channel 4 NBC. The media seemed genuinely happy to announce to the world that just because a priest was accused does not mean that he is guilty—but in fact as in my case was totally innocent; the victim of a possible conspiracy. Now, finally after a wait of over five years since that detective walked into my office that fateful day of February 8, 2003 and unjustly accused me of a horrific crime.

The dictionary defines fateful as an event controlled by fate. The dictionary defines fate as supposed power predetermining an individual's destiny—preordained. Was this supposed to happen? In order to produce an ending, that the world would finally learn about and rejoice as a kind of resurrection—I was dead and buried in the darkest place imaginable. Now I have risen from that place and am fully alive, having gone full circle, and I have come out the other side, with the unfolding of events that are mind-boggling…a journey of epic proportions. I am back from where I started; with preparations for a celebration of my retirement and the fortieth anniversary preparations that were put on hold for over five brutal, torturous years.

There will be no closure to that five year saga until that celebration is carried out and completed with God's help.

CHAPTER 77

HOMECOMING CELEBRATION

(A Hero's Welcome)

Sunday, June 8, 2008; twelve noon at St. Rose of Lima Church in East Hanover N.J. For the first time in five years, I stood at my former altar and celebrated a Mass of Thanksgiving. It was particularly poignant for me, as it brought closure to over five years of torture. At least a thousand people came out for the occasion. Many cars were turned back—there were no parking places left anywhere in East Hanover. It was an exciting, exhilarating event for the entire community. The following is the homily I preached at the Thanksgiving Mass:

"Brothers and sisters, Abraham believed that he would become the father of a great nation. It was always in God's plan that through Abraham, Esrael was going to become a great nation. They would be trapped in slavery for four hundred years and God promised they would come out with great substance. We have a God who knows how to get you back home. We have a God with a divine strategy. God is so strategic that he will use adversity to maneuver us, to put us in the right place at the right time. I could not believe that I could have served Him faithfully for forty years, and now he was abandoning me. But the bible says to rejoice when you are falsely accused; for great is your reward in Heaven. For God had a strategy to bring me out, when God sees you are taking Him for granted he will allow an enemy to afflict you. When we see the enemy coming we should rejoice. The more the enemy afflicted me the stronger my faith became.

1. I am still here.

2. Still standing.

3. I feel I was not treated fairly but I am still here.

4. I cried myself to sleep, but I am still here.

5. Somehow I have more joy than I ever had before.

6. I feel God's presence more than I ever felt before.

7. I am closer to the suffering Christ than I ever was before.

8. Satan meant it for evil, but God meant it for good.

9. Isn't it funny – the more that is taken away from us, a deeper relationship we have with God.

10. Isn't it funny – when a person loses their sight, their hearing increases. It's strange how God allows something to be taken away from us, but then allows another thing in our life to become more valuable.

11. So without grieving for what we have lost, we begin to appreciate what we have left.

12. God has something better for me than the situation I have been struggling with.

God allows trouble to come to us to bless us. In fact, we can't have victory without conflict. God always has an exit strategy. He told Abraham, 'I wasn't going to bring you into it, if I wasn't going to get you out.'

Lazarus was dead four days and entombed before Jesus came. Jesus said, 'Remove the stone.' Lazarus's sister said, 'By now he stinks!' Jesus said, 'Did I not tell you, if you believe, you will see the glory of God?' Then Jesus said, 'Lazarus, come forth.' He told the disciples to untie him and let him go.

Jesus had an exit strategy for Lazarus. He was trapped, now he was free. Can you imagine what it is like for the innocent fish in the blue ocean playing in the reef and the coral and suddenly the fisherman drops his net and they are trapped? Can you imagine an innocent bird flying freely in the sky looking for a place to land? Suddenly he lands on a spot, in the wrong place at the wrong time, and is trapped in the snare of the fowler. Feathers fly and it is the end of a beautiful song. An awful thing to be trapped; when you're trapped you are in trouble. Your soul slips down to the bowels of the earth.

In New Orleans, in the Katrina debacle, all the people were jammed into the Superdome. Trapped, water all around; can't get out; no food, no restrooms; laying on feces and urine... 'Trapped!' ... Innocent people. On 9/11, two planes crash into the twin towers and all those people were trapped. It's an awful thing to be trapped...trapped in the fowler's snare, trapped in the fisherman's net, trapped in the Superdome, and trapped in the Twin Towers.

One day I went into my apartment and found it infested with cockroaches. In my clothes, bed, kitchen, ceiling...the maintenance man sprayed and told me to get Clorox, mix it with water, and sprinkle it about. I went to the hardware store—they gave me a box and I sprinkled it around and in two days the cockroaches were gone. I went back to the hardware store and bought several boxes, knocked on several apartment doors and gave them a box. Soon, the entire block was free of cockroaches. They now call me 'The Terminator... hasta la vista, baby.' God provided an exit strategy.

Have you ever been trapped? I was viciously attacked by a false accusation that destroyed my good name, my health, my reputation. I felt helpless—I was trapped. The attack on me had a ripple effect—like dropping a stone in a pool that ripples—going out and out scandalizing the children in our beautiful school run by our wonderful principal, Sister Rita, and then it spread to our child care center directed by the extraordinary, wonderful director, Irene Monteleone. And then it spread to the children in our CCD program under the leadership of the very capable Diane Miller. Then it spread to our youth program under the leadership of Michele Froisland—then it spread to our excellent administrator, Jean Beyer; and finally wounding the parish at large. All these people trapped by this terrible false accusation.

The greatest pain of all came when I would hear through the grapevine that some people who I knew, loved, and helped in the past, had stated: 'He is guilty!' Like Jesus, I felt betrayed. But like Jesus I would say, 'Father, forgive them for they know not what they do.' But thank God, the vast majority never stopped believing in my innocence and longed for this day of triumph. Just last week, at the priest jubilee party, my former bishop came all the way up the hall and embraced me saying, 'Congratulations—it's a resurrection.' Then there were close friends who circled around me and called me day and night to make sure I was still alive, since I lived alone and they worried about me. I miss those of my friends who died while I was in exile, like Jim Fahey, Ed Hansen, Gus Aurmuller, Paul McGuire, Marge Yatchintson, and others that slip my mind right now.

While separated from my parish family, every night before I would go to bed I would fall on my knees and plead with God to take me home while I slept, so I would not wake up to another day of pain and suffering. To lull myself to sleep I would keep repeating: 'Father, into your hands I commit my spirit—receive my soul O Lord and commit me to God the most high.' But I would wake up and find myself trapped; to live another day of suffering and pain. I would take refuge before a picture of the Sacred Heart of Jesus saying: 'Dear Jesus, you said, 'Come to me all you who find life weary and burdensome and I will refresh you. For I am meek and humble of heart,' Then I would drive a half hour to the shore to find some solace in the ebb and flow of the tide. That was my life for five years…trapped. Someone's financial life is dead, someone's emotional life is dead, and it's been dead so long…like Lazarus, that by now it stinks. Have you ever been tapped in a sticky situation – can't get out, can't get free, can't talk about it? By now, it stinks!

The diocese delayed in setting up a canonical trial. Larry Colisordo wrote a letter to Bishop Serratelli and within days, the bishop ordered a trial to be set up by the tribunal of three judges from outside the diocese. A prosecutor for the accusers and a canon lawyer for me. Presided over by the chief canonist of the diocese, the prosecutor wanted the trial to be dismissed as inconclusive and not provable. It was up to the bishop to decide what measures to take and to legislate whatever he decided should be done. I insisted on a trial – so the trial finally started. It was a long drawn out, complicated, brutal process. I was eventually exonerated unanimously without one dissenting voice. God had provided an exit strategy so I could say, 'I'm out …I'm out of the darkness, out of my dungeon, out of the snare, out of the trap of a false accusation, out of the depression.'

I have reached the top of the mountain and like Peter, James, and John, I have seen Jesus transformed before me. His face shown like the sun and His garments were as white as snow. Like Peter, I cry out: 'Lord it is good for me to be at the altar again.' Let me never again be separated from my Bride, the Church, and let me go down the mountain from here to reach out to other priests who are falsely accused. Let me reach out to victims who have been abused by priests. John Paul II said, 'There is no room in the church for priests who hurt children.' Priests who are suffering and trapped in an Obsessive Compulsive Disorder—a mental condition. The Church had no understanding of this condition twenty or thirty years ago…sent them for counseling…they did not know it was incurable.

Jesus came back to Jerusalem riding on a donkey. I came back to Saint Rose of Lima riding in a limousine provided by Joe Lionardis. Not to my funeral but to my resurrection from the grave of darkness. From the darkest place I have ever been in. When God brings you back…it is in style. I left a victim and returned a victor. For five years I have gone down life's most dangerous road under a cloud of a false accusation. During those dark times, I would see a light at the end of a tunnel, only to discover it was the headlights of a freight train that came crashing down on me and crushed me to the ground. I had to pick myself up and go on ahead. A man walking covered with scars, no matter how hopeless.

At one of my darkest moments while I was driving my car on the Garden State Parkway, I looked right in front of me and there was a bumper sticker.

The saying was: 'Don't give up five minutes before the miracle happens.' Sure enough, a short time later, everything was resolved. Rome spoke and God had given me an exit strategy. God said, 'I wasn't going to bring you into it if I wasn't going to bring you out of it.' As I said before, we have a God who knows how to get you back home.

I am out, I am out, I am out!!! I was trapped for five long years and now I am free, I am free, I am free. Free at last; thank God Almighty I am free at last."

* * *

I had clawed my way out of that dark hole of a conspiracy brought on by that long ago false accusation. I had finally returned in triumph to my parish to a magnificent thunderous celebration. As one of the young people, Gary Gerber, said to his mother: "Mom, Monsignor McCarthy was like a rock star."

* * *

DON'T GIVE UP

Twixt failure and success the points so fine
Men sometimes know not when they touch the line
Just when the pearl was waiting one more plunge
How many a struggle has thrown up the sponge
Then take this homey from the bitterest cup
"There is no failure save in giving up."
       — Author Unknown

FALLING DOWN

[EXCERPTED]
The world all around me was falling down
And when it crumbled I saw higher ground
Something happened inside of me
I stepped into my identity.
       — Dr. Michael B. Beckwith

45TH ANNIVERSARY — Msgr. William McCarthy, a retired diocesan priest and former pastor of St. Rose of Lima Parish in East Hanover, recently celebrated a Mass in St. Rose of Lima Church to mark the 45th anniversary of his ordination. With him are (from left) Msgr. Paul Knauer, pastor of Our Lady of the Lake Parish in Sparta, and Msgr. Robert Carroll, pastor of Our Lady of Fatima, Highland Lakes. *Submitted photo*

Can you believe it? Five years in the waiting…What should have been my 40th was instead my 45th Anniversary celebration at St. Rose of Lima Parish. Assisting me in performing my first public mass in five years, with over 1000 in attendance, were my faithful friends throughout my ordeal, Monsignor Paul Knauer (left) and Monsignor Robert Carroll (right).

After five years of exile, St. Rose of Lima welcomed her falsely accused pastor home, exonerated, and with the mother of all welcomes. I returned in triumph to the cheers of 1000 people. It was a day the parish will never forget. Free at last, free at last, thank God Almighty, I am free at last!

CHAPTER 78

POSTSCRIPT

Shortly after my exoneration, on June 3, 2008, the Priests' Jubilee Luncheon was held in the restaurant of the Madison Hotel. In attendance, besides myself, were over 150 priests...*and my former bishop*. I sat at a table near the front; my former bishop's table was at the opposite end of the hall.

Suddenly, my former bishop left his table and began shuffling up the hall, calling my name, "Where is Liam?" (my Gaelic name) "Where is Liam?" Again and again. Finally, he arrived at my table, reached over to me, embraced me, and began crying. In the presence of all these priests he said to me, "I am very sorry. Congratulations. It is a resurrection for you."

"Thank you," was all I said.

It was a humbling experience for him, finally admitting he had made a mistake. And he did it, *as it were*, before the whole world. For me it was at first a shock, but eventually a healing moment among many that were to follow.

Looking back at that event, I "take off my hat" to my former bishop for his courageous gesture that turned the clock back to the time when I admired him and loved him. The sheep healing the shepherd.

Later on, some friends of mine expressed surprise at my reaction, especially in light of how long it took my former bishop to apologize. But of course I forgave him. What was I going to do? I am in the forgiveness business.

YEAR SEVEN (2009)

CHAPTER 79

EPILOGUE

March 3, 2009

I wrote to the former Vicar General of the diocese, requesting an interview. I wanted to go face to face with the person who was directly responsible for my destruction (in conjunction with my former bishop and the promoter of justice). I was told he had strongly advised my former bishop to proceed with my censure.

On March 3, 2009, we both sat down in his office facing each other. I began by opening my bible to John 7:51, and read: "Nicodemus spoke out, 'Does our law condemn a person without first hearing him and knowing the facts?'"

I then asked him point blank: "Why did you condemn me without hearing me and knowing the facts?"

He replied, "Bill, we were following the system."

"What system?" I pressed.

"Orders from Dallas," he said, "when they hastily put together that charter."

I looked him squarely in the eyes and stated, "That's what they said at the Nuremburg Trials—'We were only following orders.'" When he didn't respond, I continued: "They were all convicted of crimes against humanity.

"In 2003, the diocese also committed a crime against humanity—me in particular. They did not lift a finger to help me. The diocese, particularly you as Vicar General, was reckless and impetuous in censuring me, and calling for my execution as a priest.

"You behaved badly!" I raised my voice. "Instead of prudently investigating the accusation, you rushed to judgment and as a result, you caused me extraordinary damage. You were reckless!"

Again he didn't respond.

I then asked him why the diocese retained a lawyer, a psychiatrist, and a therapist for the two sisters. He emphatically denied retaining such people.

"Now I know for sure who did," I said in a moment of revelation. "It was one of the conspirators in an attempt to control the two sisters."

"I have no idea," he stated.

After more bantering back and forth, he admitted that he never spoke to Detective Reedy. Also, he never spoke to the alleged victims, the two little sisters who were roughly six and seven years old at the time of the alleged incident, and approximately 28 years old at the time of the false accusation. And he never spoke to the accused—which was me. I asked him why I was not brought before the board that was established for that very reason—why was I not given a chance to present *my* side of the story?

He had NO plausible answer. He just shrugged and sat there looking helpless.

Being very frustrated at that point, I firmly repeated to him:

"One: You never spoke to the detective.

"Two: You never spoke to my accusers.

"Three: You never spoke to me, the accused.

"However, you proceeded in concert with my bishop and the promoter of justice to censure me. You put blind faith in the detective's report, which you received with a regular stamp, and accepted it as infallible. Reedy was in fact a rogue detective, who had been used by my conspirators..."

"Bill," the former Vicar General interrupted, "we were acting in good faith."

At that point I almost lost it, and practically shouted, "How hypocritical! You then published in the diocesan newspaper, over the entire front page, the whole sordid story which ruined my health, my reputation, my life. I suffered the humiliation of being a censured priest for five long years until finally, through the conclusion of an ecclesiastical trial, I was unanimously declared innocent." I pounded the armrest with my fist and demanded, "You have a lot of explaining to do."

I asked the former Vicar General how he could justify his behavior.

Once again, he had no answer, except to meekly offer, "Sorry, Bill, we made a mistake."

"I forgive you," I said evenly, "but I will never forget. My life is irreversibly tarnished. I suffer from chronic flashbacks and panic attacks.

"So that my suffering will not be in vain, I want you to go public with an apology to the press—and further, that you write to the apostolic delegate in Washington, D.C., Archbishop Sambi, and demand that he make a concerted effort to revise that weapon of mass destruction of our priests—that instrument known as the *Dallas Charter*."

The former Vicar General promised me he would do his best. I must give him credit for his calm demeanor and humility. I got the impression he was not just paying me lip service; and that he would indeed at least make the effort to correct the wrong that he had done. He not only acted like he knew he was guilty; he accepted the blame, which made me think that deep down, he was doing what Jesus would want him to do.

Anthology
of
Reviews
of the Book

The Conspiracy
An Innocent Priest

By

Msgr. William McCarthy

A True Story

I have just concluded your very frank and touching story and I am writing to thank you most sincerely for your courage and your candor. I am working on a Research Study of Procedural Justice for Priests - Diocesan and Religious - and I am wondering if you will be so kind as to write a Foreword to my work. I am from Adelaide, South Australia, but am presently at St. Paschal Baylon Church, Thousand Oaks, CA. Please do give an address on which I can reach you, so that I can furnish you with more information. It will also interest you to know that, thanks to you, I have contacted iUniverse Publishers and they have responded most enthusiastically. I am very heartened. I did mention that I had just concluded reading your book and felt drawn toward them as well. I eagerly look forward to hearing from you. I was truly delighted to speak to you personally, and I thank you for responding so promptly. I have just concluded the masterful and informative book of Fr. Kevin McKenna entitled *The Battle of Rights in the United States Catholic Church.* And the reason why I found it most enlightening and reassuring is the fact that I am currently completing a Research Study on ***Procedural Justice for Priests — Diocesan and Religious.*** My Research has revealed that though clearly and authoritatively delineated in the Code of Canon. Law, the rights of priests have been flagrantly denied with woeful consequences to countless individuals and to the Catholic Church.

To be personal, I have served as a priest in the pastoral ministry over the past 42 years and in two archdioceses — Bombay, India and Adelaide, South Australia. Never have I been informed of my rights, thereby exposing me to repeated and hurtful injustices. I was alone, defenseless and helpless. My Research confirms that this has been the identical experience of countless priests all over the world with lamentable and irreversible consequences. What has exacerbated such unfortunate and inexcusable incidents is the callous disregard of Procedural Justice as clearly, authoritatively and unmistakably outlined in Canon Law. The recent sexual abuse crisis has challenged one and all to do some serious introspection and to honestly examine what can personally and collectively be done to regain the lost trust and credibility and to facilitate the progressive implementation, as prophetically envisioned by Blessed Pope John Paul II (September 12, 2004) "...of a pastoral style (by each bishop) which is even more open to collaboration with all." It is to this end that my Research Study is directed. In the memorable words of the late Fr. James Keller, Founder of the Christopher Movement, *"It is better to light a candle than to curse the darkness."* As I am in the process of seeking a publisher, I am writing to request you, Monsignor, to write a Foreword to my Research Study. I will most gratefully appreciate your comments and recommendations so that I can better meet the expectations of readers, both clerical and lay, and so enhance the overall efficacy of this very cogent and important work — a vital and pressing need for every priest throughout the world. With every good wish and eagerly looking forward to hearing from you.

—Fr. James Valladares

From *The Catalyst*
The Catholic League
THE CONSPIRACY: AN INNOCENT PRIEST
Monsignor William McCarthy

The Conspiracy chronicles the monumental struggles of an innocent priest, Monsignor William McCarthy, falsely accused in 2003 of molesting two young sisters more than 23 years earlier. On the eve of his retirement from a stellar career as a priest and pastor, he becomes the victim of an anonymous complaint. Over the next five years, he struggles to prove his innocence to the Church and community. His own bishop and a friend of 40 years abandons him; and the Monsignor has only his faith to give him the strength to prove his innocence. *The Conspiracy* is a book that demonstrates how one's faith can overcome even the worst injustices perpetrated on any human being.

The Conspiracy: An Innocent Priest is available on Amazon.com
RECONSIDERING THE DALLAS CHARTER
Fr. Michael E Orsi

The following recounts what happened to an innocent priest from New Jersey in the wake of the bishops' conference that took place in 2002. Just a few months after it was exposed that the Boston Archdiocese was deeply involved in a cover-up of priestly sexual abuse, the bishops assembled in Dallas. The June meeting was held in a hostile environment: calls for quick and lasting reforms were made from many quarters, and the media had a field day with it. While much good came out of the meeting, it is clear now that on some very important matters, there was a rush to judgment. Nothing was more hastily considered than the due process rights of accused priests. One of those victims was Msgr. Bill McCarthy.

Justice demands that the guilty pay, but it also demands that the innocent not suffer. On June 15- 18, the bishops will meet in Seattle, and one of the items they are expected to address is the issue of accused priests and fairness in dealing with them. It is only fitting that the documented case of Msgr. McCarthy be given due consideration. Sadly, he is not alone.

Bill Donohue
The Catholic League

Monsignor William McCarthy is a retired priest from the Diocese of Paterson, New Jersey. After a stellar, four-decade pastoral career, he is a priest in good standing. However, for almost five years he wasn't. In *The Conspiracy: An Innocent Priest, A True Story,* McCarthy recounts the ordeal that resulted from a false accusation that he abused two young girls.

A 2003 complaint—made anonymously some 23 years after the incidents were alleged to have occurred—subjected McCarthy to the provisions of the *Dallas Charter for the Protection of Children and Young People,* enacted by the United States bishops in 2002 to address the highly publicized and damaging reports of child abuse. He is straightforward in his negative assessment of this draconian measure. He also criticizes the ineptitude of some bishops, the unchecked bureaucracy of diocesan chancery offices, the vendettas carried on by some of the laity against priests, the corruption of some law enforcement officers, and the arduous process and long wait faced by priests seeking justice from the Church.

On the other hand, he is complimentary toward Cardinal Joseph Ratzinger (now Pope Benedict XVI), who refused the request of McCarthy's former bishop to laicize him immediately. Instead, the future pope ordered a canonical trial at which McCarthy was completely exonerated.

Some of the situations addressed in this book are chilling. About the vindictive nature of some people who have a gripe (real or imagined) against a priest, McCarthy writes:

> "Leaders of even simple ordinary positions such as pastors of local churches are not without their adversaries who will go to any extent to hurt them. During the 'pedophile' eruption in the USA, the media was inundated with countless accusations of priests. People were bombarded with this phenomena, it was in the 'air' as it were. Consequently, anyone with a grudge against a priest was motivated to seize the opportunity to make a hit."

The motive of an accuser (or a purported witness) should be thoroughly investigated as part of the inquiry process whenever an allegation arises. Yet, this is rarely considered a top priority. Instead, ever since the Boston debacle caused by Cardinal Bernard Law's mismanagement put the issue of recidivist abusers in the nation's headlines, accused priests are automatically presumed guilty by their bishops, with very little scrutiny of those making the accusations.

The judgment of guilt is generally affirmed in the court of public opinion, since the priest has already been removed from his ministry. Out-of-court payoffs to plaintiffs, which have become a common practice, exacerbate the problem. People assume that the exchange of money automatically proves there was something wrong, creating a no-win situation even for a priest who is ultimately found to be innocent.

Therefore, unless incontrovertible evidence can be shown that abuse occurred, each case should be litigated aggressively by the priest's diocese (this is as true in the case of dead priests). The system, as it stands now, encourages false accusations, has led to bankruptcy in many dioceses, and left the Church, its bishops and priests more vulnerable than ever.

McCarthy paints a dreary portrait of his former bishop and chancery staff that is, unfortunately, all too common. Instead of an organization guided by Christian principle, we see a group of confused and desperate people whose behavior illustrates such key insights from business management as, "Personnel is policy," and "Like brings on like." Concerned only with self-protection, they are only too willing to throw a priest "under the bus." As McCarthy explains:

"In my case, my former bishop writes an official letter to the Pope demanding my immediate laicization, ex officio; this time not even a trial or personal discussion of any kind. No recourse of any sort was allowed me. No communication was possible—I was shunned by the diocese and my brother priests. My name erased from the official records. My life was essentially evaporated."

Infuriating as it may be, Canon Law enables bishops to act as little potentates in their dioceses. Inadequate bishops, fearful of public opinion, tend to isolate themselves from those who think differently than they do, and confront issues in a dictatorial manner. Bishops who allowed known serial pedophiles to continue in the priesthood should have been removed. So too those who sacrificed innocent priests for expediency, hiding behind the non-binding *Dallas Charter*. But the Vatican has no mechanism for removing them (even for evaluating them), unless immoral behavior, heresy, or financial mismanagement can be proven. And so, many of them continue to exercise their office in good standing. No wonder the outrage!

It seems to be part of our psychological make-up to trust law enforcement personnel and think of them as good people. We also tend to believe that telling the truth will clear us of an allegation. McCarthy jarringly demonstrates that this trust is misplaced. He chronicles the emotional abuse suffered at the hands of a police detective, and discusses the use of such dubious investigative practices as a rigged lie detector test and proposing "suppressed memories" to alleged victims. He recounts the testimony given by a police detective at his canonical trial:

"Then [the detective] testified—the one who began this whole shamble. The one who convinced the girls that 'Father McCarthy molested you when you were children,' even though they denied having any memories whatsoever of such a thing happening. He invoked the technique prevalent in the seventies called 'suppressed memory.' He had said to them, 'You don't remember it because it was so painful and awful that you just buried it...but he did molest you.' After several intense barrages at them, they allowed themselves to become convinced those awful things actually happened to them."

McCarthy rightly advises any priest facing a sexual abuse charge to get a civil and canon lawyer before answering any questions, either from the bishop or from the police—especially the police. He notes how the conviction of an abusive priest is viewed as a feather in a police officer's cap career-wise.

So much is said about abuse victims—and rightly so—but little is said about the priests falsely accused, either those living or those who have died. Least discussed of all is the truth that, in some cases, Satan is acting on the minds and imaginations of those people who lend themselves to the task of destroying an innocent priest. The Evil One knows that to cripple the priesthood is to strike at the heart of the Church. That's why every effort must be made to protect the innocent, for their good and for the good of the Body of Christ.

> *McCarthy has performed an invaluable service by giving us his story in the form of an insightful memoir.*

McCarthy shows his readers the entire process, civil and canonical, which he endured. His story is an invaluable education for those not familiar with the usual course of events involved in these cases. He says:
"Unquestionably there needs to be positive meaningful change to the ecclesiastical tribunal system. They have never been truly challenged. It is time for priests around the world to speak out for major reform. It needs to change so that innocent priests like me can get a fair shake—and I'm going to keep fighting until it is done. If I don't keep up the struggle, my life's work will be in vain."

McCarthy acknowledges the importance of his lay friends and brother priests who supported him during his long ordeal. They were, he says, essential to his survival. He praises his new bishop for treating him with dignity and respect, and reports a reconciliation with his now-retired bishop and the Vicar-General who processed the case against him. McCarthy says he has forgiven all those involved in his crucifixion but, he says, he will never forget. Nor will anyone who reads McCarthy's account.

The Conspiracy is a combination diary, spiritual journal, and exercise in self-analysis, and it includes a bibliography of other books McCarthy found helpful during his ordeal. It is self-published, and so doesn't have all the polish of a work edited and produced by a major publishing house. In a sense, that enhances its effectiveness. This is a raw account of one man's ordeal, capturing both the torment inflicted on an innocent priest and the joy of his vindication.

Despite the successful outcome of his case, the physical and psychological wounds McCarthy sustained have left permanent scars. Yet the depth of spiritual growth which he reports has enabled him to identify with the innocently crucified Lord. Perhaps that's the most important point the book makes.

This story should be read by every priest and every lay person, because the priest scandal is a sad episode in the history of the Church which effects everyone. McCarthy has performed an invaluable service by giving us his story in the form of an insightful memoir. His account puts the sensationalism surrounding the crisis in a different light, bringing into focus those priests who are being abused by an unjust system. And he offers words of hope to any of his fellows who may be experiencing the pain he endured:

"Finally, may I dare say, if there is one message I want to leave from this journal, it is if there is a priest out there who is falsely accused, I want you to know, that you are not alone, and with perseverance and hopefully with patient endurance, you can make it to the other side of darkness."

Fr. Michael P. Orsi *is*
Chaplain and Research Fellow in Law and Religion
Ave Maria Law School.

This is the true story of a man who has been grossly wronged, and of his day-to-day and even hour-to-hour feelings in this situation of a wrongful distortion of facts that literally has destroyed his reputation. He presents the accusations, his dismissal from the church by a hierarchy that was hastily responding in an almost panic reaction to attacks brought against members of the Catholic Church and the disastrous effect it had upon him both mentally and physically. It recalls periods of his early life, his pleasure of being ordained and his love for his work, his teaching, counseling, ministering to his parishioners and his utter devotion to his way of life. And it recalls the people who helped him to fight the accusations over months and years to eventually ferret out the truth and to ultimately prove his innocence.

The CONSPIRACY no doubt has provided a catharsis for the Monsignor, but he also has set forth probably one of the most unique pieces of literature I ever have read. Every living person no doubt has experienced some incident in their lives in which they have been wrongly accused of some action and can equate with numerous of the trains of thought expressed. He quite aptly has provided a description of the scrambled thought patterns that a person experiences when caught in such unbelievable situation. There are the swings from thoughts of home and early family and happy times to farther mundane daily activities to pertinent phrases from readings or visual performances, to the vicious accusations, from disbelief to the depths of despair — all of these thought patterns a wrongly accused person experiences. And these experiences uniquely have been set forth by a dedicated man of the church — the last person one usually would think of in such a situation. Because the story is by and about a Monsignor of the Catholic Church many readers will think of it as a read most appropriate to members of that faith. To do so is a mistake. This story is most timely and one that everyone might well benefit from reading. It looks at an ugly situation that relatively recently has been brought to light and of the typical reflexive overreaction that such a situation elicits. Much can be learned from this fact alone. Additionally the monsignor provides two quotes that are most thoughtful and would be helpful for anyone to keep in mind. The first, perhaps more prevalent for Christians: *"You never know that God is all you need until God is all you have."* The second *"Don't give up five minutes before the miracle happens."*

—John H. Manhold

I saw your story in The Catalyst and I will definitely buy your book. Like you, I was falsely accused back in 1998. 1 was a teacher here in Abington, PA and I was arrested, handcuffed, and did the 'pro' walk in front of all the television news cameras in the Delaware Valley. My family and I suffered immensely. I was suspended from my teaching position without pay and it took nine long months before the Montco D.A. found that the female, who I had taught twelve years before, was lying and later found to be mentally unstable. My story was the focus of a December 1998 NBC Dateline show. My wife and I are trying to get a law passed in Pennsylvania that would make the false reporting of serious crimes into felonies. Presently I am supporting the case of Father Gordon MacRae who sits in a N.H. prison now for sixteen years. I am convinced he is totally innocent. Also, one of my old scouts from when I was a Scoutmaster in Philly is one of the falsely accused priests in our archdiocese (John Bowe). He is being represented by my attorney who was responsible for my exoneration. I will definitely buy your book. You are one courageous individual, and I should know having gone through the nightmare myself.

—galla17@comcast.net
www.msgrwilliammcearthy.com

Reading *The Conspiracy* brought much sadness to my heart as I experienced Monsignor McCarthy's pain in this long five year trial of his soul. People are weak (even those in the church hierarchy who we expect more from) and will always disappoint, but I thank God for the graces given Monsignor so that he persevered with this heavy cross. This book should be read by all those who so loosely ridicule and unfairly accuse our good priests — and there are so many good and holy priests that I personally know and many many more who need our support. I only met Monsignor after his spiritual scourging was over and he was completely exonerated. He was living in the same town trying to keep body and soul together while enduring this trial and I didn't know him then. How I wish I had, for I would have befriended him in a heartbeat and been part of those faithful friends who stood by him encouraging him to stand tall and persevere. I thank God he did and we are blessed now to have him in our lives. God is good.

—Mary Majkowski

In *"THE CONSPIRACY, An Innocent Priest,"* Monsignor William McCarthy takes the reader into his world where false allegations stripped him of his priesthood. Prayers and the love of his friends who were convinced of his innocence helped him to survive his unjust hell. The priest who helped my wife and me live through the pain of losing our daughter to breast cancer was finally exonerated. The reader will feel his pain during his nightmare and will applaud his innocence and return to the priesthood he so desperately missed.

—Hilton Otero

Just a note to tell you how much I received as I read your book "*The Conspiracy.*" I received anger, peace, love and hate, outrage and calm..." could go on and on.... Remember, I was there working for you for over 24 years, and as my friend, I felt your pain, despair, hopelessness, and finally, vindication, all due to your writings. I must admit that while reading, you as the author, brought me to my knees several times during your trials. I, myself; also had trials to deal with, and still do, but I refer to 'highlighted' portions in the book and I find my own peace through your writings. Besides the birth of my children, that day in May was the most emotional one of my life, your vindication! In a way, your writings saved your life, and mine too. God Bless You,

—Diane Miller

Many, many thanks for keeping me informed of your latest project. I am amazed by your energy and creativity. Please be assured of my prayers. I always enjoy hearing from you. Have a Happy Easter.

—Most Reverend Arthur J. Serratelli, S.T.D., S.S.L., D.D.,
Bishop of Paterson

For this week I'd like to focus on national broadcast radio and focus again on national and local TV. Please, do not hesitate with any questions, comments, or concerns. Thank you for your time, Msgr. McCarthy.

—The Washington Post

I enjoyed reviewing the screenplay that you forwarded to me. God bless you for sharing this with me!

—Bishop Paul Bootkoski

I have just finished your book and could identify with so many of your emotions. I am a Catholic school teacher and last year, in my 32nd year at the same school, I was falsely accused by a former student from 1994. I don't know how you lasted for 5 years! It only took 3 months for the DA to find there was no evidence to support a case, but the diocese of Fall River, MA immediately released my name to the press and removed me from the school. The damage was done and there is no way to get my reputation back. I returned to the classroom in January. The pain continues… and the anxiety increases as I prepare to return to school in just 10 days. I just want you to know that it is not only priests who are affected by the fear of the bishops. I am a single laywoman who has served the Church faithfully. I would like to ask you if you ever sued the diocese, the detective, or the women who concocted the story in the first place. I am hoping that you respond.

—Jean Revil

Thanks for the book ***"The Conspiracy... An Innocent Priest"***. It was, indeed, a mighty read. It was very engaging, engrossing and intriguing. Your endurance and suffering through the false allegation is a story of amazing grace in faith, prayer and perseverance. Your tenacity in winning the fight and the war through the long, dark night of suffering and pain is, again, a triumph of grace in little David against the Goliath of the institutional Church.

Liam, I am quite sure that as you look back from the mountain top experience of exoneration, you must sometimes find yourself wondering how you came through the valleys of self doubt, despair and hopelessness that was so clearly a part of your psychological state as you hung on against the onslaught of evil. I like the quality of your literary style and your brutal transparency in sharing the journey of those terrible years. Beyond the Liam McCarthy that I knew in seminary days, your book revealed to me another Liam: A man who is a giant in pursuing the truth and articulating clearly your "dark night of the soul." I was very, very impressed by your use of quotes from so many other different sources and their relevancy to the story. Your love for the priesthood is profound and humbling and stamped throughout the pages of the story. It must be obvious to you that I found your book inspiring, challenging, revealing, most instructive, and enlightening on the gifts that can too easily be taken for granted. It is again obvious to me that your brought your suffering to the cross and you anchored it all on the cross and you were led to ultimate triumph and resurrection.

I am most grateful for your thoughtfulness in sharing your story with me and I look forward to a personal dialogue with you sometime when we might be together in person. Perhaps you may want to make a visit here to Tucson and come as an honored guest and a friend of many years. Your story makes a gigantic contribution to truth and integrity and is certainly great material for presentation through the medium of film. I stand in admiration and awe of the God who brought you through this immense trial and in admiration and awe of your love for priesthood and your personal response.

Thanks for the recent photographs that recalls so vividly the road of memory and of our Carlow days. Mickey Flynn seems to have done very good for himself with his wife and family. I passed your book on to Msgr. John Cusack who knew you in the Diocese. He was very keen to get a read of the book. Liam, I hope you continue to enjoy your retirement now and that the trauma of the past years is receding more and more in your memory, even though it will all always leave a residue of hurt, which can be a call to God's grace and blessings upon you. Thanks, Liam, for your thoughtfulness. Prayerful and grateful good wishes, Your friend out west,

— Monsignor Tom Cehalane

When I heard that your book was available, I placed an order and was eager to sit quietly and read it cover to cover. It is not that type of book, it took me longer to read each page, longer than usual for me, as I found it a difficult and slow read as I took my time to ponder over certain statements and paragraphs. I read one-third of the book then our lives went full throttle, full speed ahead. Company came for a few weeks then we did quite a bit of traveling out of state, no quiet time to read. While I was away, a friend asked if she could borrow my book. What I would like to comment on is the portion of the book that I have read. It is very powerful but, at the same time, very sad, indeed, to see the depths of despair that entered your life. At times, it was quite emotional and I had to put the book down to think and to pray. I can't imagine anyone having to go through such an ordeal. I must tell you that a friend of mine who is going through a very difficult time in her life, told me that she found your book inspirational ... you gave her another way of looking at life, which was hope-filled. I asked her to contact you to let you know how you are helping her during these very confusing, sad and hurtful days. I look forward to collecting the book from my friend and continue on your journey through those very difficult years, Fr. McCarthy. I will be in touch again and, in the meantime, please know how much I admire your perseverance in restoring your good name. Somewhere I read, the real meaning of peace does not mean to be in a place where there is no noise, trouble or hard work. Peace means to be in the midst of all those things and still be calm in your heart. I bid you peace for the rest of time, Fr. McCarthy. Love and prayers,

—Ann Marie

It almost feels appropriate that I have finished your book: *"The Conspiracy, an Innocent Priest,"* as we begin the period of Lent wherein we are ask to recall the trial, passion and death of Our Lord Jesus Christ. As I read your book, your words seem to describe a similar passion, trial and spiritual demise. I had heard of your accusation but was not totally informed of what had gone on. Now I am sorry that I was not so informed for I would have made an effort to be of support to you. I am so sorry for all that you had to suffer unjustly by this accusation. I, like yourself, do not have the greatest of patience, but I admire yours throughout the past five years in which you, have been asked by God to have a mountain of patience with all those involved. I was saddened to read of how you were initially treated by Bishop Rodimer, the Vicar General, and the Media. It made me happy to read that there was a reconciliation with both Bishop Rodimer and Msgr. Tillyer, and that Bishop Serratelli had been so supportive of you throughout. It only speaks of the humanness of the

Church and how fallible all of us are. Congratulations on composing your book and relating your struggles and triumph of innocence. It was so good to read of all the prayers and support you received from your parishioners, priest friends and others. Now you have begun a new chapter of your priestly life. May it resound with much happiness and priestly joy. You deserve both! Truly, as the endorsers of your book claim: "It is a must read for all Catholics and non-Catholics alike." Fraternally yours,

—Monsignor Elso Introini

I hope that you are well and that you are enjoying the holiday season. I am writing to let you know that I just finished your book *The Conspiracy.* I am so sorry that you experienced the trauma and despair that these women put your through. Your life was in such turmoil for those long years. The unknown and the inability to take control of such a horrible situation must have been horrendous. However, (and I don't mean that lightly) your book will be an inspiration to many who are in the same or similar situations. You have shown how important **hope** is because without it there is nothing for the distressed. Your reference to Biblical quotes, your own sayings (the one that I remember best is.. The mind is its own place, it can make a hell out of heaven or a heaven out of hell), your use of relevant current events (i.e., Terry Schiavo case and September 11) and your reference to other writings, make it a book that I will recommend to people and reread myself. Thank you for sharing so much of yourself. Love,

—Betty (Tunny) Bodenweiser
(daughter of Jim and Betty Tunny - Chatham)

Many, many thanks for your kind note. It is so good to hear from me. I hope you are doing well. You are an extremely courageous man. God bless. Sincerely yours in Christ,

—Most Reverend Arthur J. Serratelli, S.T.D., D.D.
Bishop of Paterson

I wish to acknowledge the receipt of your book and also for your kind letter. As you retrace the suffering and pain that you went through, I am hoping that in the process, the Lord will bring you to greater healing and wholeness. Be assured of my continued prayers. Sincerely yours in Christ,

—Most Reverend Arthur J. Serratelli, S.T.D., S.S.L., D.D.
Bishop of Paterson

I just recently finished your book. I could never begin to visualize just what you went through without reading this account of your suffering. As I told you in my phone call, it was so upsetting to read how my dear friend Monsignor McCarthy suffered, died and was buried. I can't tell you how many nights I went to sleep crying and praying for you because of your horrible ordeal. Thank God your book has a happy ending. It is so good knowing you are fully resurrected back into the priesthood that you love and lived every day of your life for. I just say I wonder whatever happened to Mrs. Murphy's daughter and Mr. Cain and also Detective Reedy. Did they all just walk away after having done this horrible thing to your life? I know I tell you this in every conversation and letter I have ever had with you but you, Monsignor McCarthy, made an impact on my faith in God more than any priest I have ever known You are the one who taught me to know and love the Holy Spirit in a new way which changed my life forever. I will always be thankful to you for this gift and I pray God will bless your life abundantly just as you have touched so many lives and brought Christ to them. You are the one who taught me to know and love Jesus as my Personal Friend and Savior. You are a wonderful priest and wonderful man and I will always admire you and even more so after reading your book. Thank you for being my favorite priest and for being the wonderful Good and Faithful Servant you are. Love and Blessings. PS: I have bought 4 books so far and I'm sending them to two of my former pastors. The others will be circulating.

—Rita DeRiancho

I should like to congratulate you on your exoneration and escape from those most vicious accusations. Your endurance is exemplary and the results most gratifying. I have enclosed a copy of the review I have done on your book and truly believe you have provided a step by step account of the manner in which most unjustly accused persons react to such a situation. It is something from which many readers can profit. I also appreciate from a very personal standpoint, more than you can imagine, the two phrases you quoted and I, in turn, have quoted. For me, especially, you provided them at a most appropriate time, and I thank you. Sincerely,

—John H. Manhold

When I got your letter a few weeks back announcing that your book was now published I decided that I needed to read it. I found it appalling in some measure-especially in the way your accusation was handled by the diocese- but it also brought out clearly your struggle to remain positive through the whole ordeal. You were not afraid to bear your soul in the book, to share your time of depression, the endless days when little of note occurred in your life and the lack of energy you felt on many days. There must have been days when you felt that it would never be resolved in your favor, days in which you did not want to go on. I just read a book called "Unbroken" by Laura Hillenbrand, about Louis Zamparini, a runner in the 1936 Olympics in Berlin for the USA. He was captured by the Japanese in the Pacific in 1943 and his story and that of a few more men is worth reading. The brutality they experienced was shocking but Louis and a few more survived the brutal beatings in the POW camp and came back to the U.S. He had an addiction to alcohol which almost destroyed him; however a visit to a Billy Graham Crusade helped him find the light. You would find it inspirational I'm sure. Your battle went on for five long years. It was too bad that our Ordinary and the VG did not handle it better. There was a rush to judgment and an inability to examine the nature of the accusation and the motives of the two women involved. How you kept all of that from your family in Ireland is beyond me. It was wonderful to read the last section after you were exonerated and you finally were able to return to St. Rose for the celebration. You have a very valuable lesson to teach us, all of us still in active ministry, and in the trenches. I still try to be as open and accepting of children as possible but I make sure their parents are close by. I thank you for writing the book; it took great courage to do so. I hope it has been selling well and that you have received feedback from many guys. I was happy to see that Arthur was instrumental in breaking the case open and helping you to get your life back. I wish you many more years in priestly ministry. Many Blessings,

—Father Chris Muldoon

Recently I saw an article in one of our Catholic press publications regarding your book, *The Conspiracy.* Immediately it piqued my interest. (I haven't as yet read your book as I am on a waiting list at the local library). The article I read gave me enough information to know that you have first hand knowledge of what my family has been through. Several years ago my priest-brother was falsely accused of sexual misconduct. He stayed with me while he was not allowed to represent himself as a priest. He has since been exonerated of all charges and returned to active duty in his parish. The false allegations have never allowed his reputation to be as it once was. For many years he had been very active in scouting. Because the diocese paid the accuser up front there is still a mark against his name regarding scouting. Now to get to the main reason for this correspondence. Shortly my brother will be going to the Youth Day in Spain with others from his parish. Needless to say he needed to get the proper credentials from the Bishop so he could celebrate Mass while on this trip outside the diocese. We were absolutely astounded to find the papers contained a notation regarding the false sexual accusation against him. It did however state that he had been fully exonerated of all charges. In my opinion this is a total injustice to my brother, just giving reason to further scrutinize his every action. He has talked about checking this out with his legal counsel but to date has not done this. I am trying to give him some space on this but it makes me ill to think our Church can act in this way. Have you had this experience? If so, would you be willing to share this information with me so I can either lay this to rest or call the Archbishop? I thank you for taking the time to read this letter. I wish you the best . I pray for all priests daily. Thank you for your years of service for the Lord. Sincerely,

—Marjorie M. Walsh

I received your package mail in late afternoon on Tuesday, April 12th. And 1 read the contents with the letter by Father Ken Gumbert, OP from Providence College and the accompanying draft of the Hollywood Treatment of your story of being falsely accused of abuse. I just finished reading it at midnight and found that it was well depicted. Not knowing how it will finally be demonstrated for the screen and who would play the important characters makes me withhold my final judgment. I too believe that the media should do a better job of notifying the public about those found innocent of abuse claims. They do such a dramatic job of placing judgment on those accused without further evidence etc. which may include the hierarchy of our church. That hurried reaction by the Bishops of the United States to have the policy of "one strike you are out" without proper evidence or hearing does not speak well for an institution that vows to promote justice, peace and love. I admire your courage and your willingness to do this. I would hope that Fr. Culbert would engage those who have been similarly accused and been found innocent to know of your willingness, and then have them join you in this effort. Bill, be prepared for what may be its outcome. Some will applaud your effort and others will be negative, not wanting to view anything more about priests and abuse. You have been strong in the past with fighting for justice, perhaps this is the armor that will be the encouragement for doing what you deem best for all concerned. You have my prayers!

—Monsignor Elso

Thank you for sending your book *The Conspiracy* to me. It is a very powerful account of your own intense trial and testing. I would indeed like to come down to New Jersey or wherever sometime in the second half of June to interview you about your story for my documentary film about falsely accused priests. I have made contact with a number of falsely accused, but most all of them are afraid to speak with me on camera about their stories. There is still so much fear and psychological damage to those who have experienced this trauma. I understand the hesitancy to get involved in this. But it would greatly help the public to know that there are indeed many cases of falsely accused priests out there. However, no one to my knowledge has said this yet in the media. I'm hoping my film will be able to convey this message. Please let know if you would be willing to be interviewed and where and when we could meet. Wishing you peace during this season of Lent. Sincerely,

—Rev. Ken Gumbert, OP
Providence College

Was so glad to hear from you and hope that the words written express my view of your book. You have been through much, but thank God you have overcome to continue to help us all with your experience. We all need to know that our lives will always encounter difficulties but you showed us that we can overcome our problems. Thanks for your many years of services to help us always.

—Vickie Yannuzzi

I am very excited about how the book has progressed. I am on schedule to release it in January 2012.

Your ordeal is a very valuable section of the book and I am hoping it leads to more sales of your book, *The Conspiracy.* I have enclosed a draft of my Introduction, as well as a draft of the chapter about your ordeal: Written words that open your heart to help us know the joys and sorrow that could be captured in *"The Conspiracy of an Innocent Priest".* It is a true account of the depths of darkness that was brought about into his life -- like lightning that strikes with no control. May the written words bring you into his moment of despair and hope that he lived and that you will come to know the Monsignor desired to express and know that he is now able to share the events that were brought into his life. He is now able share with the many who were touched by his priesthood, the joy of his redemption, and able to continue his life to serve God's people.

—David Pierre

My name is Maura. I am sure you remember me. While at the parish you were always very good to me and my family. I must say I never doubted your innocence. I bought your book and was so happy you wrote it. If you have time, love to meet you or if you can write back to me. Thank you for this wonderful book. Your friend Sincerely,

—Maura

Today I finished reading your book: *"The Conspiracy."* It was excellent; I could not put it down!

I had tears on more than one occasion as I read about your torture and ordeal. My heart broke for you and the painful moments, months and years you endured. May these prayers help to heal the wounds and bad memories so you can feel inner peace. I really appreciated all the wonderful quotes and reference in your book – so poignant. You m ay not remember me but my parents were Aldo (now deceased 3-9-11) and Chetty Angelino. My sister is Diana Torna and I was in a prayer group with her and other young moms which you were a part of on occasion. I also taught at Vacation Bible School 3 summers around the time my daughter went to St. Roe preschool. Even though my husband and children belong to OLBS in Roseland we participated in Adoration and many morning Masses. We enjoyed your 45th Anniversary Mass and celebration and are all so grateful for your exoneration. It was interesting to learn of your hand in EWTN's infancy. My husband and I listen to it regularly and get a lot out of it. I also enjoyed the biographical aspect of the book and can see that you come from an exemplary family. God bless you always. Thank you for sharing so much through your writing. It is a treasure of wisdom and inspiration. We all have painful times that we an relate in a small way to some aspect of your suffering. I am so glad it is behind you. I did not believe the allegations and am thankful for your ministry to all of us. Fondly,

—Mary Angelo Murray

Thank you so much for the autographed copy of your book *"The Conspiracy."* What a surprise it was to find it in our mailbox. Your book is so moving. I couldn't put it down and finished it in an afternoon. Don is now reading the book and enjoyed seeing two of the photos he took in it. We are very happy all your pain and suffering has passed and hopefully time will ease the memories of the whole ordeal. You are a special person and always in our prayers. Best Regards,

—Don & Debbie Deignan

I have finished reading your wonderfully written book. At times I could not stop reading it and at other times I had to run away from it! Your very deep and personal descriptions of the pain you suffered just blew me away. Words cannot describe how sorry I am that this devastating injustice happened to you. You suffered more than most would, because you have a sensitive and gentle heart; the very attributes, among many, that make you such a special priest. Never, in this life can we know the "why?" of it. There are so many "favorites" of mine in your book but #1 is when you write "God gave me my hearts desire. He gave me what he didn't give to the angels, the power to make him present in the Eucharist and to forgive sins in the Sacrament of Reconciliation." The last two chapters, the postscript and the epilogue were a triumph, carried out with such dignity, especially your personal meeting with the former Vicar General. Those that know and love you do not see your life as "irreversibly tarnished" but rather as a shining star. You have become a warrior and I so proud of you! I always knew you would not disappoint me or any of us at St. Rose. "May the peace of God which transcends all understanding, guard your heart and mind." With great affection and prayers always, Your sister in Christ

—Doris

Just wanted to let you know how much I enjoyed reading your book. Through your words and feelings I felt your pain but your scriptural, music and book quotes touch me very much. I am so happy for you now, and we know that the Lord in his time gave you the victory. Thank you for touching us with your wonderful words. Happy and Peaceful Thanksgiving! We all have so much to be thankful for as we can just look at the amazing world made by our Creator. Peace,

—Carolyn Imposimoto

The book is a triumph. The last few chapters were superbly handled. Congratulations and thank you for the complimentary copy. Sincerely in Christ,

—Father Jack Catoir, J.C.D.

Thank you for sending me a copy of your book! Your ordeal was truly frightening and remarkable. It should be made into a movie! I hope to speak with you as I near completion of my next book on falsely accused priests. Peace,

—David Pierre (author of "Double Standard)

I hope that God has granted you the peace you have yearned for throughout the hard and terrible years of the **"*Conspiracy.*"** Your beautiful words and insights I know will be of comfort to me as I live these days of widowhood. My husband of 56 years passed away in March and I am adjusting to many new responsibilities. Thank God for my beautiful family and friends.

—Chetty (Mrs. Concetta Angelino)

Dear Tom:

Your letter is one of the most uplifting of letters I have ever received. You have made a major contribution to healing my mind, body and soul. I have always looked up to you with admiration and respect, a gentle giant. Your letter is beyond anything I ever expected from my peers and classmates. You made me feel ten feet tall when during my dark days I felt very small indeed, ashamed of even been associated with such a despicable accusation, thinking I could never recover from such a terrible attack on my character, especially with my classmates. Now you have become the wind beneath my wings, my savior. A special thanks for your invitation to Tucson as your honored guest. How special you make me feel! Hopefully I can do that some time in the future. With a grateful heart, Your friend,

—Liam

Above is a humorous cartoon depicting Monsignor William McCarthy at the altar in an amusing way. It was presented to him by Irene Monteleone, Director of our preschool in 1985. Monsignor said, "I loved it and the children loved it. It was a child's concept of what I was all about."

The Catholic Church was challenged with a tsunami of issues relative to pedophilia in the late 1990's, culminating in a meeting of the United States Catholic Conferences of Bishops in Dallas Texas, in the year 2002. Against this backdrop of activity, a simple retirement of a priest was complicated by baseless accusations in 2003. After many years of devotion and inspiration to both community and church, the retirement of Liam McCarthy from St. Rose of Lima in East Hanover New Jersey was anything but peaceful and ceremonious. In his book, Conspiracy and the Innocent Priest, Liam McCarthy describes in vivid detail his formation into Catholicism and the false accusations that caused much agony in his later years. I have personally known Liam McCarthy since he presided as pastor at St. Rose in 1980, the better part of thirty plus years. His story is one of remarkable forbearance and courage in face of adversity that was not deserving of a dedicated man of the cloth. I was convinced, and still contend that no accusation would, in the end, tarnish such a great priest and Monsignor of the Church.

—Carmine M. and Eileen M. Fischetti

The Conspiracy walks you through the life of a priest in total despair after being falsely accused of child molestation. The author, Monsignor William McCarthy in his book goes from present to past; you will be moved as he shares his inner most thoughts and emotions, his torment and sufferings and his anger and forgiveness. He takes you with him from the beginning... the accusations, the unfaithfulness of his Bishop, his perseverance, his unending powerful prayer, the survival tactics he used to get through each day, his ecclesiastical trial... to the end of his long and painful journey when he was finally exonerated by the Church, six long years later. The different passages used by the author will inspire you. You will be absorbed in this unbelievable true story of a conspiracy against an innocent man. Monsignor McCarthy is a most remarkable man; you will see him as I came to know him, a man of great faith, gentle and humble, with untiring and unconditional love and devotion for his family, friends, parishioners and Church. This book is a symbol of faith and definitely a must read for everyone, especially in these days of pedophile priests. In the end we have a priest whose life was shattered, may never be the same, but not destroyed... he is "still standing" in his unfailing faith and love, with his bride, his beloved Church.

—Marie and Jerry Carlone

I would be remiss if I did not present myself to you most gratefully. I am Mother Antonia & I was very deeply & humbly touched by the words that you have written about me as a 'rising star'. My prayer is to not only to serve the 'least of Mine', but I consider myself, the 'least of Mine'. Thinking of what Jesus said about John the Baptist being the greatest man on earth & still & all, less than the least in heaven. Those words are enough to give us thought & put those thoughts into action to serve the Lord. I have only done my work, & that, poorly. However, Father, your beautiful words made happy, all my Sisters & family & Associates & me. Pray for me please, Father, that I learn only the two things that Christ asked me to learn, "to be meek & humble of heart". Be assured of the place you have in my prayers. My hope & my joy at the thought of being in yours. God bless you, Father. May His light shine upon you & in you, that you be a light in the world. Peace, Love, Mercy,

—Mother Antonia Brenner, E.S.E.H.

MAB:samm

I pray this letter finds you well. Gerry and I were so happy to see you, if even for a moment, at the Memorial Mass at St. Rose for Sr. Dolores. Your eulogy to her was very special. I am sure she was delighted. I was so pleased to see that many of her friends were able to attend in view of the weather that day. We will truly miss her friendship as well as her frequent visits with stay overs to our home. You and Sr. Dolores were a great team and I know that she thought you were a wonderful holy priest and a good friend. She always talked about the marvelous years working with you at Sr. Rose even in her last days when we visited with her in PA. Dear Fr. McCarthy, as you asked, Gerry and I put together the enclosed review of your book. I hope that you will be pleased with it; however, you certainly are free to change it, add to it or just file it away. We did not want to make it too long, .although we had so much to say. I pick up your book to read often and each time I do, I find that I come across something that I did not "see" or "come upon" in the previous readings. And each time I reread .... My heart goes out to you more and more; my respect and admiration for you as a holy and caring priest grows deeper and deeper. A while ago, when your book first came out, as you know, I purchased ten copies to give to friends. I don't think I ever told you this before, but one book was given to Fr. Louis, now the Superior General of the Vocationist Fathers. Fr. Louis told us many times that he thought your book was excellent and he used several of your passages when giving a homily, speech and religious instruction to the novices. As a matter of fact, one night when we had Fr. Louis, Bishop Marconi and Bishop da Cunha at our home for dinner, I brought up the subject of your book. I went to get a copy from the bookcase and came back to the table to hear Fr. Louis telling all that they should read this excellent book. He also did mention that fact of using the passages. The Bishops had only good things to say about you and were happy that your ordeal was over. It was an impromptu event, but next time we will let you know to see if you would like to be here with us. Well, I guess I should close for now. Please stay well. Gerry and I would like to take you to lunch. Is Rooney's convenient for you? Or would. you prefer another place? Talk to you soon. Love,

—Marie & Gerry too!

Thanks for the book *"The Conspiracy... An Innocent Priest"*. It was, indeed, a mighty read. It was very engaging, engrossing and intriguing. Your endurance and suffering through the false allegation is a story of amazing grace in faith, prayer and perseverance, Your tenacity in winning the fight and the war through the long, dark night of suffering and pain is, again, a triumph of grace in little David against the Goliath of the institutional Church. Liam, I am quite sure that as you look back from the mountain top experience of exoneration, you must sometimes find yourself wondering how you came through the valleys of self doubt, despair and hopelessness that was so clearly a part of your psychological state as you hung on against the onslaught of evil. I like the quality of your literary style and your brutal transparency in sharing the journey of those terrible years. Beyond the Liam McCarthy that I knew in seminary days, your book revealed to me another Liam: A man who is a giant in pursuing the truth and articulating clearly your "dark night of the soul." I was very, very impressed by your use of quotes from so many other different sources and their relevancy to the story. Your love for the priesthood is profound and humbling and stamped throughout the pages of the story. It must be obvious to you that I found your book inspiring, challenging, revealing, most instructive, and enlightening on the gifts that can too easily be taken for granted. It is again obvious to me that your brought your suffering to the cross and you anchored it all on the cross and you were led to ultimate triumph and resurrection. I am most grateful for your thoughtfulness in sharing your story with me and I look forward to a personal dialogue with you sometime when we might be together in person. Perhaps you may want to make a visit here to Tucson and come as an honored guest and a friend of many years. Your story makes a gigantic contribution to truth and integrity and is certainly great material for presentation through the medium of film. I stand in admiration and awe of the God who brought you through this immense trial and in admiration and awe of your love for the priesthood and your personal response. Prayerful and very grateful good wishes for ongoing healing, Your peer from almost a half century ago,

—Monsignor Tom Cehalane

I am a priest of the Diocese of Kansas City-St Joseph. I am a subject of a lawsuit claiming I did things to someone 32 years ago. It involves a "suppressed" and now recovered memory. It is totally false, and the story does not hold together. I am confident the suit will be dismissed, but in the meantime I don't have faculties. I am thinking of starting some sort of group, maybe a defense league or anti-defamation league. I have read your book and am familiar with both guilty and innocent priests. I'd love to talk with you about your thoughts on this. Blessings,

—Father Tom Cronin

In *"The Conspiracy"*, Msgr. McCarthy weaves the rich experiences of a priesthood serving the parish family that he loved for over 40 years, with the pain of his five year ordeal of being wrongfully accused of molesting two young sisters along with spiritual insight that he discovered during his journey into the "dark night of the soul." Like most priests, Msgr. McCarthy's story is one of a young man, joyful in giving his life to serve the Lord in every way he could. He left his family and all those he knew in Ireland to start a new life here in the US, happy to serve God and to serve the needs of thousands who became his new family. We see the wit and wisdom of a man who ministered and shared in the experiences of men, women and children of all ages through the joys and the sorrows of life. And finally, at a time when he anticipated experiencing and serving God in his retirement, he was given the most challenging ordeal of his life. But in his struggle, he found in himself newfound strength and new insight in how our Lord works good from that which is evil. Through his ordeal, he has been able to capture and include in this book inspirational stories, prayers, and insights from a multitude of sources, including his own, that I believe he was meant to share with others. I plan to make his book a resource that I will use in my ministry. Msgr. McCarthy's concluding message, perhaps, is the most meaningful of all — that of forgiveness, and a desire to help others who may find themselves trapped in similar circumstances. Ultimately, his message is intended for us all, but particularly to those in leadership positions — it is a plea for personal integrity; always to seek truth, for in seeking truth we seek God Himself.

> *"Truth must be sought at all costs, but separate isolated truths will not do. Truth is like life; it has to be taken on its entirety or not at all. ... We must welcome truth even if it reproaches and inconveniences us — even if it appears in the place where we thought it could not be found."*
> — *Archbishop Fulton Sheen*

—Deacon Ron Forino

FALLNG DOWN

A surge of life pulled Me from the dead
I gave up mental contamination
And started building a spiritual foundation
The world all around me was falling down
And when it crumbled I saw higher ground
Something happened inside of me
I stepped into my identity.

—Dr. Michael B. Beckwith

Our Priests

Words & Music: Bridget Hylak & Joseph Lee Hooker
© 2009 J.L. Hooker, All world rights reserved

In this world of darkness, still there shines a light
Standing with God's people to show them what is right
They carry on the wisdom that God has handed down
They are truly diamonds in our Savior's crown

CHORUS
Our Priests!! They are treasures!
Their hands, our saving grace…
Instruments of God, they must never be disgraced…
our priests…

The world calls and taunts them, yet they firmly stand
Bringing light to darkness at the Lord's command
Serving Bread of Angels to the hungry lambs
Their voice of truth will lead us to the Promised Land
(Chorus)

Eyes upon the Savior, guided by their vow
Strongly must they shepherd, yet humbly must they bow
Shining light from heaven, teaching truth sublime!
Reaching for perfection, touching the divine (Chorus)

Our priests, our saving grace, Our priests!!
Never be disgraced.. Our priests… our saving grace…

You brighten and enlighten my weekends each time you have Mass at OLV. You have no idea how the people in the pews perk up and smile when they see you walking through the aisle. Not to downgrade the importance of the Mass, but introductory jokes set the pace for a more positive reflection of the service As I once told you leaving church (which I know you could not recall since so many people complement you) I can't wait to go home to tell my husband your jokes. You're the kindest, sweetest, gentlest priest I've ever known -- I've known many. I'm sure you knew Monsignor Dalton - he brought tears to my eyes each homily – he never failed to say to us – "By the way, have I told you all that I love you." It was beautiful and forever lasting and you have made such an impression of love to the parishioners of OLV.

Well enough about how much I love and respect you. I read your book (I am not an avid book reader) and couldn't put it down. I can't express the sadness I felt for you and what you had to endure so many years. I would feel for anyone experiencing anything like this – but it magnified to think it could have happened to someone so sweet and religious as you. I don't know how you survived except for your faith in God. Now I see you in a totally different perspective in a more positive manner than I ever had before reading the book and you were then even on the highest pedal of love and respect There's no question you've got the best seat in heaven. (But don't try to sit for a long time!) It's difficult to comprehend your pure existence all those years and the spiritual strength you had to have to survive each and every day. Each time I see you, the book facts run through my mind and I hold an even deeper respect for you, not only as a loving priest but also as a strong human being. I guess by now you're wondering when this letter will end. I could probably continue for pages expressing my respect and love for you but I think you've gotten the message. I wish (and I know many people feel the same) we knew you earlier at OLV, but we're all looking forward for many more years of being blessed by your presence at Mass and your loving greeting walking out of church. Stay well, I know you'll stay strong, and have a wonderful peaceful life! Love and respect,

—Lillian Martin

Thank you for coming to our 50th wedding celebration and renewing our marriage vows. It meant a lot to us and you did a good job. I know it was noisy and very crowded but we got through it. Thank you for the blessed rosary beads and the beautiful Nuptial Blessing. I will frame it and hang it for everyone to read. These things were very thoughtful of you. You're a good man. I'm reading your book, and I'm sorry about all of the suffering you went through. Depression and anxiety are no strangers to my family, so I can relate to how you describe it. My mother suffered with mental illness all her life – never got rid of her demons, and I suffered with (2) major depressions myself. I still take stabilizing medication. You were so right about negative thinking and having a good support system, taking care of yourself, etc. So keep on going on. We'll see you in Church – God bless!

Sincerely yours,
—Josephine

The ending of your book was the best part! Oceans of Mercy!
—Sister Kathy Bernadette Wunilla, ESTH

I just wanted you to know that I'm enjoying your book very much. You did an excellent job and I hope many people will be helped by it. I'm sure it wasn't easy revealing yourself this way but much good will come of it. I saw Sr. Catherine Degnos this week and she wants to read it too. May God bless you today and always. PS: I'm going to Medjugorje and Germany to see Kathy. I'll call when I return to the states. Pray for me and Kathy.
—Dorothy Thaller (Hurley)

This book has touched my heart like no other because it is both inspiring and heart breaking. It tells the chilling story of how someone I know and love, who selflessly devoted his entire life to the service of the church, was totally betrayed by that very church. On almost every page, there's some little detail that sticks in my mind or tweaks my heart as it offers vignettes of cruelty, cowardice, terror, compassion and courage. I am so proud of you for having the wherewithal to overcome this terrible injustice that was visited on you, a holy and totally innocent man who never lost sight of his faith and love of Jesus. I am so grateful to you for sharing this book with me and inspiring me and my family in numerous different ways. We have shared this book with many friends in Ireland who are priests and they were equally horrified at the church who betrayed you in your hour of need. I am so sorry that you had to endure this very painful and sometimes seemingly insurmountable struggle, but I am so proud and enriched by your never wavering faith and your eventual triumph. May your future be filled with an abundance of blessings.

Your loving niece,
—Finola Tobin

My name is John McCarthy and I am Monsignor Liam McCarthy's nephew. I live in Cork City, Ireland with my wife and two children. One spring morning I received a book in the post from Liam instructing me to read it. When I saw the book cover and the title I was shocked. I was the first in the family to receive the book and hadn't realized what Liam had gone through following his retirement. Reading the book I learned what Liam had suffered, from looking forward to a happy retirement, being falsely accused, to being fully exonerated. It was hard to read this painful chapter in Liam's life; I was delighted that he got closure. I enjoyed the religious analogies and his recollection of family stories from his youth. Having good friends means so much. After reading the book Liam informed the rest of the family and I was so glad that he did. I said to him that he survived to tell the story and wished him all the best in the future.

—John McCarthy
Doneraile

After reading *The Conspiracy*, Connie and I felt that Monsignor suffered greatly as did Jesus during his Passion. Like Jesus he suffered loneliness, abandonment, and inner turmoil. He went through this suffering to be vindicated after five long years. Perhaps Monsignor McCarthy was chosen to be the author of this book to give courage and strength to other priests and laity who have experienced the same situations.

—Walter and Connie

I would like to say how sad I was to read your book and find what a horrendous time you have been through. I have always felt you were a very special person and after reading your book, I realize that you have an incredible faith that is an inspiration to us all. I have been brought to tears reading some of the dark moments that you endured and how your faith gave you the strength to keep going. I will always keep your book close and refer to it when I need to. I hope you are now experiencing peace of mind. Take Care.

—Your niece Yvonne

Written words that open your heart help us to know the joys and sorrows that were captured in *"The Conspiracy of an Innocent Priest."* It is a true account of the departments of darkness that were brought into his life – like lightning that strikes with no control. May the written words bring you into his moments of despair and hope that he lived and may you come to know that Monsignor desired to express his ordeal in writing and thereby was able to share the events that were brought into his life. He is now able to share (with the many who were touched by his priesthood) the joy of his redemption and able to continue his life to serve God's people.

—Anonymous

In the rush to judgment following the worldwide pedophile scandal involving a number of faithless and depraved priests, Monsignor Liam McCarthy writes a compelling and moving account of his unjust treatment and eventual vindication after a grueling five year purgatory. Just as the introduction of DNA testing has redeemed a number of imprisoned or wrongfully convicted felons, so *The Conspiracy* book proves that at least one priest was clearly innocent -- his dreadful experience so eloquently detailed proved the point. "Innocent until proven guilty" is a norm apparently ignored by the Vatican and many members of the Church hierarchy who in this case were obviously in a "Conspiracy".

—John J. "Jack" Hogan

351

Monsignor McCarthy's book is an important story for our bishops and church leaders to reflect on. Here we have an extremely dedicated and effective pastor who is literally "thrown under the bus" by his bishop because of an accusation by two vindictive women and encouraged by a dangerous detective whose badge should be taken away. How many other priests did or will meet this kind of fate? Monsignor McCarthy points out that it's crucial for the bishops to revise their methods of passing judgment when priests are accused of child abuse and dioceses need to take seriously, with undue delay, a professional review of each case that comes their way. The so called Dallas decision needs serious review to guarantee swift resolution to each case where a priest is accused. Bishops should bring on professionals and competent individuals to assist them in investigating and expeditiously passing judgment on each case where a priest is accused of child abuse or behavior unbecoming the clergy. Yes, expeditiously!

—Monsignor John B. Szymanski, P.A., V.G. Em.

"Innocent Until Proven Guilty," is a phrase I remember since my childhood. After being falsely accused of child molestation by a local detective, Monsignor William McCarthy relates his personal experiences required to prove his innocence. The book takes us from his life as a little boy growing up in Ireland to his accomplishments as Pastor of a Catholic Church in New Jersey. One can understand the loneliness and hurt Monsignor felt after the Bishop relieved him of his priestly duties soon after the accusation. *"The Conspiracy"* is a must read in order to understand one man's battle to clear his name and the struggles required to maintain one's sanity when "Guilty Until Proven Innocent" is proclaimed.

—Howard MacDonald

For us the process of law demands that guilt in a particular accusation of crime can only be determined through a painstaking sifting of evidence. Unfortunately in the case of priests, guilt is assumed by the general public to be present merely because of the accusation itself. Any of us can be accused, lay or clerical, and it would appear that the bishops do little to investigate and to protect innocent priests, even when the particular incident warrants their protection. Msgr. McCarthy, as revealed in this excellent account, is almost unique in his proclaiming his innocence through his writing of a vicious, accusing stalker, and the endless loneliness of a priest forced out of his parish and his priesthood. His only consolation was so many loyal individuals in his flock and his abiding faith in the eventual clearing of his name through the grace of our own Lord Jesus. God bless you, Father Bill, for the fortitude you exhibited in proclaiming your innocence and for giving so positive an example to other priests falsely accused.

—Frank and Mary McGuire

I can't help but wonder how many more innocent priests have been denied the opportunity to expeditiously defend themselves when accused of immoral behavior with young people. I would hope that compulsory reading of "The Conspiracy" would be included in all seminaries and as part of an education session made available to interested parishioners in all churches. As a member of the laity, I am sure some priests are guilty of intolerable behavior and should suffer the consequences. I also feel that there has been a rush to judgment in instances where vile people and their lawyers are simply looking for money and the Church has caved in as a rush to settle the matter. I commend you for writing "The Conspiracy." It's a story that had to be told. I am heartfully sorry and somewhat angry over the torment you experienced. You and those innocent accused members of the clergy will be in my prayers. I admire your perseverance to clear yourself of charges and your unconditional trust in our Lord, Jesus Christ. Respectfully,

—Bob Shaw

AUTHORS AND THEIR BOOKS

Referenced by Monsignor McCarthy
(Including Sections Deleted From The Final Version)

Adamson, Kate; *Kate's Journey*

Bombeck, Erma; *If Life is a Bowl of Cherries, What am I Doing in the Pits?*

Castaneda, Carlos; *The Teachings of Don Juan*

Chittister, Joan; *Seared By Struggle -- Transformed By Hope*

Cloud, Henry & Townsend, John; *God Will Make A Way*

Connery, Donald; *Convicting the Innocent*

DeChardin, Pierre; *The Phenomenon of Man*

Day, Laura; *Crisis*

DeAngelis, Barbara; *How Did I Get Here?*

Dickens, Charles; *A Tale of Two Cities*

Gonzales, Laurence; *Deep Survival*

Graham, Ruth; *Principles for Reflection*

Greeley, Andrew; *Confessions of a Parish Priest*

Harvey, Andrew; *The Way of Passion*

Jakes, Bishop T.D.; *Television Sermon Excerpts*

Kubler-Ross, Elizabeth; *On Death and Dying*

Kushner, Harold; *Overcoming Life's Disappointments*

Lewis, C.S.; *A Grief Observed*

Lewis, C.S.; *The Problem of Pain*

Milton, John; *Paradise Lost*

Moore, Thomas; *Dark Nights of the Soul*

Muggeridge, Malcolm; *Something Beautiful For God*

Nuland, Sherwin; *How We Die*

O'Kelley, Eugene; *Chasing Daylight*

Pitino, Rich; *Rebound Rules*

Prejean, Helen; *Dead Man Walking*

Rupp, Joyce; *The Cup Of Our Life: A Guide for Spiritual Growth*

Rushnell, Squire; *When God Winks (How the Power of Coincidence Guides Your Life)*
Sharma, Robin S.; *The Monk Who Sold His Ferrari*
Smith, Gordon; *Remembering Garrett*
Styson, William; *Darkness Visible*
Warren, Rick; *Answers to Life's Difficult Questions*
Warren, Rick; *The Purpose Driven Life*

PLAY
Keane, John B.; *Pishogue*

SONGS
Clapton, Eric; *Tears In Heaven*
John, Elton & Taupin, Bernie; *Candle in the Wind*

MOVIES
Cinderella Man (Dir. Ron Howard)
The DiVinci Code (Dir. Ron Howard)
Million Dollar Baby (Dir. Clint Eastwood)
The Passion of Christ (Dir. Mel Gibson)
Scent of a Woman (Dir. Martin Brest)
Seabiscuit (Dir. Gary Ross)
United 93 (Dir. Paul Greengrass)
Why Did I Get Married? (Dir. Tyler Perry)
The Wrong Man (Dir. Alfred Hitchcock)

ABOUT THE AUTHOR

Monsignor William McCarthy was born in County Cork, Ireland. He came to the U.S. following his ordination to the priesthood in 1963 after graduating from St. Patrick Seminary, Carlow.

His first U.S. parish assignment was St. Patrick, Chatham, NJ, where he remained from 1963 to 1968. He spent a year as associate pastor of St. Nicholas parish, Passaic, NJ. From 1969 to 1974 he served as associate pastor of St. Michael, Netcong, NJ; and from there went to St. Cecilia, Rockaway, NJ.

Monsignor McCarthy has pursued graduate courses in marriage counseling at Seton Hall University; and in theology at New York Theological Seminary.

In addition, he taught religion at Bayley-Ellard High School, Madison from 1963 to 1966; served as Assistant Diocesan Director of Scouting, 1965-68; was a member of the Diocesan Ecumenical Committee, 1969-1972; Knights of Columbus chaplain in Netcong, Chatham and Passaic, NJ; Director of Upper Morris CYO, 1970-75; and member of the Diocesan Personnel Board in 1973. He also was a member of the Role of the Priest Committee of the Diocesan Priests Senate.

Father McCarthy served as pastor of Saint Rose of Lima Church in East Hanover, NJ from 1980 to 2003, and currently holds the title of Pastor Emeritus.

Made in the USA
Middletown, DE
31 July 2019